Korea

Division, Reunification,
and U.S. Foreign Policy

Korea
Division, Reunification, and U.S. Foreign Policy

Martin Hart-Landsberg

Monthly Review Press
New York

© 1998 by Monthly Review Press

Hart-Landsberg, Martin.
  Korea: division, reunification, and U.S. foreign policy / Martin Hart-Landsberg.
    p.   cm.
  Includes bibliographical references and index
  ISBN 0-85345-928-2. — ISBN 0-85345-927-4 (pbk.)
    1. United States—Foreign relations—Korea. 2. Korea—Foreign
relations—United States. 3. United States—Foreign
Relations—1945-1989. 4. United States—Foreign relations—1989-
5. Korean reunification question (1945-) I. Title.
E183.8.K6H388 1998
327.730519—dc21   98-13451
                                                          CIP
Cover art courtesy of National Museum of Contemporary Art, Seoul

Monthly Review Press
122 West 27th Street
New York NY 10001

Manufactured in the United States of America

10 9 8 7 6 5 4 3 2 1

Contents

For Sylvia

Acknowledgments

Many people on both sides of the Pacific aided my investigation into the history and significance of the division of Korea. In South Korea, Kang Jeong-koo, Lee Su-hoon, and Lim Young-il were especially generous with their time and insights. I also wish to thank the Sejong Institute for hosting me as a visiting scholar during the summer of 1995. In the United States, Norm Diamond, Ed Reed, David Satterwhite, Hyuk-Kyo Suh, and Chong-Ae Yu deserve special mention. I am also grateful to the Korea program of the American Friends Service Committee for giving me the opportunity to travel in Northeast Asia in 1992-93, exploring issues related to Korean reunification. Finally, I wish to acknowledge Bruce Cumings, Sylvia Hart-Landsberg, Hyuk-Kyo Suh, and James West, all of whom read earlier drafts of this book and offered helpful suggestions for improving it.

Portland, Oregon
January 1998

Introduction

This book aims to explain how and why U.S. foreign policy has under-mined Korean efforts to create a democratic, egalitarian, and independent Korea, and to encourage Americans to work for a new policy toward Korea. This is no trivial task, since most Americans believe the "official" history of U.S.-Korean relations, which takes an opposite position. For example, a U.S. State Department publication describes U.S. and UN actions in Korea after the end of the Second World War as follows:

> At the moment of liberation [from Japanese colonialism] the United States, as one of the occupying powers, looked forward to cooperation with its Allies and the Korean people in the creation of a new Korea—united, democratic, and free of all foreign domination. This purpose, which has also been that of the United Nations, has been only partially achieved. . . . [T]he people of South Korea, under UN observation, freely chose their representatives and successfully established a democratic republic. The people of the North, to whom the Communist occupying power denied the free expression of their own will, were instead forced to establish a rival regime which subsequently launched an unprovoked surprise attack on the South. At great cost of life and property, this aggression was repelled through UN action; and unceasing efforts have been made by the United Nations and its members since that time to realize the continuing aspirations of the Korean people for unity in a single, free, and independent nation.[1]

The willingness of the U.S. government to send soldiers to fight in the Korean War under the UN flag continues to be cited by many officials and commentators as one of the most important examples of the U.S. govern-ment's deep commitment to democracy. Those who take such a position usually also point out that in the case of South Korea this commitment has been amply rewarded, as South Koreans have used their freedom to create one of the most dynamic and prosperous countries in the world. In short, according to the conventional view, few acts of foreign policy have been so idealistically motivated or successful.

The continuing historical and ideological importance of the Korean War is well reflected in the political speeches surrounding the July 27, 1995, opening of the Korean War Memorial in Washington, D.C. In his remarks at the celebration, President Bill Clinton offered the following description of the significance of U.S. participation in the Korean War: "By sending a clear message that America had not defeated fascism to see communism prevail, [Americans] put the Free World on the road to victory in the Cold War." South Korean President Kim Young Sam, who also attended the celebration, made the same point: "The blood and sweat shed by the U.S. and the UN troops proved to be the prime mover behind the realization of freedom throughout the world after the war. . . . [In that sense the Korean War] was a war that heralded the collapse of the Berlin Wall and the demise of communism."[2]

The two presidents, appearing later at a joint news conference, also made their case for a continuing U.S. military presence on the Korean peninsula. "Forty-two years have passed since the Korean War ended," said President Clinton, "but for the people of South Korea, the threat is present every day. . . . [Therefore] I reaffirm our nation's pledge to keep American forces in Korea, as long as they need them, and the Korean people want them to remain." President Kim added, "President Clinton and I reconfirmed that maintaining and strengthening a firm, joint Korea-U.S. defense posture is essential to guarding the peace and stability not only of the Korean peninsula but also the Northeast Asian region."[3]

The Korean War Memorial is dominated by nineteen slightly larger-than-life statues of U.S. soldiers on patrol; the soldiers look tired but are on guard against a surprise attack. It is only a few hundred yards from the Vietnam Memorial but, according to many journalists, the difference between the two is striking. Charles Krauthammer explains:

> The Vietnam Memorial thrusts you into war's aftermath, its legacy of loss; the Korean Memorial thrusts you into war's actuality, its crucible of fear and courage. The one memorializes death, numberlessly multiplied; the other struggle, faithfully rendered. . . .
>
> The Vietnam Memorial was a vessel for saying: This is war. Never again. The Korean Memorial, dedicated thirteen years later, reflects a different sensibility. In the interim, the horrors of Rwanda and Bosnia have made even those once

most adamantly antiwar rethink and indeed reverse themselves. Thirteen years later, we are not so sure that "learning war no more" is a good idea. Thirteen years later, we agree: There are battles worth fighting, they should be chosen with great care and fought with great purpose, but there are purposes worth fighting for. Korea was one.[4]

There is no denying the sacrifices made by the hundreds of thousands of Americans who fought in the Korean War. More than 54,000 soldiers died in Korea, almost as many as the 58,000 who died in the Vietnam War, but in less than one-third the time. What is open to challenge, however, is the interpretation of that war and how it has shaped U.S. policy toward Korea. In fact, the very inscription on the Korean War Memorial should make us cautious about embracing the official history highlighted above. That inscription reads: "Our nation honors her uniformed sons and daughters who answered their country's call to defend a country they never knew and a people they never met."

There is, of course, a sad truth to this inscription. Most Americans at the time of the Korean War knew little about the forces leading to the war or the reasons for U.S. intervention. Nevertheless, while the inscription is supposed to emphasize the altruism underlying U.S. foreign policy, it unintentionally raises an important question: how well do most Americans now, almost fifty years later, understand the causes and consequences of the division of Korea, the Korean War, or U.S. foreign policy toward Korea? The answer is: not very well.

Perhaps the primary reason for this unfortunate state of affairs is that U.S. and South Korean leaders and opinion-makers continue to present a misleading picture of U.S. motivations and actions, past and present, as they concern Korea. The many speeches and newspaper articles that praise the U.S. government's unshakable commitment to defend democracy on the Korean peninsula fail to mention the 1905 Taft-Katsura Memorandum. In this secret agreement, the U.S. government pledged to recognize Japan's hegemony over Korea in exchange for Japan's promise that it would not interfere with U.S. colonial interests in Hawaii and the Philippines. Nor do they tell of U.S. and Japanese opposition to Korean attempts to present their case for independence to the world community at both the Paris Peace Conference in 1919 and the Washington Conference of 1921-1922, which dealt with Asian affairs.

Standard commentaries on U.S.-Korean relations also overlook the historical evidence that would place primary responsibility for the division of Korea with the United States. After the Japanese surrendered ending the Second World War, the U.S. government unilaterally declared that Soviet forces fighting the Japanese in northern Korea should stop at the 38th parallel. This would allow U.S. troops, which would not arrive in Korea for several weeks, to receive the Japanese surrender south of the 38th parallel, a division that would place approximately two-thirds of the country's population and the capital in what would later become South Korea. This declaration served not to achieve Japanese disarmament or Korean independence, but to secure U.S. influence on the Korean peninsula and advance U.S. political and economic interests in Northeast Asia.

When U.S. forces finally arrived in Korea, they found a working, socialist-oriented Korean government, the Korean People's Republic (which preceded the post-division Democratic People's Republic of Korea [DPRK] in the North), maintaining order and production throughout the country through popularly run people's committees and associated mass organizations. The United States forcibly destroyed these popular committees and organizations in the south and, in their place, imposed its own military-run government. This policy was responsible for setting in motion separate political processes in north and south Korea, eventually leading to the establishment of separate Korean governments, each organized around radically different political structures and visions, and each claiming to be the only legitimate government of Korea.

Seen from this perspective, the Korean War is best understood as a civil war fought to reunify a divided nation. Even the U.S. ambassador to the United Nations admitted as much in October 1950, when he called the 38th parallel dividing Korea an "imaginary line."[5] Given the unpopularity of the U.S.-backed South Korean government, there is every reason to believe that this civil war would have ended quickly if the United States had not intervened. Those who supported the Korean People's Republic would have had another opportunity to build a democratic Korea. However, the United States did intervene, and its military effort succeeded in maintaining the status quo of a divided Korea.

The continuing division has turned the Korean peninsula into one of the most potentially explosive areas in the world. U.S. commentators and government officials frequently warn of the dangers posed to the people of northeast Asia by North Korean militarism, in particular the alleged North Korean nuclear threat. But significantly, they generally omit that the United States introduced the nuclear threat to the peninsula when it threatened to use nuclear weapons against North Korea and China during the Korean War. Nor do they mention that it was the United States, in violation of the terms of the Korean War armistice, which first introduced nuclear weapons onto the Korean peninsula in 1957. And none mention that the United States regularized the nuclear threat when it began annual war games in South Korea in 1976. Moreover, they fail to call attention to the fact that it is the North, and not the United States, which consistently seeks to negotiate a peace treaty to bring the Korean War to a formal conclusion.

There is good reason to question the commitment of U.S. military, political, and corporate leaders to promoting the peaceful reunification of Korea, much less to reducing tensions on the peninsula. That is because the existence of a hostile North Korean regime serves some U.S. interests quite well. As a case in point, it is no accident that North Korea became a major nuclear threat to the peace and stability of northeast Asia only after the collapse of the Soviet Union. Support for high levels of military spending and an aggressive foreign policy had rested heavily on national acceptance of Cold War ideology. With the collapse of the Soviet Union, the United States was forced to craft a new post-Cold War military strategy justifying its activities in the region. In *The Bottom-Up Review: Forces for a New Era*, the Department of Defense concluded that the United States needed an army capable of fighting two regional conflicts against mid-sized third world countries with large modern armies.[6] The greatest danger cited to U.S. interests was simultaneous military actions by Iraq and North Korea. Thus, the North Korean "threat" has become one of the primary justifications for maintaining U.S. military spending at roughly Cold War levels.

Political and corporate leaders have been quick to capitalize on this new military strategy. The North Korean threat has enabled them to renew their push for a Star Wars missile defense system. Funding for this program had fallen from a peak of $1.9 billion in 1992 to $400 million in 1994. But, as *Business Week* explains, the campaign to revive Star Wars once again went into high gear in 1995:

Big industrialists and conservative politicians see the project as perfect for their aims. With a stream of disturbing reports as their ammo, Reaganites in conservative think tanks have publicized the threat from such rogue states as North Korea and Iraq. Republicans, relying on polls and focus groups, think voters will go ballistic if Democrats block efforts to provide a defense blanket. Meanwhile, arms makers such as TRW Inc. and Lockheed Martin Corp. could reap a bonanza from one of the Pentagon's few growth areas.[7]

Working hard to ensure that Americans take the North Korean threat seriously, some intelligence officials claim that the western United States could conceivably be within range of new North Korean missiles (still under development) by the year 2000. One U.S. senator commented, "if the information is even close to the truth, it presents for the first time a very serious and relatively quick challenge to U.S. sovereignty."[8] We can only guess at the new weapons systems being designed to counter this potential "challenge."

By providing justification for a strong U.S. military presence in the Asia-Pacific region, the North Korean threat offers potential economic benefits to businesses outside of military production, as well. One analyst explains the tie between military and economic strength as follows:

A senior Pentagon official told Thomas Friedman of the *New York Times* that during the Cold War years Taiwanese businesses gave preference to U.S. firms over Japanese firms because the U.S. was protecting them. In the post-Cold War world evidently a successful U.S. police action has the same effect. In October 1993, after the U.S.-led victory in the Gulf War, Saudi Arabia signed a $6 billion contract for jetliners with U.S. corporations, Boeing and McDonnell Douglas. A European consortium, Airbus Industries, which had hoped for a fifty-fifty split, complained that Washington had pressured Saudi Arabia "which has come to rely on the United States for its security."[9]

The current connection between U.S. military deployment and business interests in the Asia-Pacific region is not hard to document. Admiral Charles R. Larson, then commander of U.S. forces in the Pacific, noted in an October 1993 speech that foreign deployment of U.S. military forces was being cut back worldwide *except* in the Asia-Pacific region. The reason, said Larson, was that U.S. trade with Asia was now greater than that with either Europe or Latin America. Referring to the Clinton administration's vision of a "New Pacific Community," Larson argued that forward deployment of U.S. forces was the key to the military security necessary to support that community and guarantee America a dominant role in it.[10]

At present, South Korea and Japan provide the main locations for U.S. forces in Asia, and it is the North Korean threat that provides the main justification for their presence. When Okinawans responded to the 1995 rape of a twelve-year-old girl by three U.S. soldiers by demanding the removal of U.S. troops, Secretary of Defense William Perry argued that removing troops from Japan "would not serve the function of providing security and stability in the Western Pacific. They are not located here because it is convenient for us to have them located here. They are located here because this is where they have to be to provide security in the Asia-Pacific region."[11] The reason: "All of our planning depends heavily on proximity to North Korea."[12]

While the division of Korea, and by extension the North Korean threat, has offered a number of important benefits to U.S. military, political, and corporate leaders, giving U.S. policymakers strong incentive to oppose better relations with North Korea and the reunification of Korea, there are signs that the consensus for a hard-line position against the North may be weakening. For example, the U.S. government chose negotiation rather than war to settle its nuclear standoff with North Korea. The October 1994 agreement signed by the United States and North Korea included, among other things, a U.S. commitment to help North Korea transform and modernize its nuclear energy program and to improve relations between the two countries. Moreover, in 1996, the U.S. government responded positively, over South Korean objections, to North Korean requests for emergency food aid made necessary by devastating rains and flooding. But it would be premature to conclude that these developments represent a fundamental change in U.S. policy toward Korea. Many government and military officials openly reject even these first steps toward improving relations with North Korea. At the same time, however, these inconsistencies in policy provide hope that we are entering an historical period when popular pressure can, in fact, succeed in forcing such a change.

There are certainly many reasons for Americans to want to change the current policy. It has been costly for them: tens of thousands of U.S. lives were lost in one Korean War, and many more could be lost in another. It also serves to justify a large military budget at a time when social programs are being slashed in the name of budget-balancing.

The current policy has also caused Koreans much suffering. Millions lost their lives during the Korean War, and Koreans, like Americans, continue to live under the threat of a new war. More directly, U.S. determination to secure the survival of a "friendly" regime on the peninsula has led the U.S. to oppose democratic movements in the South in favor of military dictatorship. This was the situation in 1980 when the U.S. government chose to support military actions against the citizens of Kwangju who were opposing a new military coup.

The governments of North and South Korea have also used the tensions generated by the continuing division to maintain tight social control over their respective populations. We read and hear much about the lack of freedom in the North. But we hear very little about South Korean governmental repression, allegedly for national security purposes, of teachers who try to offer their students an open learning environment, workers who seek more democratic workplaces, and students who speak out for reunification and national independence. For all of these reasons a new U.S. policy toward Korea is needed, one that is dedicated to creating an environment where Koreans can freely and peacefully begin erasing the "imaginary line" that continues to cause so much harm and suffering.

I. EMPIRE
AND RESISTANCE

CHAPTER 1

The United States and Korea

Korea, forcibly colonized by Japan in 1910, was liberated with Japan's August 1945 defeat in the Second World War. Four days before U.S. military forces were to land in southern Korea in September 1945, ostensibly to accept the surrender of Japanese troops, the commander of U.S. forces informed his officers that Korea was "an enemy of the United States" and should be treated as such.[1] Many Koreans had fought the Japanese as best they could. They were among the many victims of the war. What had they done to warrant such a characterization? The answer is simple: U.S. plans for regional dominance included exercising control over Korea. Because many Koreans were as opposed to a U.S.-dominated future as the Japan-dominated past, U.S. officials considered them enemies.

U.S. troops did not appear in Korea solely to support Korean efforts to create "a new Korea united, democratic, and free of all foreign domination," as declared by State Department ideologists.[2] The troops arriving in southern Korea were primarily an instrument for carrying out U.S. foreign policy objectives. In order to understand U.S. policy toward Korea in the period following the end of the Second World War, which remains the starting point for most studies of U.S.-Korea relations, we must therefore first examine the prior evolution of U.S. imperialist ambitions and actions, the ways in which an expansionist foreign policy long predating the Cold War set the stage for the division and subjugation of Korea.

BRIDGING THE PACIFIC:
HISTORICAL ORIGINS OF EMPIRE

Early American experience was defined by the westward movement of people and expansion of power. In 1790, there were 3.9 million people in the United States, most of them living within fifty miles of the Atlantic Ocean. The 1803 purchase of the Louisiana Territories from France doubled the size of the nation, extending the western frontier from the Appalachians across the Mississippi to the Rocky Mountains. The population increased to 13 million by 1830, and by 1840, some 4.5 million people had crossed the Appalachian Mountains into the Mississippi Valley. This expansion was made possible by what was then called "Indian Removal"; in 1820 there were 120,000 Native Americans living east of the Mississippi Valley, but by 1844 there were fewer than 30,000.[3]

Native Americans were not the only victims of U.S. westward expansion. Southwest of the Rocky Mountains was Mexico, which then included Texas, California, New Mexico, Utah, Nevada, Arizona, and part of Colorado. With support from the U.S. government, Texas declared its independence from Mexico in 1836 and became a state in 1845. Soon after, President James Polk sent federal troops to the Rio Grande and ordered them to defend the territory north of the river as the border of Texas. This was a deliberate challenge to Mexico since the territory being defended was 150 miles south of the border previously agreed upon.

As expected, Mexican forces attacked the federal troops and Polk quickly received congressional approval to wage war against Mexico. Federal troops invaded California, then considered the main prize, and New Mexico. They also headed into Mexico and attacked Mexico City. Overwhelmed, Mexico surrendered and, under the terms of the 1848 Treaty of Guadalupe Hidalgo, ceded nearly half of its territory, including California, to the United States. For the U.S. elite, the march west was a natural consequence of what newspaper editor John O'Sullivan called "our manifest destiny to over-spread the continent allotted by Providence for the free development of our yearly multiplying millions."[4]

U.S. interest in California had been stimulated by, among other things, a growing commercial interest in the Pacific. Early in the nineteenth century, U.S. traders and whalers made Hawaii a port of call; by the middle of the century, U.S. business interests had come to dominate Hawaiian politics. U.S. whaling vessels also regularly fished along the Japanese coast and wanted access to its ports for repair and supplies. As commercial activity increased in the region, business groups envisioned using Japan as one of the key stops along a Pacific steamer route linking California and China.

Although China was the biggest commercial attraction in the Pacific, Britain had difficulty selling sufficient goods to the Chinese to balance its bilateral trade. One of Britain's most successful exports to China was Indian opium. Thus, when China moved to ban its sale, confiscating and destroying opium stored in warehouses and demanding that foreign merchants pledge not to bring opium into China, Britain responded with force. It fought and defeated China in the Opium War of 1840 to 1842.

The resulting Treaty of Nanking began the "treaty port system," requiring China to open five ports to British trade and consular supervision. Britain also claimed Hong Kong as a base for protecting its interests. A second treaty was signed in 1843, giving Britain extraterritorial rights, including consular courts in which British subjects could be tried under British law. It also introduced the most-favored-nation clause, establishing a system of cooperative imperialism, whereby China was forced to give Britain the benefits of any new treaty it might sign with another country.[5]

Following Britain's lead, the United States forced China to sign a treaty in 1844 with greater concessions beyond those acquired by Britain. Britain, however, voiced no objections since the logic of cooperative imperialism ensured that it also enjoyed the benefits of the new Chinese concessions.

The Chinese people, already suffering oppression and poverty, found their situation worsened by the tremendous financial burden these treaties imposed on the Chinese state. Nine years after the Opium War, the Taiping Rebellion occurred. Peasants overran the south of China, destroying land deeds and loan contracts, giving land to those who worked it, and ending such practices as the binding of women's feet and the sale of brides. The Taipings set up a separate state which, for a time, governed more than half of China's population.

The Western powers took advantage of the situation to make new demands on the Chinese government. This led to a second Opium War and to a new round of unequal treaties in 1858 allowing the Western powers to designate any area of China, even inland areas, as open treaty ports. Having achieved their aims, the British and French openly, and the United States covertly, helped the ruling Manchus defeat the Taipings; the Taiping state fell in 1864.

In contrast to its follower status in China, the United States took the lead in forcing Japan to accept the treaty port system. Japan's de facto ruler, the Shogun of the Tokugawa house, had forbidden contact with any foreigners except the Dutch and Chinese, who had been allowed to stay in Nagasaki since the 1630s. This Japanese policy was originally implemented to reduce foreign cultural and social influences, particularly Christianity. But after the European powers began their humiliation of China, Japan continued the policy for economic and political reasons as well. It ended, however, after four U.S. warships sailed to the entrance of Tokyo Bay in July 1853 and Commodore Matthew C. Perry demanded that the Japanese sign a treaty of friendship and commerce. Japan agreed the following year to open two ports and allow the appointment of an American consul. The British and Russians quickly followed, negotiating similar treaties in 1854 and 1855, respectively.

The U.S. consul arrived in Japan in 1856 with instructions to reopen negotiations to secure special trade rights. Having no military leverage, he initially found the talks difficult. However, after the British succeeded in capturing Canton during the second Opium War, his threat that a similar attack could be organized against Japanese cities produced an agreement with Japan in July 1858. Within two months, Japan was forced to sign treaties with Holland, Russia, Britain, and France.

Encouraged by its success with China and Japan, the United States turned its attention to Korea. In August 1866, the U.S. warship *General Sherman* sailed, uninvited, up the Taedong River to Pyongyang in search of trading opportunities. Hostile crowds along the way provoked the crew into launching an attack. The crowds retaliated by burning the ship and beheading surviving crew members.[6] Five years later, the U.S. Asiatic Squadron was ordered to Korea. When a survey party from the fleet was fired on by cannons from a Korean fort, U.S. ships fired back and demanded an apology. With no response from the Korean forces, the U.S. officer in charge ordered five forts destroyed; 350 Koreans were killed or wounded, and the expedition eventually left, failing to make official contact with the Korean government.[7]

The U.S. government's growing involvement and interest in Asia convinced policymakers of the desirability of formally establishing authority over Hawaii. In 1875 the U.S. government pressured Hawaii into granting it exclusive commercial privileges. It is worth noting that in China, where it held a relatively weak position, the United States supported the open door policy of the treaty port system. But in Hawaii, where U.S. power was largely unchallenged, the United States sought exclusive control. A renegotiated treaty in 1884 granted the United States the right to build the Pearl Harbor naval base. An annexation treaty was finally concluded in 1897; Hawaii lost its independence on August 12, 1898.

Perhaps the key event promoting U.S. regional aspirations was the 1898 Spanish-American War. Cuba's impending victory in its independence struggle against Spain provided the initial motivation for the war. While U.S. elites were glad to see Spain defeated, they did not want to see Cuba independent. Taking advantage of a mysterious explosion that destroyed the battleship Maine in Havana Harbor, the U.S. government charged Spain with authorship of the deed and declared war. The resulting conflict with Spain began in April, lasted three months, and extended from the Caribbean to the Pacific. Commodore George Dewey's major victory over the Spanish fleet in Manila Bay on May 1 had the effect of turning business attention beyond Cuba to Asia. In a move to win government support for the permanent occupation of the Philippines, the business community initiated a major publicity campaign, with the slogan "Bridge the Pacific."

U.S. involvement in Asia was now driven by economics in particular, the desire for access to foreign markets. As the State Department explained in 1898:

> It seems to be conceded that every year we shall be confronted with an increasing surplus of manufactured goods for sale in foreign markets if American operatives and artisans are to be kept employed the year around. The enlargement of foreign consumption of the products of our mills and workshops has, therefore, become a serious problem of statesmanship as well as of commerce.[8]

China was considered at the time to be one of the most promising markets for U.S. products. However, the other Western powers that dominated China were beginning to reject the treaty port system which guaranteed open markets, in favor of nationally controlled spheres of influence. For example, by the end of the decade, sixteen of China's twenty-one provinces were under foreign domination. With these obstacles in mainland China, U.S. leaders saw control over the Philippines as the most effective way to establish a competitive position for penetrating the Chinese market. As Senator Albert Beveridge explained:

> Mr. President, the times call for candor. The Philippines are ours forever . . . and just beyond the Philippines are China's illimitable markets. We will not retreat from either. . . . We will not renounce our part in the mission of our race, trustees, under God, of the civilization of the world. . . .
>
> The Pacific is our ocean. . . . Where shall we turn for consumers of our surplus? Geography answers the question. China is our natural customer. . . . The Philippine gives us a base at the door of all the East.[9]

The treaty ending the Spanish-American War was signed in December 1898. Spain, reluctantly bowing to U.S. demands, turned over Guam, Puerto Rico, and the Philippines, for a payment of $20 million. The United States allowed Cuba to become independent, but not before securing political control over the island.

Spain, of course, did not consult with the Filipino people before handing over the Philippines to the United States. The Filipinos had fought against Spain for their independence; now they had to struggle against the United States. A bloody war lasting three years saw the deployment of some 70,000 troops before the United States could declare victory; some 16,000 Filipinos died in combat and another 200,000 from war-related disease or hunger.[10]

As this condensed survey makes clear, early U.S. foreign policy was guided consistently by the aim of westward expansion, a policy that led U.S. forces to take land from Native Americans and Mexicans; prop up an undemocratic Chinese government; force open Japanese ports; annex Hawaii; and colonize Guam, Puerto Rico, and the Philippines. Korea escaped Japan's fate only because its economic value was not considered great enough to sustain U.S. interest.

The Japanese Challenge to U.S. Interests

The U.S. government's forced opening of Japanese ports in 1858 triggered debates, assassinations, local rebellion, and, in 1868, civil war. One reason for the intensity of Japan's response was that Japanese elites were aware of what Western imperialism had done to China. The Japanese civil war brought to power a coalition of regional leaders, with the Emperor Meiji providing a unifying nationalist framework. The new government moved quickly to promote domestic industry and commerce and, as one historian explains, "Within a generation [the Meiji Restoration] had dismantled feudalism, substituting an emperor-centered bureaucratic state; created a modern army and navy; instituted legal codes and education of the Western type; and taken the first major steps toward industrial development." [11]

The Imperial Charter Oath of 1868 embraced the slogan "rich nation, strong army." The Meiji government, having watched Western practices, drew from history the lesson that domestic activity alone would not be sufficient to generate the wealth required for national defense and independence. Control over foreign markets and resources was also needed. Korea was the obvious first target. It was close, not under the control of other Western powers, and it was the gateway to the resource-rich areas of Manchuria and northern China.

Taking advantage of the West's obsession with China, and worried by Russian moves toward Manchuria, the new Japanese government quickly initiated its own colonialism. It deliberately sent a survey fleet into Korean waters in 1875. When Korean coastal batteries attacked, Japan rushed troops and a naval squadron to the area, demanding both an apology and a trade agreement. The 1876 Treaty of Kanghwa gave Japan access to three ports and permission for coastal surveys, required payment of indemnities, and declared Korea independent from Chinese suzerainty.

The Korean court, in a move to keep Japan at arm's length, followed China's advice and signed trade agreements with other countries. The United States was the first to sign in 1882, followed quickly by Britain and Germany, and later by Italy, Russia, and France. This strategy proved costly; in addition to the indemnity owed Japan, the Korean government was obligated to exchange diplomatic missions and construct modern transportation facilities, all of which translated into higher taxes. The higher taxes, as well as increased imports, made a bad situation worse for Korean peasants. This led to the Tonghak Uprising in 1894. Although the Tonghak leadership pledged loyalty to the king of Korea, their demands for social and economic equality and national independence alarmed him. Rather than choosing to negotiate, he called on China to send troops. China's forces soon arrived. So did Japan's, however, under the pretext that they were needed to guard Japanese property. Although the Tonghak quickly ended their rebellion, the Japanese government refused to withdraw its troops. Japan argued that Korea's instability posed a threat to Japan's security and demanded that China grant Japan authority to restructure the Korean government and supervise its activities.

When Korea, with the backing of the Chinese government, refused Japan's demands, Japan declared war on China in August 1894. Within two months Japan succeeded in taking control of Korea and its government. The Chinese were defeated easily and forced to sign a peace treaty in April 1895. China was forced to recognize Japan's authority in Korea, sign a new commercial treaty giving Japan full rights in the treaty port system, pay an indemnity, and cede control over Taiwan and the Liaotung peninsula in Manchuria.

Japan's gains were short-lived, however. Russia opposed Japanese influence in Manchuria, an area it wished to dominate. With the backing of Germany and France, Russia succeeded in forcing Japan to give up control over the Liaotung peninsula and to adopt a lower profile in Korea. The Russians, French, and Germans then demanded, and received, extra compensation from China for their support against Japan.

China's hopeless situation led to the anti-foreign Yi He Tuan Uprising, known in the West as the Boxer Rebellion. By June 1900 the Yi He Tuan had gained control over Beijing and were laying siege to its foreign legations there. Eight countries, including the United States, put together a military force to suppress the uprising; Japan contributed the most troops. The uprising was put down, but at great cost to the Chinese government in the form of new unequal treaties and indemnities. Russia took advantage of the resulting chaos to further strengthen its economic and political position in Manchuria.

Both the United States and Britain were alarmed by Russian gains. Their interests in China were best served by keeping the entire country open and accessible, but Russia's actions were leading to the formal separation of Manchuria from China, and Russian dominance over northern China. Both countries wanted to roll back the Russian advance, but neither were in a position to take the necessary military action to do so. Japan was in such a position, however, and received support and encouragement from both the United States and Britain.

The first Anglo-Japanese Treaty of Alliance, signed in January 1902, recognized the special interests of both Britain and Japan in China, as well as Japan's special interests, "politically as well as commercially and industrially in Korea. The alliance called for joint action in defense of those interests if they were threatened by the aggressive action of any other power."[12] Reassured that it could count on British assistance to offset German or French intervention in a Russian-Japanese war, the Japanese demanded that the Russians pull their troops out of Manchuria. When the Russians refused, the Japanese launched a surprise sea and land attack against Russian positions in southern Manchuria in February 1904. At great human and financial cost, Japan won a series of victories in the heavy land battles that followed.

The United States encouraged Japan by providing financial support for its war effort. Equally important, it gave its blessing to Japanese control over Korea. Right before the fighting began, the U.S. foreign minister to Korea stated that although he was "no pro-Japanese enthusiast," it was obvious that "Korea should belong to Japan by right of ancient conquest and tradition. I think our government will make a mistake if it tries to have Japan simply continue this fiction of independence."[13] After the war, W. W. Rockhill, a China specialist for the State Department, said that Japanese annexation of Korea was "absolutely indicated as the one great and final step westward of the Japanese Empire."[14]

Rockhill's statement can best be interpreted as wishful thinking. The United States had originally sought to punish Russia for trying to upset the status quo in China. Japan's overwhelming success in the war was an unpleasant surprise. It meant that Japan was now a potential threat to U.S. interests in the region. In fact, fearful that Japan might seek to widen its own regional sphere of influence at U.S. expense, President Theodore Roosevelt sent Secretary of War William Howard Taft to Tokyo in July 1905 to negotiate a secret agreement with the Japanese prime minister. In the resulting Taft-Katsura Memorandum, the United States recognized Japan's right to control Korea in exchange for Japan's acceptance of U.S. hegemony over the Philippines.

The Japanese-Russian war ended in August 1905 with Japanese armies in control of Korea, Manchuria, and Sakhalin. The Portsmouth Peace Conference, organized by the United States, produced a treaty recognizing Japan's rights in Korea in almost the same terms as had the Anglo-Japanese Treaty. The Portsmouth treaty also required Russia to transfer to Japan its controlling interest in the South Manchuria railway system and its rights to various economic concessions in Manchuria. China had little choice but to agree.

During the war, Japan forced the Korean government to accept control of its finance, foreign affairs, and local police. At the war's conclusion, Japan immediately took steps to turn Korea into a protectorate. The Korean king objected, but to little effect. On November 17, 1905, the Japanese themselves applied the royal seal to the necessary documents. Japan formally annexed Korea on August 22, 1910, completing its transformation from an independent country into a Japanese colony.

In spite of U.S. hopes, Japan's gains at Portsmouth did not satisfy its imperialist ambitions. Japan soon began tightening restrictions on other countries economic activities in Manchuria. It also signed an agreement with Russia that resulted in Inner Mongolia becoming a Japanese sphere of influence and Outer Mongolia becoming a Russian sphere of influence. Japan and Russia also negotiated a power-sharing arrangement for North China.

Concerned by these developments, the U.S. government initiated new negotiations with Japan, resulting in the November 1908 Root-Takahira Agreement. The United States reiterated its recognition of Japanese dominance over Korea and acknowledged Japan's new central role in Manchuria. In return, the United States received Japan's pledge to limit its expansion into the rest of China. The Japanese elite, especially the military, viewed the agreement with disdain. They saw no reason to limit Japan's territorial ambitions in China so that the United States and European powers could satisfy their own. But not yet strong enough to openly challenge the West for control over China, there was little Japan could do but wait until the regional balance of forces changed in its favor.

That moment came with the First World War. Since it was primarily a European war, the First World War forced the European powers to concentrate their resources and attention regionally. The U.S. government attempted to convince Europe and Japan to agree to respect the status quo in China, but Japan refused. It declared war on Germany in August 1914 and immediately seized control of Germany's leasehold in China (the Shantung peninsula), as well as a number of German-held islands in the Western Pacific. In 1915 Japan presented the Chinese government of Yuan Shi-kai with its Twenty-One Demands. The demands called for China to give Japan all of Germany's concessions, greater political control in Manchuria and Inner Mongolia, exclusive mining and industrial privileges in the Yangtse Valley, and the power to exercise supervisory control over China's social and political institutions. As a package, these demands would have turned Manchuria and Inner Mongolia into Japanese protectorates and China into a Japanese dependency.

At the time, China was in the midst of civil war. A nationalist revolution led by Sun Yat-sen, which sought to overthrow the corrupt Manchu government, had begun in October 1911. The Western powers, including the United States, opposed Sun's movement, fearing that its success would lead to limitations on their economic freedoms in the region. They pressed the Manchu emperor to reform his government and select Yuan Shi-kai as prime minister and commander in chief. Yuan had helped suppress the Ye Hi Tuan Rebellion and so enjoyed the confidence of the West. However, Yuan betrayed the Manchu government in 1912, making a deal with Sun Yat-sen to form a new government over which he would be president. This government ended more than 2,000 years of rule by monarchy, but collapsed one year later when Yuan broke with Sun and declared himself emperor. Sun and his Kuomintang (Nationalist Party) established a rival government in the south. With European governments occupied by the First World War, Yuan was forced to face Japan alone. Reluctantly, he accepted most of Japan's economic demands. As a result, Japan was able to greatly increase its exports to China and secure a steady supply of important raw material inputs (coal and iron) for its rapidly growing heavy industries.

Although greatly upset by Japan's actions, President Woodrow Wilson decided to let them go unchallenged. U.S. attention was focused on events in Europe, largely for economic reasons. The United States was in recession when the First World War began. At the time most U.S. business and political leaders believed that a return to prosperity required greater access to foreign markets. Events were to provide support for their belief: by 1915, war orders from England, France, and Belgium had helped boost U.S. growth. By April 1917 the United States had sold these countries more than $2 billion worth of goods.[15] Realizing that the United States faced the possibility of economic crisis if the Allies lost, Wilson decided to involve the country in the fighting in April 1917, when it appeared that the German-led Central Powers might win.

As it turned out, events engendered by the war in Europe actually promoted a temporary U.S. alliance with Japan. In May 1917, one month before the first U.S. troops were to arrive in Europe, a revolution in Russia overthrew the tzar. The Allies supported the new Russian government headed up by Alexander Kerensky, largely because they thought it would enable Russia to remain in the war. The war had taken a terrible toll on the country. More than 3.8 million Russians had been killed in the first ten months. By 1917 the economy had collapsed and there were food riots. People were desperate for an end to the fighting, but the Kerensky government disappointed them by yielding to Allied pressure and keeping Russia in the war.

Another revolution broke out in November, led by the Bolsheviks, who had demanded an immediate end to the fighting. The new Soviet government issued a Decree of Peace which called for the immediate opening of negotiations for a just and democratic peace. V. I. Lenin, the new head of state, gave content to the decree when he spoke out strongly against secret diplomacy and forced annexations.

The Allies were horrified. Not prepared to end the war short of total victory, they feared that a unilateral Russian decision to stop fighting would allow Germany to concentrate its forces on the western front. They also feared that a successful socialist revolution in Russia might trigger similar revolutions throughout Europe. Their response was to offer financial and military support to reactionary Russian generals whom they hoped would topple the new revolutionary government. That support included an organized invasion of the Soviet Republic by troops from fourteen nations.

Although the United States and Japan were rivals in China, their shared opposition to communism led them to jointly participate in the invasion. The United States sent 7,000 soldiers to Vladivostok in August 1918 and an additional 5,000 to the Russian port of Archangel in September. Japan, fearing that Soviet anti-imperialist propaganda might strengthen China's resistance to its activities in Manchuria and northern China, sent 70,000 troops to northern Manchuria and the Russian far east.

The internationally organized intervention caused great suffering in Russia, but did not succeed in destroying the revolution. Most Allied soldiers were tired of war and many were sympathetic to the revolution's aims. The Russian generals selected by the Allies for leadership also proved unable to offer an action program that could win popular support. In near mutiny, U.S. troops in Archangel refused to move to the front in March 1919. They were withdrawn by the end of June. The war did not go well in Siberia either: U.S. troops withdrew from Vladivostok in April 1920. The Japanese held on as long as they could, eventually withdrawing from Siberia in 1922 and later from Sakhalin in 1925.

When the Paris Peace Conference began in January 1919, the victorious Allied powers, with the Russian Revolution very much on their minds, tackled three important questions: how to punish Germany, stop the spread of communism in Europe, and divide the spoils of the war. They quickly resolved the first two by rearranging borders. The answer to the third was complicated by the Soviet peace offensive. In an effort to counteract Lenin, the Allies encouraged Wilson to craft an alternative statement of principles for achieving a just peace. Wilson complied, issuing his Fourteen Points in January 1919. The points included a call for freedom of navigation, removal of economic barriers to trade, reduction of armaments, the establishment of the League of Nations, and, most importantly in terms of U.S. relations with Korea, "a free, open-minded, and absolutely impartial adjustment of all colonial claims."

Koreans responded to the Fourteen Points with great excitement and hope. Koreans in Japan, China, and Hawaii began organizing in an effort to gain international support for Korean independence. A delegation of overseas Koreans was sent to address the Paris Peace Conference. Within Korea, nearly a million people peacefully demonstrated for independence. Beginning on March 1, 1919, the demonstrations (known as the "March First Movement") lasted for several months.

Wilson was not interested in challenging global power relations. Therefore, he took the position at the Paris conference that discussion of colonial claims should be limited only to those territories that had been taken from the defeated powers. Since Japan was one of the victors, a discussion of the status of Korea was inappropriate. The United States joined with Japan in blocking the attempt of the Korean delegation to address the Peace Conference. As for the activity in Korea, the State Department informed the U.S. ambassador in Japan in April 1919, "The Consulate [in Seoul] should be extremely careful not to encourage any belief that the United States will assist the Korean nationalists in carrying out their plans and that it should not do anything which may cause Japanese authorities to suspect American Government sympathizes with Korean nationalist movement."[16] Japan violently suppressed the March First Movement, and, true to its word, the United States remained silent.

The U.S. government's working relationship with Japan did not include the acceptance of Japan's activities in China. The United States tried unsuccessfully to use the Peace Conference to undo Japan's gains and restore China's territorial integrity. But because several countries, including Australia and New Zealand, wanted to annex German possessions, the United States could not force Japan to relinquish control over its newly acquired German holdings in China.

Determined to get its way, the United States organized the Washington Conference of 1921-1922 with one aim in mind: to reduce Japan's influence in China. The agenda included two simultaneous discussions. One addressed disarmament, the other addressed social and political concerns. The disarmament discussions lasted from November 1921 to February 1922 and culminated in a naval treaty signed by the United States, England, Japan, France, and Italy. The treaty limited the total tonnage of each country's ships and gun caliber in proportions favoring Britain and the United States. Another treaty resulted from the discussions on social and political concerns. Nine countries signed a formal statement pledging, among other things, "not to support any agreements . . . designed to create Spheres of Influence" in China. As a result of the treaty, Japan was forced to renounce the concessions it had won from China during the war. The limited nature of U.S. concerns was made clear when it blocked a delegation of Koreans from raising the issue of their independence.

The U.S. diplomatic victory was short-lived. No international agreements could stabilize the political situation in China as long as imperialism continued to exploit the country. Angered that the nine-country statement did not call for an end to the unequal trade treaties, extraterritoriality, or Japanese rule over Manchuria, Sun Yat-sen sought and received support from the Soviet government in 1923. That same year the Kuomintang joined forces with the Chinese Communist Party to establish a provisional all-China government in Canton, in opposition to the U.S.-recognized government in Beijing.

Sun's plan was to create a revolutionary army and make a Northern Expedition "not only to overthrow warlordism, but also to drive out imperialism upon which the warlords in China depend for their existence."[17] The Northern Expedition began in 1926, under Chiang Kai-shek's leadership, and despite Sun's death. Although the expedition initially enjoyed great success, Chiang was uneasy about working in alliance with the Communists. The Communists were committed to ending foreign domination of China. Chiang, on the other hand, wanted only to establish himself as ruler of a united and powerful China. Hoping to break the alliance for their own reasons, Western business interests and governments, as well as many wealthy Chinese, offered Chiang their financial and political support if he would break with the Communists. Chiang readily agreed and, in March 1927, his Kuomintang army turned its guns against the workers and Communists of Shanghai who had only weeks before helped him liberate the city. Similar massacres followed in Canton and Nanking. According to a 1949 State Department white paper on China, the purges in Shanghai and Canton "involved several hundred thousand deaths."[18]

Chiang established his own government in Nanking which quickly won foreign recognition. By 1929 it ruled over most of China, with the exception of Manchuria and some areas in the south which were still under Communist control. In the summer of 1929, Chiang, with the support of the local warlord, attempted to eliminate the remaining Soviet presence in northern Manchuria. He closed Soviet consulates in four cities, took over railway lines, and arrested hundreds of Soviet workers. But fighting broke out between the two countries, and after being badly beaten in several military encounters, Chiang agreed to restore the status quo. Chiang also launched a massive campaign in 1930 to defeat the Communists who had established their own government in Kiangsi province in the southeast. His Fifth Extermination campaign, which started in 1933, finally succeeded in driving the Communists out of the region. It did not, however, break their organization. From 1934 to 1935, Mao led the communists on their famous 6,000-mile Long March to northwest China, where he set up a new base in Yenan.

Chiang's ambitions were troubling for the Japanese. They could accept a unified China as long as its leadership respected Japan's special position in the country. Manchuria and Inner Mongolia were different; the Japanese viewed them as separate from China and wanted them under their own direct control. Thus, neither Chiang's attempt to unify China (including Manchuria) under his own rule nor the reassertion of Russian influence in northern Manchuria were acceptable.

In September 1931, the Japanese army decided to settle the issue of who controlled Manchuria. They drove out Chinese garrisons and seized control of the major south Manchurian cities. The League of Nations, with U.S. support, tried to force the Japanese to withdraw, but they refused. Instead, Japan began extending its operations from the south to the north of Manchuria. By early January 1932, Japan was in control of all of Manchuria. On February 18, it announced the transformation of Manchuria into the sovereign state of Manchukuo. Emboldened by their success in Manchuria, the Japanese extended their offensive and pushed into Mongolia in January 1933. Then, they invaded China proper, forcing Chiang to accept a demilitarized zone south of the Great Wall.

Alarmed by the rapid expansion of Japanese power, the U.S. government decided to resume diplomatic relations with the Soviet Union in 1933. One year later, worried about Japanese designs on the Philippines, it offered the Philippines independence, but only after a ten-year probationary period during which time the Filipino commonwealth (established in 1936) was to remain under U.S. supervision.

Although the Chinese soviet republic had declared war against the Japanese in April 1932, Chiang adopted a no-engagement policy. He remained far more concerned with defeating the Chinese Communists than resisting the Japanese. This policy was very unpopular among Chiang's troops, especially those that had been forced to withdraw in the face of Japanese aggression in Manchuria and northern China. Under the direction of their former warlord, Manchurian troops kidnapped Chiang when he visited the region in 1936 and forced him to join a united front with the Communists against Japan. The agreement, as it turned out, had little effect on Chiang's actions.

The agreement also did little to stop Japan's advance. In July 1937 Japanese troops on illegal midnight maneuvers near Beijing claimed they were attacked by Chinese railway guards. The Japanese rushed 10,000 troops to the area and made a number of demands on the Chinese government, including ones that would have turned North China into a Japanese protectorate. When Chiang refused to accept the demands, the Japanese launched an all-out invasion of the country. In December, the Japanese captured the capital, Nanking. The battle lasted some forty days, during which time Japanese troops engaged in numerous atrocities, including rape and the murder of some 300,000 Chinese civilians.

Chiang did not surrender. Rather, he withdrew with his armies to Chungking, in the southwest. This allowed the Japanese to easily take control over the eastern part of the country, with the exception of the northeast, where they encountered stiff Communist resistance. Chiang actually became distressed at the success of the Communists and initiated a blockade of the areas in which they were active.

The Western powers, including the United States, did little to aid China. Japan had once again made its move when Britain and France were concerned with European affairs, specifically the ambitions of Germany and Italy, and once again the United States was not prepared to risk war against Japan to save China. One reason for caution was that U.S. business with Japan far exceeded that with China. Approximately 19 percent of U.S. foreign trade from 1931 to 1935 was with Asia. Of that total, 43 percent was with Japan, 18 percent with the Philippines, and 14 percent with China. Japan was, in fact, America's third largest trading partner. It was also the largest Asian recipient of U.S. investment.[19]

Japan's decision to pursue a more aggressive policy toward Manchuria, Mongolia, and China during the 1930s was largely motivated by economic concerns. The collapse of world trade in 1929, with the onset of the Depression, triggered the formation of regional trading blocs. Japanese exports fell by 43 percent in value from 1929 to 1931, leading Japanese policymakers to conclude that the country needed to form its own regional economic bloc.[20] Japanese efforts focused on creating a tight inner ring of dependencies including Korea, Manchuria, and North China. The latter two had became major suppliers of coal and iron for Japan's heavy industry. Japan actually created a five-year plan for 1937 to 1941 that covered Japan, Manchukuo, and North China and specified production and import goals for key industries such as iron and steel, oil, coal, armaments, and shipbuilding. Korea remained an important producer and exporter of food to Japan. From 1935 to 1939, Korea exported about 40 percent of its rice crop to Japan. Korea also functioned as an important mining and manufacturing center. By 1941 it was producing significant quantities of iron and steel as well as light metals, chemicals, and magnesium.[21]

In spite of its regional success, Japan was not satisfied. Communist-led resistance, among other factors, kept northeast Asian production below expectations. Moreover, there were many important resources that the region could not supply in the quantities desired by the Japanese. Oil was one. Japan depended on the United States for 55 percent of its imported oil and Indonesia for another 20 percent.[22] To ensure a relatively self-sufficient economic system, Japanese planners realized as early as the mid-1930s that they had to expand their reach into southeast Asia. Japanese planners also realized that this expansion would be the most dangerous yet. Most southeast Asian countries were European colonies. British interests, in particular, would be directly threatened. Recognizing that war with the West was a possible outcome and using anticommunism as a pretext for military alliance, Japan signed its Anti-Comintern Pact with Germany in 1936. A 1940 treaty between Japan, Italy, and Germany obligated each country to come to the help of the others if any were attacked by a country "not involved in the current struggles." Taking advantage of German military victories in Europe, Japan began moving south in 1940.

The United States could no longer ignore Japan's regional challenge. Japanese actions in the context of European events posed a serious threat to U.S. interests worldwide. As the historian W. G. Beasley explains:

> [A]s Japanese moves toward Southeast Asia were becoming a factor in Britain's ability to resist the Axis powers . . . the United States began reluctantly to intervene. In September 1940 the American ambassador in Tokyo commented in a telegram to Washington that "American interests in the Pacific are definitely threatened by her [Japan's] policy of southward expansion, which is a thrust at the British Empire in the East." Given that the existence of the British empire was an element in America's own security, "we must strive by every means to preserve the status quo in the Pacific, at least until the war in Europe has been won or lost."[23]

The U.S. government responded to Japan's southward expansion with economic pressure. In 1940, it began limiting the export of scrap metal and petroleum to Japan. In 1941, it froze Japanese assets and embargoed all exports of iron and steel, brass, copper, zinc, and oil. Unwilling to reverse course, the Japanese government concluded that war with the United States was unavoidable. It launched a December 7, 1941, surprise attack on the Pearl Harbor naval base, hoping to weaken U.S. military capabilities.

U.S. Hegemony and Korea

The U.S. war effort in the Pacific began slowly. Although U.S. forces engaged the Japanese in a number of important battles during 1942, priority was given to winning the European war against Germany and Italy. This strategy meant that China had to face Japanese aggression for an unknown period of time before it could expect any direct and substantial U.S. assistance.

The United States continued to see China as the key to stability in the Pacific. President Franklin Roosevelt believed that it was China's weakness that led to the Pacific War, but that a renewed China, in alliance with the United States, could create a stable postwar Asia. Anxious to keep Chiang from making a deal with the Japanese, Roosevelt offered him enticements. In 1943, at U.S. urging, the Western powers agreed to terminate their rights to treaty ports and accept China as an equal power. The United States also invited China to participate in the 1943 Cairo Conference with Britain. The declaration ending this conference included a pledge that the three countries would continue to fight until Japan was defeated. The declaration also contained the first official wartime statement regarding Korea's postwar future: "The aforesaid three powers, mindful of the enslavement of the people of Korea, are determined that in due course Korea shall become free and independent."

After leaving Cairo, Roosevelt and British Prime Minister Winston Churchill met with the Soviet leader Joseph Stalin in Teheran. While explaining to Stalin his plan for Korea, Roosevelt clarified what he meant by "in due course." In the words of the Korean scholar Bong-youn Choy: "Roosevelt expressed his view that the Far Eastern colonial people would need some length of time for an education period to learn the art of self-government before full independence might be attained, as he had experienced to be true in the Philippines."[24]

Prior to the attack on Pearl Harbor, the U.S. government allowed Japan free reign in Korea in an attempt to secure Japan's recognition of U.S. interests in the Philippines and China. The Pacific War shifted the balance of power, leaving the United States and Japan in a struggle for supremacy in the region. Although Korea was not key to the outcome of this struggle, Roosevelt, looking to the future, understood that control over Korea, with its strategic location near Japan, China, and the Soviet Union, would significantly strengthen the U.S. government's ability to mold a postwar Asia responsive to U.S. interests.

Convinced that the time had come for the United States to put forward its claim to shape Korea's political future, Roosevelt initially preferred to create a Korean trusteeship solely under U.S. jurisdiction as he had done for the Philippines. However, the political-military realities of the struggle against Japan forced him to settle for indirect control through an international trusteeship. The United States desperately wanted the Soviet Union to join the war and take on the powerful Japanese armies in Manchuria and Korea, while U.S. forces carried the war directly to the Japanese home islands. There was no reasonable way for Roosevelt to convince the Soviets to undertake such a difficult task and then deny them a role in deciding Korea's postwar future. Soviet troops would likely be there on the ground; U.S. troops would not. An international trusteeship, where the Soviet Union's voice would be one of many, was thus as good a device for achieving U.S. aims as could be imagined. And at Teheran, the United States won general Soviet agreement to both entering the war against Japan and joining a trusteeship for Korea.

Roosevelt raised both war and trusteeship issues again in February 1945, when the leaders of Britain, the Soviet Union, and the United States met at Yalta. This time, Roosevelt was more specific about his trusteeship idea. It was to be a four-power trusteeship involving Great Britain, China, the Soviet Union, and the United States that would last anywhere from twenty to thirty years. "The shorter the period the better," Stalin is reported to have said.[25] Stalin also renewed his promise that the Soviet Union would enter the war against Japan, this time adding that because of the need to build up forces in the East, the likely date would be three months after the defeat of Germany. The three leaders also agreed on how to treat Germany after the war, including its division into occupation zones and reparations arrangements. Yalta represented the high point of U.S.-British-Soviet unity.

This unity did not last long. German armies were beginning to collapse and Churchill, no longer worried about the outcome of the war in Europe, soon began pressing Roosevelt to end the alliance with the Soviet Union.

In his opinion, Soviet-supported socialism was now the biggest threat to U.S. and British postwar interests. Roosevelt took a somewhat different position, believing that he could protect U.S. interests without an open break from the Soviet Union. However, after Roosevelt died in early April 1945, he was succeeded by Harry Truman, who held the same views as Churchill. After Truman conferred with his top advisors in April, Admiral Leahy, his chief of staff, summed up the general consensus as follows: "The time had arrived to take a strong American attitude toward the Soviet Union and that no particular harm could be done to our war prospects if Russia should slow down or even stop its war effort in Europe and Asia."[26]

The tide of battle in the Pacific had turned in favor of the U.S. forces. In the summer of 1944, they easily took Saipan, Tinian, and Guam. Iwo Jima was taken in the last week of March 1945, although with many casualties. The United States, seriously planning for a December invasion of Japan, stepped up its bombing campaign. A March 1945 air attack on Tokyo was estimated to have killed some 125,000 people.[27] After bombing raids in May and June, the Joint Chiefs of Staff predicted, "Japan will become a nation without cities, with her transportation disrupted, and will have tremendous difficulty in holding her people together for continued resistance."[28]

Germany surrendered on May 8, 1945, but from the perspective of U.S. policymakers its defeat left an unfortunately complex postwar political situation in Europe. The Soviet Union had emerged from the war with great prestige and a significant armed presence in Central and Eastern Europe which could not be ignored. In Asia, however, things were different. The Soviet Union had not yet joined the war against Japan. If the United States could defeat Japan without Soviet participation, it would be in a strong position to dictate postwar Asian politics. The stakes were high, as acting Secretary of State Joseph C. Grew made clear in May, when he wrote, "Once Russia is in the war against Japan, then Mongolia, Manchuria, and Korea will gradually slip into Russia's orbit, to be followed in due course by China and eventually Japan."[29]

U.S. intelligence had broken Japanese military codes and learned that although Japan's leaders realized they could not defeat the United States, they were willing to keep fighting in hopes of winning an acceptable negotiated end to the war. Most importantly, this meant a guaranteed postwar role for the emperor. However, the United States also learned that

Japan would reconsider this position and surrender unconditionally if the Soviet Union entered the war. Thus U.S. foreign policy imperatives, seeking to prevent Soviet participation in the war while aiming for Japan's unconditional surrender, required U.S. forces to either invade Japan or, if it became possible in time, drop an atomic bomb on Japan to force a speedy conclusion to the war.

Churchill wanted a meeting with Stalin and Truman in May or June 1945 to attempt to settle European affairs while U.S. troops were still present. Truman, however, delayed the Potsdam meeting until July. The reason was the bomb; it would not be ready for testing until then, and Truman did not want to meet with Stalin until he knew its status. The first U.S. atomic test took place in New Mexico on July 16, 1945, one day after the start of the Potsdam Conference. On July 21, Truman received a detailed report about the bomb's enormous destructive power. From that point on, he aggressively confronted Stalin, who knew nothing about the bomb, demanding changes in past agreements. For example, the United States and Britain had previously agreed to recognize Soviet influence in Bulgaria and Romania in exchange for Soviet recognition of British dominance in Greece. Now, Truman told Stalin that he would not recognize the newly formed Bulgarian and Romanian governments. Truman also backtracked on agreements made at Yalta concerning Germany, in particular those dealing with Soviet rights to reparations.

Truman had little desire to negotiate with the Soviets and was eager to end the Potsdam Conference as quickly as possible. The only formal document to come out of the conference was the Potsdam Declaration of July 26, 1945, which spelled out the Allied terms of surrender for Japan. Signed by the United States, Britain, and China, the declaration demanded the unconditional surrender of Japan, offering no assurance about the future status of the emperor. Moreover, at U.S. insistence, the Soviet Union was excluded from the drafting of, or mention in, the final declaration. With this strategy, the United States hoped to continue the war without Soviet involvement until it was ready to win it by dropping the bomb.

The Japanese, still hoping to negotiate an end to the war, and puzzled by the absence of a Soviet endorsement of the Potsdam Declaration, made no formal response. The U.S. government eagerly took Japan's diplomatic silence to mean rejection and on the morning of August 6, dropped an atomic bomb on Hiroshima. On August 8, the Soviet Union declared war against Japan, exactly three months after the defeat of Germany. The following morning, Soviet troops crossed into Manchuria and Korea. Later that same day, the United States dropped an atomic bomb on Nagasaki.

On August 10, the Japanese government sent word through its Ministry of Foreign Affairs that it would accept the terms of the Potsdam Declaration with one condition: the emperor was to be protected. On August 11, the United States sent back a carefully worded statement which treated Japan's statement of surrender as being unconditional while also suggesting a willingness to negotiate a continuing role for the emperor. The U.S. position on preserving the emperor had changed; now the emperor could be permitted to remain as a figurehead, so as to ensure both a quick Japanese surrender and compliance with U.S. dictates.

While the United States waited for Japan's official announcement of surrender, Soviet troops were on the move in Manchuria and Korea. The U.S. government now had reason to fear that war's end would find the Soviet Union in a position to exert strong influence on postwar developments in China, Manchuria, Korea, and thus Japan. Edwin Pauley, U.S. special ambassador on assignment in Moscow, cabled Truman that "quick action in the Far East to prevent Russian excesses" was needed. He recommended that the United States "occupy quickly as much as possible of the industrial areas of Korea (the north) and Manchuria."[30] Averell Harriman, U.S. ambassador to the Soviet Union, gave the same advice, calling for "American landings [to] be made to accept surrender of the Japanese troops at least on the Kwantung Peninsula and in Korea."[31]

The State-War-Navy Coordinating Committee held several long sessions to decide what to do. The Soviets were in possession of most of Manchuria but had previously agreed to respect Chinese authority there. Korea was the real question. Dean Rusk, who was at the time a colonel on the War Department General Staff described what happened:

> The Department of State had suggested that U.S. forces receive the surrender as far north as practical. The military was faced with the scarcity of U.S. forces immediately available and time and space factors which would make it difficult to reach very far north before Soviet troops . . . could enter the area.
>
> [The War Department] asked, on August 11, Col. C. B. Bonesteel III, and me, to come up with a proposal which would harmonize the political desire to have U.S. forces receive the surrender as far north as possible and the U.S. forces ability

to reach the area. We recommended the 38th parallel . . . because we felt it important to include the capital of Korea in the area of responsibility of American troops.[32]

Truman accepted the recommendation. General Order No. 1, a U.S. document setting the overall terms for the surrender of Japanese forces, included a statement that U.S. forces would accept the surrender of Japanese troops in Korea south of the 38th parallel. The Japanese formally announced their surrender on August 14, and the following day Truman sent a copy of General Order No. 1 to the leaders of other key countries. It was formally issued on September 2. Much to the surprise of U.S. planners, neither the Chinese nor the Soviets objected to the U.S. plan for the "division of Korea."

U.S. political leaders claim that it was the atomic bombings of Japan that brought the war to a successful conclusion, thus saving millions of American lives. But that is not true. Even at the time, few in the U.S. military thought that the bombings were necessary. An official study by the U.S. Strategic Bombing Survey, published less than a year after the bombings, concluded that Japan would most likely have surrendered in 1945 without the dropping of the atomic bomb and without the U.S. invasion of Japan.[33] Admiral William D. Leahy came to a similar conclusion, writing in his 1950 memoirs that "It is my opinion that the use of this barbarous weapon at Hiroshima and Nagasaki was of no material assistance in our war against Japan. The Japanese were already defeated and ready to surrender."[34] The bomb was used twice (causing some 300,000 deaths, about as many as were caused by all the conventional bombing), not for military reasons but because Truman wanted to exclude the Soviet Union from participation in the war and the surrender negotiations, and because he thought its use would be an effective way to signal to the Soviet Union that the United States was prepared to respond to any Soviet challenge with unmatched force.

Along with the long history of U.S. political and economic expansion in the region, this determination to achieve global hegemony provides the appropriate context for understanding post-1945 U.S. interest in Korea. The United States was determined to limit Soviet influence in China and Japan. Holding onto Korea, or at least part of it, was key to this wider Asian strategy of U.S. policymakers.

On September 7, 1945, General Douglas MacArthur issued Proclamation No. 1, which established a U.S. military government in south Korea; the next day U.S. troops arrived to take control. Trusting Korea's future to Koreans was not on the U.S. agenda. Truman made this clear on September 18, 1945, when he said that the "assumption by the Koreans themselves of the responsibilities and functions of a free and independent nation . . . will of necessity require time and patience."[35]

Chapter 2

The Korean Struggle for Independence and Democracy

An expansionist U.S. foreign policy bent upon securing Korea as an outpost for regional dominance in Asia is only half the background contributing to the profound conflicts that erupted following the 1945 arrival of U.S. forces in southern Korea. The other half lies in Korea's own political and economic history. North and South Korean historians today disagree on many things. They do agree, however, that foreign intervention was "the main distorting factor in the country's modern fate."[1] Korea's pre-liberation history offers considerable supporting evidence for this statement. It also offers many examples of popular resistance to foreign oppression and struggles for independence and democracy. Finally, it provides insight into why Truman's special ambassador, Edwin Pauley, thought, "Communism in [postwar] Korea could get off to a better start than practically anywhere else in the world."[2]

Foreign Intervention and the Decline of the Choson Dynasty

Korea was ruled by the Choson or Yi dynasty from 1392 to 1910. Yi Song-gye, its founder, inherited a political economy that was designed to maintain a stable agrarian social order. The king, while having title to all the land, was, in most cases, obligated to collect and share a percentage of the harvest produced on it. High officials, for example, were paid a fixed percentage of the harvest from designated "stipend lands." The more important the official, the larger and better his land holdings and the greater his stipend. Similarly, the king enjoyed rights to a share of the harvest from his own royal estate land, while local government functionaries, soldiers, public agencies, schools, and temples were each supported by a harvest tax collected on their own specially designated lands. In a very real sense, the king functioned primarily as a rent collector. The very highest-ranking officials enjoyed the only major exception to this pattern. They also received "merit land," on which they could set and collect their own rent.

There were tensions in this arrangement. Wealthy families often battled each other to gain influence with the king in order to secure top positions in the bureaucracy and obtain the associated land benefits. To maintain peace, the king was often forced to both increase the number of officials and the amount of land designated as stipend or merit land. This, in turn, reduced the revenue available to support state functions, leading to a higher tax burden on the peasant farmers working the land. When the burden became too great, the peasants would rebel, sometimes taking up arms and at other times leaving the land. Over time, the balance of power in Korea shifted in favor of the aristocracy, leaving the state short of funds and the peasants heavily exploited.

When Yi took power in a military coup, his first act was to destroy all the registers of public and private land as part of a sweeping land reform designed to undermine the aristocracy. At the same time, he began to appoint members of the literati to high positions in the state. They were paid with a harvest tax from the newly created category of "rank land," that was limited to an area around the capital. The rest of the country's land was designated as state land to be used only in support of state activities.

In the short term, Yi's actions did create a more stable revenue base for the state. But over time and under successive kings, the literati were able to increase their land holdings and transform themselves into a new ruling class, known as the *yangban*. By the mid-sixteenth century, as increasingly more public land fell under *yangban* control, the Choson state faced its own serious fiscal crisis.

During this period of economic strain in Korea a new leader, Toyotomi Hideyoshi, came to power in Japan. An expansionist, he organized an attack on Korea in 1592. As the Japanese easily pushed north toward Seoul, the king and high officials took flight. The Japanese advance was halted, however, when Korean Admiral Yi Sun-sin employed the world's first iron plated fighting ships to attack and destroy the Japanese fleet, making it impossible for Japan to reinforce or supply its troops. Within the country, farmers and slaves formed guerrilla armies. In concert with some 50,000 soldiers sent by Ming China, these grassroots forces succeeded in driving the Japanese back to the southeast coast. A period of peace negotiations followed until Japan launched a new attack in 1597. This time, the Korean and Chinese armies had little difficulty stopping the Japanese land offensive. Admiral Yi again defeated the larger Japanese fleet. Hideyoshi died in mid-1598, and by the end of the year Japan agreed to peace terms.

The many years of fighting took its toll on the Korean peasantry. By disrupting farm production, it also weakened the government's tax base. Taking advantage of Korea's difficult situation, the Manchus, who now ruled China, invaded the country in 1627. They easily overwhelmed Korean forces, leaving the Korean king with no choice but to sue for peace. Not long after, the Manchus demanded that the king acknowledge the Manchu emperor's suzerainty. When the king refused, the Manchus invaded again in 1636. The king quickly capitulated and Korea was required to pay tribute to the Manchu rulers, leading to even greater hardships on the farming population.

Unable to stabilize living conditions or defend the nation, the Choson state slowly began to lose its legitimacy. Many peasants left Korea, immigrating to Manchuria or Siberia. Others rose in protest, often led by the so-called "fallen *yangban*," members of the elite by birth who were unable to secure government employment due to the shortage of bureaucratic positions. The largest and most important uprising took place in 1862. Farmers armed with bamboo spears killed local government officials and burned government buildings.

It was at this time that Ch'oe Che-u began the Tonghak religion, a blend of Confucianism, Buddhism, Taoism, Catholicism, and Shamanism. Ch'oe Che-u preached the unity of humans and god. Since the human spirit was a replica of god, serving god meant serving people. In other words, according to the Tonghak religion, each person had an obligation to join with others to right social wrongs. This religion attracted many peasants and quickly became the foundation for a broader social movement for change. Ch'oe Che-u predicted that there would be a major revolutionary upheaval in 1864. The government responded by arresting him in 1863 and executing him the following year.

A new king was inaugurated in 1864, but since he was still too young to rule at only twelve years of age, his father, the Taewon'gun (or regent), actually ruled. The Taewon'gun succeeded in rebuilding the revenue base of the government through a series of tax reforms and used the funds to strengthen the country's military. Aware of what happened to China, the Taewon'gun rejected any contact with the West. He launched a major anti-Catholic campaign in 1866 that left nine French missionaries and some 8,000 Korean converts dead. In retaliation, the French sent warships, disembarked their troops, and tried to march toward Seoul. They were repulsed, however, and forced to withdraw.

In 1871 the U.S. Asiatic Squadron sent five warships to Korea, in part to avenge the 1866 killings of the crew of the *General Sherman*. After being fired upon, U.S. Marines attacked forts on Kanghwa Island, which guarded the river entrance to Seoul. Unable to make contact with the Korean court to gain either an apology or commercial treaty, the fleet soon withdrew. After that victory, the Taewon'gun placed stone markers on main streets in Seoul and at other important points in the country reading, "Western barbarians invade our land. If we do not fight, we must then appease them. To urge appeasement is to betray the nation."[3]

Korea had managed up to this point to keep the West at bay. This was a result of Korean determination, but it was also a result of the preoccupation of France, the United States, Britain, and Russia with other countries. "Opening" Korea was not a priority for any of them. But Japan was in a different situation. Facing its own threat from the West, Japan viewed domination of Korea as vital to its national interest. In September 1875, Japan created an incident that would give it the opportunity to assert its interest in Korea. A Japanese survey fleet was sent into Korean waters where it successfully provoked an attack by Korean coastal batteries. Japan then sent a naval squadron to demand that Korea sign an (unequal) treaty of "friendship, commerce, and navigation." After some hesitation, the Korean government, with encouragement from China, agreed and signed the Treaty of Kanghwa in February 1876. Hoping to dilute Japan's influence, the Korean government negotiated similar treaties with the United States in May 1882, Britain and Germany in June 1882, Russia in 1884, and France in 1886.

The new treaties created possibilities for Korean scholars and officials to visit other countries. Many went to Japan and were impressed by the country's rapid industrialization; they advocated that Korea follow Japan's practices. The Korean government concurred, introducing a number of similar economic reforms and employing Japanese advisors. This pro-Japanese drift led to strong anti-Japanese sentiment among many Koreans who felt that their government was falling under Japan's influence. The result was the 1882 Imo incident; soldiers rose in revolt, attacked Japanese facilities in Korea, and tried to overthrow the ruling family. The king was forced to call upon Chinese forces to suppress the uprising, and China took advantage of the situation to reassert its political position in Korea.

China's intervention greatly angered those Koreans who supported the earlier Japanese-influenced reforms. In what is known as the Kapsin incident, Korean rebels attempted to seize power in an 1884 palace coup but were defeated by Chinese troops after three days of fighting. The Japanese minister in Korea had initially offered the rebels assistance, but at the last minute he changed his mind. Embarrassed by the outcome, the Japanese government proposed that Japan and China simultaneously withdraw troops from Korea and that each government notify the other if it planned to send troops in the future. China accepted.

The king, now worried about the extent of China's influence, sought to increase Russia's involvement in Korean affairs. When the British and Japanese blocked this strategy, the king turned to the United States in an unsuccessful attempt to gain protection. The result of this maneuvering was that China remained the dominant power in Korea. But the political situation was far from stable. The foreign penetration of the Korean economy and corruption among the Korean aristocracy led to heavier financial burdens being placed on the peasantry. The following couplet, popular at the time, provides some feeling for the extent of their dissatisfaction:

As the drips of the candle on the banquet table fall, so do the tears of
  the people;
and as music swells in merry-making, the outcry of the discontented
  masses becomes the more clamorous.[4]

Growing numbers of Koreans, moreover, had continued to embrace the Tonghak religion in spite of the execution of its founder. The Tonghak called for an end to foreign interference, including expulsion of all foreigners; better treatment for peasants including equitable distribution of farmland, fair taxes, and cancellation of existing debts; and administrative reforms including the firing of corrupt officials.[5] In 1894, Chon Pong-jun, a regional Tonghak leader, decided that action should be taken to improve the lot of the peasants. He led an armed uprising in Cholla and South Ch'ungch'ong provinces under the banner "sustain the nation and provide for the people." Later that year, Chon called for a march on Seoul to demand that the king adopt the Tonghak program.

Alarmed by this popular mobilization, although it was not aimed at toppling the monarchy, the king sent a battalion of his elite troops to stop the march. When it was defeated by the growing Tonghak army, the king turned to the Chinese government for help. China sent troops, as did Japan, under the pretext that they were needed to protect Japanese lives and property. Realizing that his actions had placed his rule in danger, the king offered, and the Tonghak agreed, to discuss their differences peacefully. He also encouraged the Chinese government to propose to Japan the simultaneous withdrawal of Chinese and Japanese troops from Korea, but Japan rejected the proposal.

After a period of unsuccessful negotiations, Japanese troops seized the Korean palace in August 1894 and then attacked the Chinese forces. The Chinese were badly beaten and driven out of Korea by October. The Tonghak took up arms again, this time against the Japanese forces, but they too were defeated. The war between China and Japan ended in complete victory for Japan. Under the terms of the 1895 Treaty of Shimonoseki, China acknowledged Korea's independence, ceded the Liaotung peninsula and Taiwan to Japan, and agreed to pay an indemnity and negotiate a new commercial treaty with Japan. Japan did not get to enjoy the full fruits of victory, however. Russia strongly opposed the agreement, in particular Japan's move into Manchuria. Joined by France and Germany, Russia pressured Japan into renouncing its Manchurian claims, weakening Japanese prestige in Korea.

Anti-Japanese leaders in Korea now eagerly turned to Russia for salvation. With the backing of the influential Korean Queen Min, many pro-Russian Koreans were appointed to positions of authority in the Korean government. Unwilling to accept the resulting loss of influence, the Japanese minister to Korea encouraged sympathetic Koreans who, in October 1895, assassinated the queen in a failed attempt to take power. The king, fearing for his life, took up residence in the Russian legation for an entire year. Popular anger against Japan grew so strong that "righteous armies" were formed throughout the country to attack Japanese troops and pro-Japanese reformers. Most Koreans also strongly disapproved of their king living in a foreign legation, dispensing favors to foreign governments and corporations. One group sought to restore a sense of national dignity by forming the Independence Club in 1896. Led primarily by intellectuals who had lived and studied in the United States, the club mounted successful fundraising campaigns to build an Independence Arch and Park. The members also pushed for social, economic, and political reforms without, however, challenging the authority of the king. In fact, they encouraged the king to declare himself an emperor, thereby making him equal to the Chinese ruler. Sensing widespread support for these independence-related activities, the king returned to the palace and arranged for the recall of his Russian advisors. Initially, he supported the efforts of the club leadership, but when their criticism of his rule became too sharp, he had them arrested, and the Independence Club was dissolved in December 1898.

Within two years, Korea's independence was again threatened by international developments. Western and Japanese forces were sent to Beijing to stop the anti-foreign Yi He Tuan Uprising. Russia, taking advantage of the chaos, sought new economic concessions in both Korea and Manchuria, where it sent additional troops. The following statement from the Japanese minister at St. Petersburg indicated Japan's concern:

> Russia, stationed on the flank of Korea, would be a constant menace to the separate existence of that empire, and in any event it would make Russia the dominant power in Korea. Korea is an important outpost in Japan's line of defense, and the Japanese consequently consider the independence of Korea absolutely essential to her own repose and safety. . . . Japan possesses paramount political as well as economic and industrial interests and influence in Korea which, having regard to her own security, she cannot consent to surrender to, or share with, any other power.[6]

Japan, with British and U.S. support, demanded that Russia withdraw its forces from Manchuria. Russia refused, and in February 1904, when negotiations proved fruitless, Japan carried out a surprise attack on the Russian forces in southern Manchuria. During this time, Japan also went on the offensive in Korea, forcing the king to sign agreements that removed all constraints on Japanese military operations in the country and gave Japanese advisors oversight power in the Ministries of Finance and Foreign Affairs. In the midst of the war, Japan reduced the size of the Korean army and took control over all postal and telegraph services. By 1905, the Russians were defeated, and by the terms of the Treaty of Portsmouth they were forced to acknowledge Japan's "paramount political, military, and economic interests" in Korea.

Korea was now completely vulnerable, without a foreign "protector" powerful enough to challenge Japan. The only two possible candidates, Britain and the United States, had already pledged to recognize Japan's hegemony over Korea in exchange for Japan's recognition of British inter-ests in China (in the Anglo-Japanese Alliance of 1902) and U.S. colonial interests in Hawaii and the Philippines (in the Taft-Katsura Memorandum of 1905). Unchallenged, Japan waited only two months after the end of the war to forcibly establish a protectorate over Korea.

To ensure that Korea would remain a low-cost, trouble-free colony, Japan kept the monarchy but ruled Korea through a resident-general, a position created under the terms of the protectorate treaty. Japan, in fact, sought to project itself as a civilizing agent in Korea, hoping in this way to demon-strate the superiority of its brand of imperialism over that practiced by the West, and thus to weaken potential Asian opposition to its broader plans for regional expansion.

Many Koreans resisted Japan's authority. The king publicized the fact that no Korean official agreed to the protectorate treaty and declared it illegal, and some of the aristocracy organized new "righteous armies" to fight the Japanese troops. Embarrassed by this opposition, the Japanese leadership forced the king to abdicate in favor of his son, who agreed to a new treaty in 1907. This treaty gave the resident-general greatly expanded powers that he immediately used to disband the Korean army. But rather than return quietly to their homes, the soldiers kept their weapons and joined the "righteous armies," greatly improving their effectiveness. The number of Japanese casualties in encounters with these armies rose from 3 killed and 2 wounded in 1906 to 75 killed and 170 wounded in 1908. The Korean death toll also rose, from 82 in 1906 to 11,562 in 1908.[7]

Popular resistance led the Japanese government to seek direct control over Korea through annexation. This decision was also prompted by U.S.-Japanese emigration problems. Japan had promised the United States to restrict Japanese immigration to California. Korea was to be the alternative destination. Japan first increased its military presence in Korea and then negotiated a treaty of annexation with the powerless Korean prime minister. On August 22, 1910, the Choson dynasty and Korean independence came to an end. Fearing negative Korean public reaction, the Japanese kept news of the treaty secret for one week; they used that time to arrest leading Korean nationalists and disband Korean patriotic organizations.

Korea Under Japanese Rule

The direct instrument of Japanese rule in Korea was a colonial government headed by a military officer, the governor-general, who was appointed by the Japanese emperor. Because Korea was geographically close, the Japanese government set out to create "a tight, highly centralized governance for Korea. This was not a remote colony, far removed from the daily concerns of Japan proper. The Japanese conceived their presence in Korea as vital to the general strategic and economic fortunes of the homeland."[8] The governor-general was thus given enormous power to direct a large and ever growing colonial bureaucracy which had as its objective the control of all significant economic and political activity in Korea.

Ultimately, of course, Japanese rule rested on repression. The governor-general suspended all Korean newspapers, disbanded all Korean political organizations, and made public gatherings illegal. Resistance was met with force as the number of military and civilian police rose from 6200 in 1910 to 20,800 in 1922. By 1941, there were more than 60,000 policeman, or 1 for every 400 Koreans.[9] The police had considerable authority, including oversight rights in education, religion, and tax collection. They even had summary power with regard to misdemeanors. One measure of their activity was the number of police arrests, which rose from 50,000 in 1912 to 140,000 in 1918.[10] Significantly, the Japanese also recruited large numbers of Koreans to serve in the colonial police force. In fact, about half the force was Korean. As a result, Koreans who resisted Japanese colonialism usually came face to face with a system of repression within which Koreans themselves played an important role.

Japan's immediate economic interest in Korea was as a producer of food and raw materials. Thus one of the colonial government's first actions was to initiate a comprehensive land survey from 1910 to 1918, the purpose of which was to establish the land relations necessary to guarantee the desired export of food and primary products to Japan. The survey involved mapping all existing plots of land, classifying them according to their type and productivity, and most importantly, establishing ownership.

As part of the survey process, the Japanese created a complex system in which Koreans were required to document their ownership; those who could not or did not understand the requirements of the registration system had their land seized by the colonial government. This happened to many small farmers. The system also allowed the colonial government to legally seize all lands that had previously been classified as public or royal land. As a result, the colonial government became Korea's largest landholder. In 1930 it held approximately 40 percent of the total land area of Korea.[11] It eventually sold some of the best land at bargain prices to Japanese development companies and individual Japanese farmers.

Not all Koreans were disenfranchised by this land program. The governor-general was more than willing to allow a small number of already powerful Korean landowners, especially those who demonstrated their willingness to cooperate with Japan, to use the survey process to expand their holdings. The flip side of this process was a marked increase in tenancy rates, some as high as 80 percent in the most fertile areas of the southwest. In addition to rents which often averaged 50 percent of the harvest, tenants also had to pay for seeds, water rights, and fertilizer. Under such conditions most peasants struggled just to survive. Tenants generally paid rent and other obligations to their landlords in rice. Landlords, on the other hand, had their taxes assessed in monetary terms. The common result was that landlords sold rice to the colonial government, which in turn shipped it to Japan. But while greater irrigation, fertilizer, and farm machinery did support an increase in rice production of approximately 40 percent from 1912 to 1935, exports rose by more than eight times that amount. In other words, Koreans were providing rice for the Japanese market at a sacrifice to themselves. Korean consumption actually fell over this period by approximately 62 percent on a per capita basis.[12]

The Japanese economy grew rapidly from 1900 to 1929, and as Japan industrialized, Japanese interest in Korea changed. In 1911, the colonial government passed a law that made the establishment of new industries in Korea illegal without the permission of the governor-general. This restriction was dropped in 1920 in response to pressure from Japanese investors. Consequently, Korea also began to industrialize. During most of the 1920s, Japanese investment was largely focused in the south and in low-wage light manufacturing, especially textiles and food preparation. This pattern of investment began to change by the end of the decade, however, as Japan began taking steps to create an integrated heavy and chemical industrial sector in northeast Asia. In 1926, for example, the Japanese began building hydroelectric power stations in the north. This was followed in 1927 by the construction of a huge fertilizer plant. This trend accelerated greatly after Japan's 1931 conquest of Manchuria. With state support, Japan's giant conglomerates or *zaibatsu* built a massive electrical-chemical complex in northern Korea which included plants producing munitions for the Japanese military.

Labor for these large-scale industrial projects was primarily provided by poor tenant farmers from the south who were brought north through government and corporate programs. Before 1937, desperate farming conditions generated migration flows sufficient to meet Japanese needs. After 1937 and the start of the Pacific War, Japanese labor demands greatly increased. "Voluntary" migration was no longer adequate; a system of forced labor mobilizations was therefore introduced.

The overall impact of Japanese policy and investment on the Korean economy was enormous. Between 1911 and 1938, Korea actually grew faster than Japan.[13] The industrial structure of the Korean economy was also transformed. The share of manufacturing (including mining and timber) in GNP rose to approximately 18 percent by 1931 and 40 percent by 1939. Within manufacturing, the share of the chemical industry rose from less than 10 percent in 1930 to 34 percent in 1939.[14]

This industrial transformation also brought closer ties between the Korean and Japanese economies. By 1931, 95 percent of all Korean exports were going to Japan and 80 percent of all Korean imports were coming from

Japan. By 1939, Korea had become Japan's main export market, accounting for approximately 34 percent of all Japanese exports. Equally significant was the change in the composition of trade between the two countries. While raw materials accounted for more than 80 percent of Korean exports to Japan in 1929, their share fell to less than 50 percent by 1939. Over the same period, manufactures as a percentage of Korean exports to Japan rose from approximately 13 percent to almost 46 percent.[15]

This Japanese-directed industrialization also had a major impact on Korea's class structure. Although Japan dominated the Korean economy, the colonial government did allow the growth of a Korean capitalist class. As a case in point, in 1938 there were 740 Korean and 804 Japanese owners of manufacturing companies and 258 Korean and 274 Japanese owners of transport/storage companies. There was, of course, a great difference in the relative size of these Korean and Japanese firms. The ratio of paid-in capital between Korean and Japanese firms was 1 to 7 in the manufacturing sector and 1 to 10 in the shipping sector. Japanese domination of mining activity was even greater.[16]

Korea's industrial labor force also grew rapidly. There were approximately 385,000 factory workers in 1932. This number rose to nearly 600,000 in 1936 and reached 700,000 in 1940. By 1943, the number of workers exceeded 1.3 million. Even these numbers greatly underestimate the increase in the number of Korean industrial workers. They do not include the tens of thousands of Koreans who worked in mining and transportation, nor do they include the hundreds of thousands of Koreans who worked in Manchuria and Japan.[17] Unsurprisingly, Japanese planners carried out their industrialization policies with little regard for the well-being of these Korean workers. Wages in 1935 were 50 percent lower than they had been in 1927. The normal industrial day was lengthened over the same period from twelve to sixteen hours. In addition, the rates for industrial accidents, diseases, and death were very high because health and safety considerations were nonexistent.[18]

Korean Resistance

Resistance to foreign rule from within Korea was slow to rebuild after the Japanese annexation. Fighters in the "righteous armies" had been forced to flee the country, although they continued to attack the Japanese from newly established base camps in the Soviet far east and Manchuria. It was not until 1919 that Koreans were again able to mount a direct challenge to Japan's rule over Korea.

Ironically, the impetus for this challenge originated in Japan. The colonial government in Korea had established a highly discriminatory education system that included separate schools for Korean and Japanese students. Because the Korean system ended at the secondary level, those students who were interested in higher education had no other alternative but to attend college in Japan. While there, many became radicalized through their contact with radical Japanese student groups. In February 1919 some 600 of these Korean students organized a demonstration where they declared Korea's independence and called for support from the Western powers attending the Versailles meeting in Paris.

Strongly influenced by the efforts of these Korean students, thirty-three religious leaders in Korea drafted and signed a Declaration of Independence. It was read publicly on March 1, and more than 2 million people ultimately participated in demonstrations in support of its message. The events of March 1 had been planned secretly and caught Japan unprepared. The Japanese, refusing to believe that Koreans could organize such an action on their own, initially blamed Western missionaries. Kim San, a youthful participant in the March First Movement, tells how his middle school teacher explained the movement's strategy to his class: "Today marks the declaration of Korean independence. There will be peaceful demonstrations all over Korea. If our meetings are orderly and peaceful, we shall receive the help of President Wilson and the great powers at Versailles, and Korea will be a free nation."[19] According to Kim San, the response of the Japanese was confused:

> They didn't know what to do. Such a movement puzzled them by its intensity no less than by its peaceableness. But they quickly decided. On the second day they arrested the leaders and up to May 21, when the movement stopped, arrested altogether 300,000 people. All the hospitals and schools were turned into prison camps. My middle school was one of these temporary prisons. Two-thirds of those arrested were freed after a short detention, after having been beaten. The other 100,000 were "legally" arrested and sent to court. About 50,000 of these were sentenced to imprisonment. Not one was executed—there was no legal excuse for this. The Korean civil law forbade this, as the demonstrators had openly and insistently announced that, "We struggle only for Korean independence and

not against Japan." Execution was legal only for murder, so the Japanese killed the people on the streets instead of arresting them—a nice Japanese technicality.[20]

Significantly, there was no outcry from either the United States or any other Western country against Japan's brutal suppression of the movement.

The defeat of the March First Movement marked a significant turning point in the development of the Korean independence movement. Many in the leadership concluded that without foreign support there could be no progress toward achieving Korean independence. Some decided that the best way to encourage that support was to leave Korea for Shanghai, where they could work with the Korean Provisional Government (KPG). The KPG was formed in April 1919 by Koreans living in Manchuria, China, Siberia, and the United States. Excited by the extent of popular participation in the March 1 demonstrations, these Koreans thought that the time was ripe to form a Korean government in exile. The KPG was initially dominated by Koreans from two groups: a conservative "U.S. group" and a radical "Siberian-Manchurian group."

The U.S. group earned its name because leading members, including Syngman Rhee, had spent considerable time in the United States and because it looked to President Woodrow Wilson to lead the fight for Korean independence. The U.S. group exercised considerable influence in the KPG in large part because most of the money that supported the organization was raised in the United States.

The leaders of the Siberian-Manchurian group had long been active in military struggle against Japan from bases in Siberia and Manchuria. For example, Yi Tong-hwi had founded a military school and army in Manchuria in 1914. He and others in this group were socialists who welcomed the Russian Revolution. In fact many Koreans living in the Russian far east joined with the Bolsheviks to fight against the invasion of the Soviet Union. Yi founded the Korean Socialist Party in 1918.

Yi and the other leaders of the Siberian-Manchurian group were willing to join with the U.S. group to advance a more powerful and broad-based armed struggle against the Japanese. Rhee and the U.S. group, however, insisted that the KPG should follow a political strategy based on winning Western support for Korean independence. Convinced that this was the wrong strategy, especially after a KPG envoy had been denied the right to make a presentation at the Paris peace talks, Yi finally broke with the KPG in 1921. He later organized the Korean Communist Party in Khabarovsk, with support from Lenin.

The KPG remained under conservative leadership and was largely ineffective. It never changed its strategy even though it repeatedly failed to win international recognition. Its leaders gradually lost contact with the struggle in Korea and little was heard from the KPG until it declared war against Japan in a meaningless gesture in 1937.

The majority of those who led the March First Movement remained in the country after its defeat. While some decided that resistance of any kind was pointless, most argued for a new strategy based on the assumption that Korea had to build its national resources before it could hope to win Western support for its independence. According to this strategy, the elite had an obligation to ensure that Japanese colonialism did not succeed in destroying Korean culture or leadership. "Cultural nationalists" began negotiating with the Japanese for expanded opportunities in education and business. They launched two major projects in 1922. The first was the National University Movement, whose goal was to raise funds for a Korean-controlled national university. The second was the Gandhi-influenced Korean Production Movement, whose goal was the creation of a self-sufficient, Korean-controlled national economy.

The Japanese government found it easy to co-opt these efforts. Having concluded that the March First Movement was the consequence of the harsh rule of the governor-general, it replaced him and declared a new era of "harmony between Japan and Korea." The new governor-general promised to end the divided educational system and build a major university in Seoul. This quickly undercut the National University Movement. He also succeeded, although it took longer, in undermining the Korean Production Movement. "At its height in the summer of 1923, the Korean Production Movement had become the most successful mass mobilization of Koreans since the March First Movement. It heightened mass awareness of economic issues, and it altered, at least temporarily, Korean consumption habits."[21] But after the governor-general banned national advertisements and marches in Seoul, lowered tariffs to make foreign goods cheaper, and (perhaps most importantly) bought off major Korean capitalists by allowing them to participate in planning committees and receive subsidies for their own enterprises, this movement also lost energy.

The cultural nationalist movement proved a failure. But Japan's success in co-opting it did not mean the end of the Korean independence movement. Instead it became radically transformed under the increasingly effective leadership of leftists, especially communists.

The Rise of the Left

Socialist and revolutionary ideas became increasingly popular in Korean intellectual circles in the early 1920s, thanks to the efforts of Koreans who had previously studied and become radicalized in Japan. On their return to Korea they set up socialist-oriented study groups, journals, and youth organizations, and worked to strengthen unions and tenant farmer groups. They also attacked both the National University Movement and the Korean Production Movement as projects designed only to benefit the wealthy.

As the ideological struggle in Korea sharpened, some of these former students joined with radicalized intellectuals and workers, as well as Korean communists who had returned from Siberia. In 1925, they formed the Korean Communist Party (KCP), the first Communist party in Korea proper. Japan's highly efficient police and intelligence network, as well as a tendency towards factionalism and adventurism, almost destroyed the KCP in the first years of its existence. It survived, however, largely because it succeeded in establishing close ties with the growing farmer, working class, and student opposition to Japanese rule.

Japan's new policy toward Korea included the freedom to form social organizations. Many Koreans took advantage of this opening to form youth, educational, social, labor, and peasant organizations. According to Japanese police records, the number of registered organizations jumped from 985 in 1920 to 5,728 in 1922.[22] It was not long before the various local organizations came together to form national associations and federations. For example, tenant-farmer groups organized the Korean Labor Mutual Aid Association, which in 1922 held the country's first-ever county-level tenant conference. In 1925, the association was reorganized as the Korean Peasant Association, and its local tenant associations were reorganized as peasant unions. In addition to defending tenant rights, these unions also supported a program of political education and campaigns for freedom of speech and assembly. Tenancy was driving farmers into political action at such a rapid rate that in 1928 the governor-general established a commission to investigate conditions. The commission's findings, note historians Stewart Lone and Gavan McCormack,

> revealed just how dire was the plight of most Koreans. . . . Seventy percent of owner-cultivators just managed to break even, and over 95 percent of all tenants, full or partial, ended the year in deficit with debts bearing interest from 12-48 percent per annum. Half a million people were identified as "fire-field" squatters, burning forest land in the mountains for bare subsistence, while nearly half of all farm households endured annual "spring poverty"—eating grass and tree bark to survive after their harvest had been spent on rent and debt repayment.[23]

In 1930 activists in the north organized Red Peasants Unions which enjoyed considerable peasant support, while also maintaining close ties to Korean Communists and leftists operating in Manchuria and Siberia. These unions were "the most militant force within the entire peasant movement, rejecting the legalistic tenant associations of the 1920s and, through political publications, theater, night schools and a semi-militaristic organization, offering a violent and revolutionary challenge to Japan's authority."[24]

As Korea's industrialization proceeded, wage-workers became organized and politicized. Women in particular played a key role in the Korean labor movement. For example, in July 1923, more than one hundred women workers from four rubber factories in northern Korea went on strike to protest reduced wages and harsh treatment by management. Two days later, women workers in another rubber factory in the same area struck in solidarity. The strike led to the formation of the Kyungseong Rubber Factory Women Workers' Union which played a leading role in the 1925 formation of the Korean Labor Federation (KLF). The politics of the KLF brought together some 150 labor and trade union organizations around a statement of mission which proclaimed:

> Our purpose is to liberate the working class and to build a completely new society.
>
> We will fight with the capitalist class with the collective power of the workers until a final victory is won.
>
> We will fight for better welfare and economic improvement of the present working class.[25]

The KLF, calling for working class unity, led numerous struggles for the eight-hour day and a minimum wage system. It also "emphasized solidarity relationships between labor organizations and other social and political organizations," including the newly organized Communist movement.[26]

Strike activity reached a peak in 1929-1930, when labor disputes took place in almost every major city. One of the most important was the 1929 Wonsan labor strike called by the dock and transport workers of the Federation of Labor Unions of Wonsan to protest low wages and poor working conditions. Workers throughout Korea sent aid, and transport workers throughout the region went on a solidarity strike. The Japanese refused to yield, however, and in the end the strike leaders were arrested, the union destroyed, and the strike lost.

The Korean Communist Party also sustained its political efforts by adopting a united front policy which included joining with moderate nationalists to form the New Korea Society in 1927. By 1930, the society claimed 386 branches and 76,939 members, and a national network that coordinated youth groups, labor and peasant groups, and intellectual societies.[27] Because the top positions were filled by moderates, the Japanese allowed the organization to function. However, the regional and local leadership positions were held by Communists and other leftists who successfully used the New Korea Society's national network to strengthen their ties with farmer and labor movements.

This political alliance was always shaky, largely because the moderates continually found themselves being identified with activities or campaigns of which the Japanese strongly disapproved. The breaking point came with the Japanese repression of the 1929 Kwangju Student Movement. A fight broke out between Korean and Japanese high school students over the way a Japanese male student had treated a Korean female student. The Japanese police ended the fighting by arresting only Koreans. Korean students from throughout the country went on strike, and it took the Japanese five months to suppress it. The moderates in the New Korea Society opposed Communist efforts to have the organization support the Kwangju Student Movement, leading in time to a mutual decision to dissolve the New Korea Society.

This period marks the high point of the struggle against Japanese imperialism within Korea. Beginning with Japan's 1931 invasion of Manchuria, the colonial government made a decision to end its more accommodating stance, known as the "cultural policy." Korea had to be secured as a stable economic and military base to support Japan's broader regional aspirations, so the colonial government began to suppress any kind of popular organizing or activity. At the same time, the Japanese advance into Manchuria created new possibilities for those Koreans willing to serve Japanese interests. The Japanese needed additional manpower to run their growing empire. Koreans were therefore allowed to occupy new positions of authority in Japanese enterprises, the colonial government, and the military, in both Korea and Manchuria. (For example, Park Chung Hee, the leader of South Korea from 1961 to 1979, graduated from both the Japanese military academy in Manchukuo and the Cadet Academy in Tokyo.) This new policy had its own contradictions, however. Growing numbers of Koreans came to see their oppression in class as well as national terms, and this, contrary to Japanese desires, strengthened popular support for the Communist movement, the only organized force fighting both capitalism and colonialism.

In 1937, just before the Japanese invasion of China, all remaining Korean social, political, and cultural organizations were ordered to dissolve. In 1938, the Japanese issued a decree making it illegal to use the Korean language in schools, public meetings, or publications. The following year, Koreans were ordered to adopt Japanese names. Under the slogan "Japan and Korean Oneness," the Japanese sought to make Koreans forget their past and embrace a new historical starting point defined by the reality of Japanese rule.

Japanese demands on Koreans continued to grow as the war expanded. In 1940, the Japanese organized all of Korea into 350,000 Neighborhood Patriotic Associations. Every group of ten households became a unit whose responsibilities included organizing visits to Shinto shrines, rationing, providing security, and giving mandatory contributions of gold, silver, and brass for the Japanese war effort. In the following years, millions of Koreans were drafted for labor activities, many working eleven-hour days, seven days a week. More than a half-million Koreans were also sent to Japan to work in factories and mines. By January 1945 Koreans accounted for more than 30 percent of the entire labor force in Japan. Koreans were also drafted beginning in 1943, and tens of thousands were sent to serve the Japanese military in an active or supporting capacity. Perhaps the most heinous crime committed by the Japanese was their forced recruitment of Korean girls and young women as military prostitutes or "comfort women." One scholar describes the experience of these "comfort women" as follows:

> The testimony of former comfort women and documents on them show how women were recruited by force, kidnapped from factories and farms, or taken away because of their rebellious attitude toward Japanese colonization. Each woman was made to serve an average of thirty to forty soldiers per day, with the soldiers waiting in line outside her small room. Women who were not submissive were brutally beaten and tortured, and escape was impossible due to strict surveillance.[28]

In spite of Japan's overwhelming intervention in and control over Korean political and economic life, Communist-inspired resistance continued. Japan was forced in 1938 to establish the Korean Anti-Communist Association with branches in every province and associated groups in almost every village and factory. In fact, in response to Japanese imperialism a regional Communist-led resistance movement arose; especially strong in Manchuria and northern China, it also continued to influence political consciousness and commitments in Korea.

Although Chinese Communists organized and led the main opposition to Japan in Manchuria, Korean Communists also played an important role in the armed struggle there. The first organized Chinese Communist army was formed in 1933. Several others were established over the following two years. Each army operated in a different area of Manchuria with Koreans making up the majority of soldiers in the Second Army fighting in eastern Manchuria, and a substantial minority in the Fourth Army fighting in northeast Manchuria. Although top leadership positions in these armies were held by Chinese Communists, Koreans served as division commanders.

Kim Il Sung, who was later to become the leader of North Korea, established his reputation as a liberation fighter in the Second Army during this period. When the various regional armies joined in 1936 to create the Northeast Anti-Japanese United Army, Kim was made one of the six divisional commanders in the newly formed First Route Army. At one point he even commanded a division named after him. After a final reorganization in 1938, at which time the First Route Army was divided into three directional armies, Kim was placed in charge of the Second Directional Army. Kim was not the only Korean fighting Japan in Manchuria, but he was one of the most important and successful; the Japanese even had a special military unit assigned to capture or kill him.

Korean and Chinese Communists also joined together in northern China to fight the Japanese. Korean revolutionaries had long been active in the Chinese revolutionary movement, participating, for example, in the Kuomintang-led Northern Expedition. After Chiang launched his counter-revolution, the Korean Communists joined forces with the Chinese Communists. Many participated in the 1934 to 1935 Long March to Yenan. Other Korean Communists made their way to Yenan after 1937, fighting with the Chinese Communists against Japan until the end of the war. Among the most well-known were Mu Chong and Kim Tu-bong; they also became important leaders in North Korea.

Liberation

By early August 1945, it had become obvious to Japanese officials in Korea that the war would soon end. Fearing for their safety (there were over 30,000 Koreans in jail, most for political reasons), they raced against time to create an interim Korean government that would be willing and able to protect Japanese lives and property. Between August 9 and 13, representatives from the colonial government pleaded with the wealthy and politically conservative Song Chin-u to head such a government. Song declined.

Desperate, Japanese officials approached a popular Korean political figure, Yo Un-hyong, who was not a member of the Communist Party but was both nationalist and left of center. The Japanese were willing to negotiate with Yo because they had run out of time. By then, August 15, it appeared that the Soviets, who had already engaged Japanese forces in the north, would soon occupy the entire peninsula. The Japanese also hoped that a progressive Korean would give them more protection from the Soviets than a conservative. Yo, perhaps with advance knowledge that he would be visited, had prepared the following conditions: the Japanese must immediately release all political prisoners, guarantee food supplies for three months, and agree not to intervene in Korean peacekeeping or independence activities. The Japanese reluctantly accepted the conditions, and Yo quickly enlisted the help of other Koreans to establish the Committee for the Preparation of Korean Independence (CPKI). The CPKI, in turn, contacted Koreans throughout the country in an effort to set up a structure for a national government. Yo had set in motion a process that went far beyond what the Japanese had originally intended, but they were in no position to object.

The response of the Korean people to Japan's surrender and the establishment of the CPKI was explosive. The prisons were emptied and many of those released, including experienced Communist organizers, immediately began organizing CPKI branches. Also helping were tens of thousands of other Koreans released from Japanese-controlled youth groups and labor camps. The result was the formation of some 145 CPKI branches by the end of August. These branches functioned as basic units of government. For example, they assumed peacekeeping responsibilities throughout the country, with the exception of Seoul, Pusan, Inchon, and Mokpo, where the Japanese military retained a dominant presence. CPKI branches also organized food distribution, welfare relief, and where possible, local production.

Equally noteworthy was the rapid revitalization of worker and peasant union activity. Days after the surrender of Japan, workers began organizing new unions in factories and workplaces all over Korea. In many instances workers took possession of their enterprises, especially the large ones that had operated under Japanese ownership, running them either directly or with hired managers. Where workers were not able to take control, they often staged strikes and slowdowns to win greater power. Numerous peasant unions also formed almost overnight, particularly in areas where rural organizing had taken place in the 1920s and 1930s. In some cases, these unions seized Japanese-held lands. In other cases, they limited their activities to organizing rice collection, storage, and distribution.

Until late August it was unclear how the Soviet army would respond to the American-issued General Order No. 1, which declared that U.S. forces would receive the Japanese surrender in Korea south of the 38th parallel. A mid-August skirmish between Japanese and Soviet troops in northern Korea had slowed the Soviet drive, so Soviet forces did not appear near the 38th parallel until the last week in August. However, at that point they halted their advance, making it clear that they would respect U.S. wishes.

This decision had a major impact on the political situation in southern Korea. Soviet forces had done nothing to obstruct the work of the CPKI as they moved down the peninsula and so conservatives in the south, assuming that the Soviets would eventually occupy the entire country, had been giving sizable donations to the CPKI in an attempt to buy protection. They now stopped. Some even began to hope for a revival of their fortunes under U.S. rule.

Determined to safeguard Korea's newly gained independence, the CPKI announced on August 28 that it would temporarily function as the national government of Korea. The CPKI already controlled national communication facilities, including the press and radio. In its statement, the CPKI pledged to work for "complete independence and true democracy." This required the destruction of feudal elements and "mass struggle against the anti-democratic and reactionary forces . . . [who] colluded with Japanese imperialism and committed crimes against the nation."[29] This statement was designed to make clear to the United States, whose forces were soon to arrive in the south, that the Korean people were ready and able to govern themselves.

Finally, on September 6, two days before U.S. troops were to arrive in Korea, several hundred CPKI activists met in Seoul and established the Korean People's Republic (KPR). They elected fifty-five leaders to staff the interim administration, forty-two of them identified with the left. The list also included well-known Koreans who were still outside the country, for example, Syngman Rhee and Kim Ku, on the right, and Mu Chong and Kim Il Sung, on the left. The decision to include conservative nationalists (as opposed to collaborators) reflected an attempt to build the broadest possible political base for the new Korean government.

To be sure, the *program* of the KPR was left in direction. In the week following its inaugural assembly, the KPR made explicit its commitment to social revolution. Its twenty-seven-point platform, presented on September 14, was a sweeping program of action that called for confiscation without compensation of lands held by the Japanese and collaborators; free distribution of that land to peasants; rent limits on nonredistributed land; nationalization of such major industries as mining, transportation, banking, and communications; and state supervision of small and mid-sized companies. The program also guaranteed basic human rights and freedoms, including those of speech, press, assembly, and faith; universal suffrage to adults over the age of eighteen; equality for women; labor law reforms including an eight-hour day, a minimum wage, and prohibition of child labor; and "establishment of close relations with the United States,

USSR, England, and China, and positive opposition to any foreign influences interfering with the domestic affairs of our state."[30] In short order, the many branches of the CPKI responded to the formation of the KPR by transforming themselves into associated people's committees. Worker and peasant unions as well as youth and women's groups all pledged their support to the KPR and its program.

Some scholars have tried to discredit the KPR and its program, dismissing it as the work of a handful of Communists who did not represent the Korean people. They are wrong to do so. As one group of Korea scholars explain:

> Standard South Korean and American scholarship has tended to view the KPR as a communist front whose popularity was directly proportional to the degree it was able to camouflage its real intentions, i.e., the establishment of a revolutionary communist state. According to this view, Korea in 1945 lacked the necessary requirements for socialism and Koreans were generally unwilling to espouse the program of the Korean Communist Party. Revisionist studies of the period, on the other hand, have suggested that the KPR represented a genuine attempt at a leftist coalition government and that it had strong popular backing. . . . The KPR's roster of cabinet officers and its platform tend to lend support to the revisionist view. Both suggest an effort toward the establishment of a workable national coalition in which the left, to be sure, would predominate.[31]

The rapid formation of the KPR produced weaknesses in its underlying governing structure. The greatest of these were the tendency of the Seoul people's committee to wield undue influence in the development of "national" programs and political strategy, and its insufficient contact with the provincial and village people's committees which were actually engaged in the hard work of governing. Yet, in a short period of time the Korean people had taken a major step toward the creation of a government that represented their interests. The people's committees were an exciting and innovative vehicle for promoting direct democracy. The existence of widespread worker ownership offered yet another important structural avenue for popular participation in decision-making. Under these conditions, it is easy to understand why, as Bruce Cumings observed, "Without foreign intervention, the KPR and the organizations it sponsored would have triumphed throughout the peninsula in a matter of months."[32]

There was, of course, foreign intervention from both the Soviet Union and the United States. It was U.S. intervention that proved decisive. The

United States was determined to maintain control over as much of Korea as political and military realities would allow, and to use that control to advance its own interests in northeast Asia. To achieve this goal, the U.S. government committed itself to a policy that led tragically to the destruction of the KPR, the division of Korea, the creation of an unpopular, conservative-dominated government in the South, and, finally, the Korean War.

II. DIVISION AND WAR

Chapter 3

From Occupation
to Division

The State Department's explanation for the division of Korea is straight-forward: "At the end of the war American troops took over control of South Korea from the Japanese, while Soviet troops did the same in North Korea. The United States then worked to fulfill the wartime pledges regarding Korea, but their execution was thwarted by Soviet policies which forced the political division of the country and fastened a communist tyranny on North Korea."[1] This self-serving explanation misrepresents the interests and actions of both the United States and the Soviet Union. Korean political aspirations threatened U.S. foreign policy objectives far more than those of the Soviet Union. The United States violently crushed all opposition in southern Korea, destroying in the process possibilities for the peaceful establishment of a democratic, unified Korea. Then the U.S. government officially pursued division, over the objections of the Soviet Union, to protect its political gains in the south.

The South Under U.S. Occupation

On August 24, 1945, John Reed Hodge was appointed commanding general of U.S. armed forces in Korea. The Soviet Union had already demonstrated its acceptance of General Order No. 1, so Hodge knew that his forces would not directly confront Soviet troops in Korea. Although General Order No. 1 implied that U.S. forces were being sent to Korea solely to accept the surrender of defeated Japanese troops, their mission was much greater: to secure U.S. control over the southern part of Korea. Since neither the Soviets nor the Japanese were prepared to challenge U.S. authority in the south, the only possible source of resistance to this mission was the Korean people themselves. The U.S. government obviously understood this; four days before U.S. troops were to arrive in southern Korea, Hodge told his officers that Korea "was an enemy of the United States."[2]

The Japanese, not surprisingly, were eager to make themselves useful to the U.S. occupation force. As Bruce Cumings describes:

> Lieutenant General Kozuki Yoshio radioed from Seoul on September 1, "there are communist and independence agitators among Koreans who are plotting to take advantage of the situation to disturb peace and order here." In other messages on that day and the next two, Kozuki warned of possible sabotage of the American landing in Korea by "Red" labor unions and told of "Korean mob violence against the police, theft of munitions, and strikes." He asserted that his position was difficult and that he "was eagerly awaiting the arrival of the Americans."[3]

Hodge, in response, told Kozuki to maintain order and had leaflets dropped over southern Korea telling the Korean people to obey the existing Japanese authority. When U.S. forces landed in Inchon Harbor on September 8, 1945, they found Japanese police lining the streets.

The U.S. decision to view the Korean people as enemies and Japanese forces as friends at first thought seems unbelievable. After all, Japan had attacked and fought the United States in the long and bloody Pacific War. However, there was a rationale for this decision. The United States was secure in its control over Japan, a country still ruled by an elite that embraced capitalism. That was why the U.S. government decided "to maintain the Japanese system of government, including emperor, cabinet, and bureaucracy. . . . Although the United States ultimately built up a large bureaucracy of its own in Japan . . . [i]t transmitted orders to the existing Japanese government, which was usually in charge of implementing them."[4] In Korea, on the other hand, the United States found no such acceptable government in place. The leftward-leaning Korean People's Republic was neither controllable nor sympathetic to U.S. interests. Even the conservative leaders of the Korean Provisional Government were considered too nationalistic and independent. Left with no attractive choices, the U.S. government simply decided, with little concern for the well-being or wishes of the Korean people, that southern Korea would be ruled by a U.S. military government. And Hodge, who was in charge of securing this rule, determined that the most effective way to do this was to revitalize the Japanese colonial system, under U.S. management.

At a September 9 surrender ceremony, Hodge announced that the colonial government would continue to function with all personnel remaining in place, even the governor-general. A major outcry surged throughout Korea, leading to political repercussions in Washington, D.C. Finding itself on the defensive, the United States made some changes for the benefit of public relations. On September 12 it replaced the Japanese governor-general with an American and dismissed all Japanese bureau chiefs. Significantly, however, it did not arrest Japanese officials or send them back to Japan but kept them on as advisors. One of their assignments was to recommend to U.S. officials the Koreans they thought best suited to replace them.

Although the great majority of Koreans objected to this U.S. policy of collaboration with Japanese officials, there were Koreans who applauded U.S. actions and were eager to serve the military government. These individuals had begun to organize against the KPR beginning in late August when it became certain that the United States, and not the Soviet Union, would exercise authority in the south. On September 16 they joined together, with encouragement from the U.S. occupation, to form the Korean Democratic Party (KDP). Most KDP members were either large landholders, wealthy businesspeople, or former officials in the colonial bureaucracy. They therefore had little trouble winning positive recommendations from the Japanese colonial officials who now advised the U.S. military government. As a result, when the occupation established an advisory council of Koreans to give legitimacy and guidance to its rule, a majority of the positions went to leading KDP members.

A few KPR leaders were also invited to join the council, but they refused. On October 9, Major General Archibald V. Arnold, the military governor, angered by this refusal, ordered all Korean newspapers to publish an official statement which attacked these KPR leaders by name and threatened the use of force if they interfered with the activities of the military government. Some newspapers defied Arnold. The KPR responded by publishing a pamphlet, *The Traitors and the Patriots*, which defended the KPR and attacked the many pro-Japanese Koreans who were chosen to participate in the council by quoting from their wartime speeches praising Japan and criticizing the United States. The U.S. military authorities responded by banning the pamphlet and all future KPR publications.

The U.S. military government appointed many KDP leaders to positions of authority, including such positions as head of the Korean National Police (KNP), chief justice of the Supreme Court, chief prosecutor, director of the Department of Justice, and director of the Department of Education. The various departments were themselves staffed mostly by the same Koreans who had previously worked for the colonial government. U.S. authorities also kept in force many of the laws and regulations that had been imposed by the Japanese. The KNP had been among the key instruments of Japanese rule in Korea. To ensure its effectiveness, the Japanese centralized its operation; all police units, whether local or regional, took their orders from a central police headquarters. The U.S. military occupation retained this structure, following the counsel of Japanese colonial authorities and right-wing Koreans who argued that a strong centralized police force was necessary to challenge the power of the people's committees. The U.S. occupation also created a more conventional military force. On November 13, an Office of the Director of National Defense with control over both police and army departments was formed. This step predates any comparable Soviet effort. As Cumings notes, "The earliest American G-2 report of Soviet activities possibly directed toward building an army came nearly six months after the American initiative."[5]

While the U.S. occupation had made considerable progress in establishing its own transformed colonial government, its efforts did little to win support for U.S. rule in the south. In fact, its reliance on Japanese collaborators and institutions only served to strengthen the legitimacy of the KPR and its associated people's committees. Aware that the U.S. position would soon become untenable without quick action to destroy the KPR, the occupation took decisive steps to remake the south Korean political environment. Among the first steps taken was an attempt to build a popular conservative alternative to the KPR. On October 16, 1945, Syngman Rhee, a past leader of the KPG, flew to Korea on one of General MacArthur's planes. Rhee had spent most of his life in the United States where, in spite of having been ousted from the KPG in 1925 on charges of overstepping his authority and embezzling funds, he had continued to call himself "minister plenipotentiary and envoy extraordinary" of the KPG to the

United States. Although the United States had not taken him seriously in the past, it now backed him because, in contrast to the KDP leadership, he was strongly anti-Japanese as well as anti-communist. The United States and the KDP, which also endorsed Rhee's return, hoped to use his nationalist credentials against the left. Rhee gave his first major speech at the October 20 welcoming ceremony for the U.S. occupation. Fulfilling expectations, he used the occasion to denounce the Soviet Union and the KPR.

Alarmed by U.S. occupation policies, KPR leaders held a national meeting of people's committee representatives in late November. Hodge had been demanding that the KPR drop the word "Republic" from its name and register with the military government as a political party. In an attempt at compromise, those at the meeting decided to recognize the authority of the U.S. occupation in the south but chose to keep "Republic" in the name. A resolution was passed stating that "as long as the American Military Government exists in Korea south of the 38th parallel, the Republic cannot and will not act as a government."[6]

This was a compromise position within the KPR as well, pushed largely by its leaders in Seoul. Since the U.S. presence in Seoul had limited the power of the Seoul people's committee, KPR leaders felt they had little to lose by recognizing U.S. authority. Outside Seoul, however, the situation was quite different. People's committees in the north and large parts of the south were functioning as official governing bodies. Representatives from these committees, seeing no reason to acknowledge U.S. authority, unsuccessfully pressed for organizational reforms that would have made the KPR center in Seoul more responsive to the opinions of people's committees in the rest of the country.

At the same time, the United States found the KPR compromise unacceptable. One reason was that Koreans were continuing to form mass organizations loyal to the KPR. Representatives of labor unions from the north and south, for example, met in Seoul in early November and established the National Council of Korean Labor Unions (NCKLU), which pledged to stand behind the KPR and its program. The NCKLU's member unions were in control of almost all previously Japanese-owned plants, so support for the KPR among workers was significant. In the following month, the National League of Peasant Unions, the Korean Democratic

Youth League, and the Women's League sprang up in quick succession, with each group declaring solidarity with the KPR.

The U.S. military government, in response, passed restrictive labor laws on December 8, including one that prohibited strikes. Then it forced workers to give up control of their enterprises and appointed new managers, many of whom were former high-ranking employees from those very same enterprises. Next the military government took on the KPR. In January, after declaring KPR activities "unlawful," the U.S. occupation began unseating those people's committees which continued to govern towns and cities throughout the south. The city of Mokpo in South Cholla province, where the people's committee controlled the city government, is an example. The military government ordered provincial police to arrest the leaders of the people's committee and to force all city department directors and most city employees to resign. Then the government installed new officials, mostly pro-Japanese Koreans.

Hoping to further undermine the political influence of the people's committees, the occupation regime scheduled October 1946 elections for a South Korean Interim Legislative Assembly (SKILA). Leaving nothing to chance, Hodge announced that he would personally appoint half the legislators and have veto power over all SKILA's decisions. The United States also gave Rhee and his allies almost total control over the organization of the election. As a result, the election produced an overwhelming victory for the right. Cheju Island voters elected the only leftists, but when the representatives arrived in Seoul they were kidnapped and killed.

Popular anger at U.S. occupation policies reached the breaking point even before the election. Determined to restore the power of the people's committees, a major peasant uprising swept through the southern provinces. As a gauge of public opinion on the U.S. occupation, this mass action was far more accurate than was the outcome of the carefully managed election. The uprising began in late September 1946, when rail workers in Pusan walked off their jobs.[7] Not long after that, rail workers in Seoul, followed by printers, electrical workers, telegraph workers, postal employees, and many others went out on strike. In addition to job-related demands—higher wages, better working conditions, and the right to organize—workers called for broader political moves, such as the release of political prisoners and, most importantly, transfer of power back to the

people's committees. The rail workers' strike was especially threatening to
the U.S. military government because police and military units moved
around the country by train. The military government and its Korean allies
mobilized thousands of strikebreakers, police, and right-wing youth group
members to attack the striking Seoul rail workers. Mass arrests of workers
followed.

Angered by the violence, hundreds of workers demonstrated in Taegu
on the first of October. Police killed one of the marchers. More workers
turned out the following day, and when the police attempted to stop the
demonstration, the demonstrators fought back, killing dozens of police and
attacking the homes of Korean officials. The military government sent in
U.S. tanks and declared martial law. While this use of force contained the
rioting in Taegu, demonstrators soon took to the streets in other cities in
North Kyongsang province, burning police stations and official buildings
and attacking, even killing, wealthy landowners. In a number of cases, the
demonstrators restored the people's committees to power. By October 6,
the authorities had imposed martial law throughout North Kyongsang.

The uprising spread to South Kyongsang province. On October 7, U.S.
forces fired on a crowd of demonstrators in Chinju, killing two. U.S. troops
and Korean police also fired on a crowd in Masan, killing and wounding
many people. Riots followed in Pusan, requiring the presence of U.S. troops
there as well. In mid-October, demonstrations began in South Chungchong
province. By the end of the month they had spread further, this time to
South Cholla province. In the first two weeks of November, clashes took
place in an estimated forty-seven cities, towns, and villages throughout the
province.

The uprising, the most important in Korea since that of the Tonghak,
failed to reverse U.S. policy. One of the most important reasons was that
the actions were largely uncoordinated across provinces. The uprising
spread across the south not because there was an overall plan uniting the
efforts of south Korean workers and peasants but largely because workers
and peasants in one province were inspired to take action after learning
about what had happened in a neighboring province. This pattern of revolt
enabled U.S. forces and the KNP to mobilize and concentrate their efforts
in one province before having to confront demonstrators in another province. Even so, the outcome of the struggle was far from certain. Without the

direct involvement of U.S. forces, the autumn uprising would likely have led to civil war and victory for those Koreans seeking the return of the people's committees and their program of radical social transformation.

The occupation's victory was a major turning point in its effort to establish control over political affairs in the south, for in the process of crushing the uprising, it greatly weakened the organizational and operational capacities of the people's committees and the NCKLU. Through violence, the United States was gradually restructuring politics in southern Korea. In doing so, it was both irreversibly laying the groundwork for the division of Korea and turning the south into an authoritarian state. Roger Baldwin, the head of the American Civil Liberties Union, after visiting there in 1947, commented, "The country is literally in the grip of a police regime."[8] There is evidence for this characterization: the number of political prisoners in the south rose from 17,000 in August 1945 under Japanese rule, to more than 21,000 in December 1947 under the U.S. occupation. By the end of 1949, political prisoners numbered around 30,000, of these approximately 80 percent charged with being communists.[9]

The North under Soviet Occupation

Soviet soldiers entered northern Korea on August 9, 1945, and the following day engaged Japanese forces at Unggi and Najin. After the war ended, the Soviets continued their march down the peninsula, entering the port city of Wonsan on August 21, and Pyongyang three days later. Soviet occupation forces accepted the surrender of remaining Japanese troops and removed all Japanese from positions of authority north of the 38th parallel.

Like their U.S. counterparts, Soviet forces were responsible for ensuring a political environment in Korea favorable to the interests of their country. In this regard, the Soviet occupation was no doubt pleased to find a population strongly influenced by the left. As a result, and in contrast to the U.S. occupation, it encouraged existing CPKI branches to continue functioning as basic units of government. For example, on August 25, the Soviet command in Pyongyang authorized the local CPKI branch to take over administrative responsibilities for the province and immediately placed under its jurisdiction all major Japanese properties.

The Soviets gave Koreans in the north substantial freedom of political action in the first months of their occupation, allowing Cho Man-sik, a political moderate, to serve as head of the Pyongyang people's committee. None of the Soviets' actions during this period suggested a goal of a divided Korea. Although they did encourage the provincial people's committees to create a Five Provinces Administrative Bureau, they never treated it as a central body. Each province retained control over its own affairs. Moreover the people's committees, as well as all social movements in the north, continued to look to Seoul as their political center. The authors of *Korea Old and New, A History* explain:

> The Soviets accepted the Japanese surrender and moved temporarily into the background, allowing the ongoing process of de-Japanization and social revolution to continue at the local level through the channel of the people's committees. . . . This relatively light handed approach to Korea by the Soviets undoubtedly reflected both empathy with the Korean revolution and a pragmatic calculation that the revolution was not contrary in any way to their own strong interest in having a friendly state on the other side of the Tuman River.[10]

Early Soviet actions in Korea were not all positive, however. As Cumings points out: "The Soviet troops who entered Korea committed depredations against the Japanese and Koreans, including rape and looting, on what appears to have been a wide scale and which went quite beyond taking revenge against the enemy and its Korean allies."[11] One reason for this behavior, according to Cumings, is that the majority of Soviet soldiers entering Korea were young, poorly trained, and had few provisions. Soviet military police were quickly sent to Korea and within two weeks this widespread misbehavior stopped.

A number of Korean communists were in the Soviet Far East when the war ended. They were anxious to return to Korea, and the Soviets, eager to use their services in the occupation, encouraged them to do so. One of the most famous returning Koreans was Kim Il Sung. Kim was chosen by his fellow guerrilla fighters in the Soviet Union to head the Soviet-organized Korean Task Force. Kim arrived in the north on September 25 and was introduced by Cho Man-sik at an October welcoming ceremony of more than 70,000 people.

Both the Soviets and Koreans in the north watched developments in the south with considerable concern. While the Soviets had moved quickly to erase the Japanese presence, the U.S. occupation had sought to maintain the structure and personnel of the Japanese colonial government. While the Soviets had supported the work of the people's committees, the U.S.

occupation had, by December, declared their activities illegal in the south. From the perspective of the north, the United States was deliberately and ruthlessly destroying the basis for Korean unity—the people's committees and their associated mass organizations.

In response to these developments, the Soviets centralized political operations in the north and promoted Communists to leadership positions in all important political bodies. In February 1946, the Soviets established the North Korean Interim People's Committee (NKIPC) to coordinate the work of the formally independent provincial people's committees; Kim Il Sung was chosen to lead it. The first local elections to fill provincial, city, country, and district positions in the people's committees took place in November 1946. And in February 1947, in clear recognition of the likelihood of division, the NKIPC was replaced by a more permanent body, the North Korean People's Assembly.

Many U.S. and South Korean scholars argue that these actions prove that the Soviets and north Koreans pursued division. But their actions must be seen in the context of developments in the south. Cumings observes that the sequence of events put the south in the role of instigator of policies leading toward division:

> The early and preemptive action toward the creation of separate regimes occurred in the south, during the last three months of 1945. It was only in the aftermath of the results of southern policies that the north began to follow suit. We could argue, of course, that a separate northern regime was inevitable. But the sequence remains undeniable: the south moved first.[12]

As the north moved ahead with its own political reforms, the split between the two halves of Korea grew wider. For example, as the north began implementing its land reform program, the situation facing peasants in the north became so different from that facing peasants in the south that the National League of Peasant Unions was forced to divide into two organizations. The March 1946 land reform was followed in June by labor law reform. In July, a new law guaranteeing women's equality was passed. The law ended, among other things, concubinage, prostitution, and female infanticide. Major industries and firms were also nationalized in July. News of these popular reforms made its way south, heightening people's anger there against the U.S. occupation and Rhee.

During 1946 and 1947, the northern regime, with Soviet support, also proceeded to eliminate political movements except for those approved by the government. By late 1946, the north had built up its own large security apparatus and purged all Koreans who collaborated with the Japanese from any position of authority. Freedom of the press also ended in 1946 as all newspapers carried only officially sanctioned news.

American studies based on interviews of prisoners of war during the Korean War paint the north Korean regime as strict but fair in its treatment of citizens. One prisoner said that the police were "severe," but "no third degree measures were ever used." As a result, the people looked upon the police as "guardians of peace."[13] More generally, these studies showed that,

> Although many respondents disliked the tight control of the regime, most were laudatory of the social revolution, which opened new careers to millions and raised the educational level of the entire population within a few years. The opening of the educational system to children of the poorest classes was frequently cited, given the importance Koreans place on education and the traditional elitism of the system. People did not cower under a totalitarian dictatorship, but tended to support the regime willingly because they got concrete status and material benefits from it; most had little understanding of "communism," but they did like to get land and jobs.[14]

Although Korean Communists worked under the shadow of Soviet officials throughout this period, they maintained their own independent political vision. For example, the north Korean Communist Party led by Kim Il Sung merged with the New Democratic Party led by Kim Tu-bong (largely made up of Koreans who fought with the Chinese communists in Yenan) to form the North Korean Workers' Party (NKWP) in August 1946. Whereas the Soviets wanted the NKWP to be small and have a largely working-class membership, Kim Il Sung created a mass party numerically dominated by peasants. Moreover, Kim often expressed his determination to build an independent Korea. In his 1947 speech on the second anniversary of Korea's liberation, Kim challenged north Koreans to build "a unified, self-reliant, independent state free of foreign interference."[15] By calling for freedom from "foreign" rather than just "imperialist" interference, Kim was deliberately cautioning the Soviet Union against meddling in Korean affairs.

In fact, while the United States described north Korean leaders as puppets of the Soviet Union, there were serious strains in their relationship with the

Soviets. Despite always praising the Soviet contribution to Korean independence, north Korean revolutionaries were well aware that the Soviets
had fought the Japanese for only one week. By contrast, guerrilla fighters
like Kim had fought the Japanese for over a decade. There were also tensions
deriving from Stalin's apparent distrust of Korean Communists and the
Korean people as a whole. In 1937 Stalin ordered the forced deportation of
200,000 Koreans from the Soviet far east to central Asia on grounds that
being "Asian," they might be pro-Japanese. He also ordered the arrest and
execution of Korean Communists working for the Comintern for the same
reason. In short, the north Korean debt to the Soviet Union was more
limited than commonly understood by Western analysts.

Korean revolutionaries in the north were far closer to the Chinese
Communist movement then they were to the Soviet Union. Both Kim Il
Sung and Kim Tu-bong had fought in the Chinese Red Army. Kim Il Sung
also sent Korean soldiers into China to fight on the Communist side in the
Chinese civil war, a volunteer army that prefigured the later use of Chinese
volunteers in the Korean War. North Korea's direct military contribution
to Mao's eventual success was significant. Approximately 30,000 soldiers
went to Manchuria under Korean command in April 1947. By May some
15 to 20 percent of Chinese communist forces in Manchuria were Korean.
Bruce Cumings and Jon Halliday cite these figures: "Several intelligence
sources put the total for all Koreans in the Chinese Fourth Field Army alone
at 145,000; this army, under Lin Biao, was the crack force of the communists, having never lost a battle as it swept southward from Manchuria."[16]
Some North Korean soldiers stayed and fought in China all the way until
the last battle for Hainan Island in May 1950. The Communist victory in
China, as well as the return to North Korea of tens of thousands of
battle-hardened Korean troops in 1949, gave Kim Il Sung a significant
degree of independence from the Soviet Union.

U.S.-Soviet Negotiations and the Division of Korea

In 1943, President Roosevelt had advocated that Korea be placed under
multilateral trusteeship for an unspecified period of time. The first official
meeting to discuss the future of Korea after the Second World War was held
on December 16, 1945, when the foreign ministers of the United States,
Great Britain, and the Soviet Union met in Moscow. At that meeting the

United States proposed that U.S. and Soviet occupation commands jointly settle all issues dealing with trade, transportation, and currency, and that a four-power trusteeship be constituted to handle executive, legislative, and judicial functions until Korea was deemed ready for independence. The trusteeship was to last between five and ten years. The U.S. proposal said nothing about the creation of an interim Korean government. The Soviets countered with their own proposal which called for the establishment of a joint U.S.-Soviet commission whose job it would be to consult "with the Korean democratic parties and social organizations" to form an interim government.

Remarkably, the final agreement was close to the Soviet position, calling for the creation of a U.S.-Soviet joint commission which would have responsibility for forming an interim Korean government. The commission would then work with that government to create a plan for the establishment of an independent Korea, which would be presented for the "joint consideration of the four powers for the working out of an agreement concerning a four-power trusteeship" of up to five years. The agreement did not make trusteeship mandatory.

Although the U.S. government gave its approval to the agreement, Hodge, fearing that it would produce an interim government politically similar to the KPR, began a campaign to oppose it. Aware that the great majority of Koreans opposed trusteeship, he made public statements equating the agreement with trusteeship. Hodge also encouraged South Koreans to believe that it was the Soviet Union that sought trusteeship for Korea while it was the United States that supported immediate independence. Finally, he promoted rumors that the Soviet army would move south to enforce the terms of the trusteeship.

Leftists were initially leery of the Moscow agreement because they too opposed trusteeship. But by early January, most were active supporters. Soviet pressure was one reason. An even more important reason was that the Moscow agreement did not make trusteeship mandatory. Because it called for the creation of an interim Korean government before consideration of trusteeship (the reverse of the U.S. position), most leftists eventually decided that the agreement offered the Korean people their best opportunity to both defend the people's committees in the south and avoid trusteeship. Unfortunately for them, U.S. occupation policies made it difficult for the left to directly and openly communicate its understanding of the Moscow agreement to the south Korean people.

With the right using the public media to proclaim that it was the only true defender of Korean independence, the left was forced on the defensive. Thanks to Hodge, the right wing in the south had finally found an issue upon which to organize. Seeking to build on this momentum, the U.S. occupation actively encouraged conservative Korean leaders in the south to form a unified political alliance. The Representative Democratic Council (RDC), with Syngman Rhee as its leader, was the result.

The U.S.-Soviet Joint Commission held its first meeting in March 1946 to decide on an appropriate mechanism for establishing an interim Korean government. The United States proposed that the commission consider the RDC as the sole consultative Korean body from the south and that the RDC be empowered to consult with groups in the north to determine who should have a position in the interim government. This was a reasonable position, according to the U.S. delegation, because the RDC was the "the newly organized Korean government," which was itself "a coalition group of all important parties."[17] The Soviets rejected this proposal. They argued accurately that the commission was supposed to consult with Korean groups, not choose a Korean group to do the consulting. The United States continued to push its position until early April, when it finally agreed to a compromise: the United States and the Soviet Union would each create a list of those groups operating on their side of the parallel that should be consulted in order to create a representative interim Korean government.

New disagreements quickly developed. For example, the United States demanded that representatives from the south be given more weight in the interim government because it had two-thirds of the country's population. The Soviets countered that only those groups which accepted the Moscow agreement and were willing to support the work of the commission should be consulted. The United States disagreed, arguing that democracy required that all political groups, regardless of their position on the Moscow agreement, should be included. The Soviets pointed out that if the United States was truly interested in a democratic process it should welcome rather than reject the participation of southern people's committees. The first session ended with no resolution.

It was not long afterwards that the U.S. government decided to abandon both the Moscow agreement and its own plan for trusteeship. Unable to ensure U.S. hegemony for all of Korea, U.S. policymakers now sought the establishment of a separate South Korea. At issue was how to achieve it. America certainly had the power to break with the Soviet Union and declare an independent South Korea. The problem with that strategy was that the south Korean political elite already suffered a lack of legitimacy. Independence achieved in such a manner would do little to strengthen domestic (much less international) support for the new regime. The U.S. military also opposed such a step on the grounds that the country would be difficult to defend in case of war with the Soviet Union. The State Department's answer to the dual concerns of legitimacy and defense was to bring the issue of Korea's future to the United Nations, an organization dominated by the United States. The State Department reasoned that if the United Nations sanctioned the creation of an independent South Korea, the government would not only gain credibility but also an international commitment to its defense.[18] However, before the United States could reasonably bring the issue of Korea to the United Nations it had to establish the futility of further negotiations with the Soviets. Therefore, it agreed to another round of Joint Commission meetings.

The second session of the commission opened in May 1947. The argument over which Koreans should be consulted began just where it ended a year earlier. Some 425 southern right-wing groups, the overwhelming majority with no mass following, had registered with the commission to establish their right to be consulted. These groups claimed a combined membership equal to 62 million, or about four times the population in the south. The U.S. position was that all of these groups deserved to be consulted and involved in the process of creating an interim government. The Soviets rejected this position, and the talks quickly deadlocked. In late August, shortly before the commission's last meeting, the United States suggested that a four-power conference be convened to resolve differences. The Soviets countered by proposing the immediate withdrawal of all foreign troops, thereby allowing the Korean people to work out their own arrangements. The United States rejected the troop withdrawal.

The United States brought the Korean issue to the UN General Assembly on September 17, blaming Soviet duplicity and determination to control all of Korea for the breakdown in negotiations. Approximately one month later, it made a formal motion to establish a United Nations Temporary Commission on Korea (UNTCOK) to sponsor and observe the election of a Korean legislative body which would be empowered to form a Korean government. The Soviet Union and its allies strongly opposed this motion, arguing not only that it violated the Moscow agreement, but also that it violated Articles 32 and 107 of the UN Charter. Article 32 required consultations with both sides in a dispute, but representatives from north and south Korea were never invited to address the UN on this issue. Article 107 denied the UN jurisdiction over postwar settlement issues. Given its overwhelming influence in the UN, the United States had little trouble winning approval of its motion; an eight-nation UNTCOK was formed, including representatives from Nationalist China, Canada, Australia, Philippines, France, India, El Salvador, and Syria.

UNTCOK delegates arrived in Seoul in early January 1948 but were denied Soviet permission to enter the north. Unable to operate in both halves of Korea, the commission concluded that it could not carry out its mandate. UNTCOK's chairman reported his views to the Interim Committee of the General Assembly (which functioned when the General Assembly was not in session): "I feel that if the Koreans are left to themselves—not merely in name but in reality—they will work out their own salvation and establish their own democratic government."[19] Then he added that it was the majority opinion of UNTCOK representatives that:

> the formation of a separate government in south Korea will not facilitate the twin objectives laid down in paragraph 5 of the resolution, namely the attainment of the national independence of Korea and the withdrawal of the occupying troops. [Thus] it [would] be unrealistic to treat any scheme of election in south Korea, even though that scheme may apply theoretically to all Korea, as national.

Under U.S. pressure, the UN Interim Committee refused to change its policy. On February 26, 1948, it ordered UNTCOK to "proceed with the observance of elections in all Korea, and if that is impossible, in as much of Korea as is accessible to it." The UNTCOK representatives took a vote and, by the margin of five to three, agreed to comply with the resolution.[20]

UNTCOK's decision to observe an election in the south alone meant that it was to participate in the division of Korea. Rhee and Kim Sung-su, a wealthy landlord who headed the KDP, welcomed this outcome. The overwhelming majority of Koreans, on the other hand, opposed the election and the division that would result. Southern political leaders, including conservatives, sent word to the north that they wanted to create a united opposition to the elections. The north Korean leadership welcomed the overture and scheduled the North-South Political Leaders' Coalition Conference for April in Pyongyang.

General Hodge denounced the conference as a Communist plot, as did Rhee. However, "a majority of the public, intellectuals (including 108 well-known writers and journalists), and newspapers in south Korea expressed their sympathy for the success of the conference," according to historian Bong-youn Choy.[21] More than 540 delegates attended, 360 from the south. The conference called for immediate and simultaneous withdrawal of foreign troops from the peninsula; expressed its opposition to dictatorship, monopoly capitalism, and separate elections; and stressed the organization of a democratic government by a national political conference.

In spite of this broad-based Korean opposition to the election, it was held on May 10, 1948. Only candidates loyal to either Rhee or Kim Sung-su participated and, as a result, their followers won 190 of the 198 seats. The National Assembly adopted a constitution on July 12 and elected Syngman Rhee as South Korea's first president on July 20. The Republic of Korea (ROK) was inaugurated on August 15.

The election and the ensuing U.S. recognition of the ROK as the only lawful government of Korea placed the UN on a slippery political slope. According to Lone and McCormack:

> None of the UNTCOK members thought of the elections as creating a national parliament, but after seven weeks' debate and continuing United States pressure, and only in the absence of the Syrian and Australian delegates, agreement was reached to declare the elections "a valid expression of the free will of the electorate in those parts of Korea which were accessible to the Commission." . . . On 12 December the United Nations General Assembly declared the new body [the South Korean National Assembly] "the only legal government in Korea," although it did not pronounce on its claims to jurisdiction over the whole of the country.[22]

The north's response to the establishment of the ROK was an announcement that it had organized a secret election in the south on August 25 which allowed southern Koreans to vote for their own representatives to the Supreme People's Assembly. In the north, the Democratic People's Republic of Korea (DPRK) was inaugurated on September 9 and promptly recognized by the Soviet Union. Korea was now officially divided into two, with each government, North Korea and South Korea, claiming to be the only legitimate government of Korea.

The Road to Civil War

U.S. foreign policy had succeeded in dividing Korea and establishing a right-wing government in the South. However, the election did little to produce the desired political stability. That was because most South Koreans refused to accept national division. After failing to peacefully stop the election process, growing numbers turned to guerrilla struggle in an effort to overthrow the Rhee regime and reunite the country.

The guerrilla war in the South began on the island of Cheju, with a population of 300,000. Demonstrations had taken place against the elections on March 1, 1948, and thousands of demonstrators had been arrested. Later, the body of one of the demonstrators, who had obviously been tortured, was found in a river. That incident, coming after a long period of police brutality, triggered an explosion. On April 3, the people of Cheju attacked police stations, destroyed bridges, and cut telephone wires. A highly mobile guerrilla army of some 4,000 fighters was formed; by early June it controlled most of the villages in the interior of the island. South Korean military forces were sent to the island to suppress the rebellion. From the end of May to the end of July, more than 3,000 islanders were arrested. The military also blockaded the island, forced people into guarded towns, and destroyed trees and bushes with defoliant. In spite of these efforts, the insurgency continued to grow, reaching its peak in March 1949. In that month a major assault by four ROK battalions finally crushed the resistance. The campaign against the people of Cheju claimed some 40,000 lives; only 170 out of the island's original 400 villages remained inhabitable at its conclusion.[23]

Another rebellion broke out in October 1948, this time in the port city of Yosu. South Korean soldiers, refusing to fight in Cheju, turned against the government, seized weapons and took control of the town. Within hours of Yosu's liberation, residents began parading through the town waving red flags. Among their first acts was the restoration of the town's people's committee and the trial and execution of a number of police, ROK officials, and landlords. The insurgent soldiers carried the revolt to nearby cities and towns. In the city of Sunchon, for example, soldiers helped organize a major rally where weapons were distributed. Speakers at the rally called for the renewal of Sunchon's people's committee and the revival of the Korean People's Republic. Some demonstrators waved the DPRK flag. The rebellion did not last long. Yosu was held for one week before a South Korean military assault overwhelmed the rebel soldiers. Other cities and towns were abandoned as more than 1,000 insurgents and many supporters retreated into the mountains. Many of the remaining townspeople were beaten and tortured. Some were shot under suspicion of having given aid to the uprising, more than 500 in Yosu alone. Park Chung Hee, later to become president of South Korea, was a participant in the rebellion. He is alleged to have received lenient treatment in exchange for agreeing to hunt down others who were involved.[24]

In spite of the fact that South Korea was now an independent country, U.S. forces played a major role in crushing the Yosu rebellion. U.S. commanders planned and directed the military operation, U.S. military advisors accompanied all ROK army units, and U.S. planes were used to transport troops. Well aware of his continuing dependence on the United States, Rhee warned the press against publishing any editorial that called for the withdrawal of U.S. troops from the South.

Although the Yosu uprising was swiftly put down, resistance to the newly established South Korean government was far from over. Those who escaped into the mountains joined with others to launch a massive guerrilla struggle aimed at toppling the government. The guerrillas destroyed rail and telegraph lines and engaged the KNP and ROK army in battle. Activists of the South Korean Workers' Party (SKWP), founded in November 1946, one month after the establishment of the North Korean Workers' Party, attempted to give the rebellion a broader political focus and in this they were joined, for the first time, by some members of the North Korean Workers' Party.

The armed struggle intensified in 1949, demonstrating that Rhee and the United States had failed to win popular support for their policy of division. Unwilling to acknowledge that there was a civil war under way in the South, both blamed the Soviet Union for instigating and organizing the fighting. "Yet," concludes Cumings, "the evidence shows that the Soviets had no involvement with the southern partisans . . . while the seemingly uninvolved Americans organized and equipped the southern counterinsurgent forces, gave them their best intelligence materials, planned their actions, and occasionally commanded them directly."[25] In short, the only significant external actor in the political struggle in the South was the United States. Largely because of this U.S. involvement, the South Korean guerrilla offensive was finally defeated by May 1950.

Even while the guerrilla war was being fought in the South, tensions between the North and South were growing. One of the first major battles between DPRK and ROK armies took place on May 4, 1949, near the southern border city of Kaesong. The fighting, initiated by the South, lasted four days and left hundreds dead. The next major battle took place on the last weekend in June on the Ongjin peninsula, approximately the same area where Korean War fighting would "begin" one year later. Perhaps the worst fighting in 1949 occurred in early August, when North Korean forces attacked ROK units which were occupying a small mountain north of the 38th parallel, again on the peninsula. Although both sides were guilty of initiating cross-border battles, even General William L. Roberts, head of the U.S. Military Advisory Group, admitted that the South was largely responsible for the fighting that summer.[26] Beginning in September 1949, the military balance of power began to shift in favor of the DPRK, as additional military supplies arrived from the Soviet Union and North Korean troops returned from China. Thereafter, it was more often the North that initiated the fighting.

The origins and significance of the Korean War cannot be understood without this history. Most South Koreans opposed the destruction of the people's committees and the division of their country. Their efforts to reverse U.S. policy were resisted by the U.S. occupation and a Korean minority, largely made up of those who had collaborated with the Japanese. The resulting struggle could hardly be contained in the South, for its outcome affected all Koreans.

Chapter 4

U.S. Foreign Policy and Korea, 1945-1950

Did U.S. actions in Korea from 1945 to 1950 bear primary responsibility for the destruction of democratic institutions and the division of Korea? Mainstream scholars hold that U.S. policy toward Korea was informed by a general foreign policy grounded in humanitarian and democratic principles. Actions inconsistent with such principles are explained away by reference to the strangeness that was Korea or blamed on the Soviet Union. For example, historian Donald S. MacDonald excuses the undemocratic consequences of U.S. foreign policy by claiming that U.S. forces in Korea "were ill prepared for their responsibility." Since U.S. forces were under orders "not to recognize any Korean group until the Korean people had an opportunity for self-determination," argues MacDonald, they had little choice but to use "the structure and the Korean personnel of the former Japanese Government-General to govern their zone."[1]

U.S. intentions and actions toward Korea are better understood by recognizing that postwar U.S. foreign policy was driven by imperialist ambitions, just as it had always been in Asia. Between 1945 and 1950, this meant constraining Soviet influence and politically restructuring Germany and Japan to create a stable, U.S.-dominated global capitalist system. This involved, among other things, allying with militarists and fascists where such alliances were necessary or useful, suppressing left-led popular movements, and, as in Germany's case, promoting division. The United States acted similarly in Korea for much the same reason. In short, undemocratic U.S. actions in Korea were the result neither of ignorance nor aberration.

Nor was their outcome unintended. They reflected the broader goals and strategies of U.S. policymakers.

Confining Soviet Influence

U.S. policymakers were aware, long before the Second World War ended, that the United States would emerge as the strongest world power. As Joyce and Gabriel Kolko pointed out, Washington was committed to using that power to "restructure the world so that American business could trade, operate, and profit without restrictions everywhere."[2] U.S. leaders also generally agreed that the Soviet Union was one of the biggest potential obstacles to achieving this goal.

The U.S. government had long considered the Soviet Union a threat to its interests. U.S. troops were sent as part of the fourteen-country effort to overthrow Russia's newly established revolutionary government. When that failed, the U.S. government settled on a strategy of isolation until 1933 when Roosevelt was forced to turn to the Soviet Union for help in blocking Japan's advances in China. The exigencies of the Second World War led the United States to form an alliance with the Soviet Union that eventually grew strained when both Western and Soviet forces moved to establish control over the territories they had liberated. Following the conquest of Italy, the British and U.S. governments created an occupation structure which effectively excluded the Soviets and their domestic supporters in the antifascist resistance; the liberation of France followed in similar fashion. The Soviets carried out the same policy in Romania, Bulgaria, and Poland. By late 1944, Europe was divided into two rival spheres. Although the United States was not pleased with this development, it chose to maintain its alliance with the Soviet Union, for three main reasons. First, the war against Germany was not yet over. Second, the United States still hoped to enlist the Soviet Union in the war against Japan. Third, the United States remained confident that Soviet needs for postwar financial aid would ultimately ensure U.S. hegemony over Eastern as well as Western Europe. As Averell Harriman, the U.S. ambassador to the Soviet Union, explained, "Economic assistance is one of the most effective weapons at our disposal . . . to avoid the development of a sphere of influence of the Soviet Union over Eastern Europe and the Balkans."[3] The Yalta Conference in February 1945 was the high point of U.S.-Soviet-British unity. Several important agreements were reached there, including subjecting Germany to four-power control and giving substantial reparations to the Soviets, who agreed to enter the war against Japan within three months of the defeat of Germany.

The unity was short-lived, however, ending less than two months after the conference. As it became clear that Germany would soon be defeated, Churchill began trying to convince Roosevelt that the Soviet Union was now the main enemy facing the West in its effort to create a stable, capitalist Europe. Roosevelt, however, rejected Churchill's call for a break, remaining confident that the Soviet Union could be successfully accommodated within a U.S.-dominated global capitalist system. But Roosevelt's view was a minority one within U.S. planning circles, and after Roosevelt's death, Truman quickly reversed the direction of U.S. policy. U.S. elites favored this change because the Soviet Union showed no sign of willingness to yield either political or economic control over Eastern Europe to the United States. Moreover, there were growing indications of a possible political crisis in Western Europe stemming from war-caused economic destruction. Harriman, aware of the political strength of the Communist parties in France and Italy, warned that these parties were well-placed to take advantage of any crisis. He therefore concluded that the United States should end its cooperation with the Soviet Union: "Unless we and the British now adopt an independent line the people in our areas of responsibility will suffer and the chances of Soviet domination of Europe will be enhanced."[4]

The independent line was adopted in July 1945 at Potsdam. According to Churchill, once Truman learned of the successful testing of the atomic bomb, he became "a changed man. He told the Russians just where they got on and off and generally bossed the whole meeting."[5] On September 19, 1945, only one month after Japan's surrender, the Joint Chiefs of Staff approved a memorandum that made the Soviet Union the main focus of U.S. military planning.[6] In September 1946, Special Counsel Clark Clifford, at Truman's request, submitted a report which offered a comprehensive policy for dealing with the Soviet Union. His recommendation, based on consultations with the secretaries of state, war, and navy, the Joint Chiefs of Staff, and the Central Intelligence Agency, was that the United States should prepare "to confine Soviet influence to its present area."[7] This anti-Soviet evolution of U.S. global foreign policy helps to explain the main features of U.S. occupation policy in Korea—the suppression of left politi-

cal activity in the south beginning in late 1945, the undermining of trusteeship negotiations with the Soviet Union beginning in early 1946, and the
promotion of Korea's division beginning in 1947.

Constructing the Global Capitalist Economy

The Soviet Union was not the only obstacle facing U.S. policymakers in
their quest to create an integrated world capitalist system. The U.S. economy sank into a depression during the 1930s, largely because of insufficient
demand. This lack of demand came in part from a fall in exports caused by
the worldwide depression and aggravated by the economic policies of major
European countries. Britain, for example, had created a sterling bloc that
largely excluded U.S. imports. Together, the various trading blocs and
restrictions left approximately one half of all world trade closed to the
United States. While war-induced demand eventually stimulated a substantial rise in exports, U.S. policymakers worried that with the end of the war,
exports might once again fall, pushing the United States back into a
depression.

There was good reason for concern. Europe's wartime devastation was
so great that even the capitalist governments felt their only alternative was
to maintain the existing systems of trade regulation. At the same time,
however, these governments, fearing a possible slide into socialism, hoped
the United States would provide the necessary financial support that would
enable the reestablishment of an open trading system. Toward this end
Britain and later France sent a mission to the United States, in the fall of
1945, to request loans of $6 billion and $4 billion respectively.

Although the Truman administration supported these requests, Congress was not enthusiastic. Congressional pressure forced Truman to offer
Britain a far less attractive $3.75 billion low-interest loan, and the French a
$650 million export-import bank credit. Even then, Congress balked at
approving the British loan. While the Truman administration defended the
loan as key to winning British support for an open world trading system,
many in Congress, reflecting the opinion of their constituents, opposed it
because they disapproved of both greater U.S. involvement in international
affairs and opening up U.S. markets. Some were also hostile to the loan
request because they objected to the British Labour Party's decision to
nationalize the steel industry. Still others were worried about the effect of

the loan on U.S.-Soviet relations; Truman had already rejected an earlier Soviet request for funds.

Significantly, the argument that finally secured the July 1946 approval of the loan was one that the Truman administration came to out of desperation—that a weak Britain would open the door to greater Soviet influence in Western Europe. Although the Soviet Union and an economically closed Europe represented separate threats to U.S. aims, Truman, who deeply hated the Soviet Union, was certainly not opposed to folding them into one interconnected menace, especially when doing so enabled him to advance U.S. global interests on both fronts. Instrumental to creating the necessary climate for this argument was Churchill's famous March 1946 "Iron Curtain" speech, in which he called for a U.S.-British alliance against the Soviet Union. Truman had seen the speech ahead of time and was present on the platform when it was delivered.

Recognizing the foreign policy benefits to be gained by exciting fear and distrust of the Soviet Union, Truman presented his "Truman Doctrine" in a speech on March 12, 1947. After accusing the Soviet Union of attempting to enslave people throughout the world, he argued that "it must be the policy of the United States to support free peoples who are resisting attempted subjugation by armed minorities or by outside pressures." He then called for giving aid to Greece ($250 million for military and economic aid) and Turkey ($150 million in military aid). This aid was explained as an emergency response to Soviet subversion in Greece and Turkey, made necessary by the fact that the British were no longer financially able to sustain their past efforts to help the people of those countries defend themselves against the "threat of communism."[8]

In reality, the fighting in Greece was a civil war between a left-led resistance movement and a repressive right-wing monarchy, with no Soviet involvement. There was no Soviet presence in or threat to Turkey. Both the Greek and Turkish governments were corrupt and undemocratic. Finally, the United States, as far back as mid-1946, understood that the British would have to reduce their presence in the Mediterranean and had been preparing to replace them as the dominant power in the region.[9]

The Truman Doctrine was more than a cover for a U.S. move to gain bases and influence in Greece and Turkey. It signaled the public rejection of Roosevelt's past policy of seeking to shape a capitalist world order without open confrontation with the Soviet Union. To be clear, the Truman Doctrine was not the beginning of the U.S. government's anti-Soviet crusade. As Cumings points out:

> Much of the security program established in early 1947 was a ratification and public airing of previous decisions, something Truman noted in April 1947 when he remarked that people seemed to think the contest with the Soviets accelerated suddenly into the Truman Doctrine, when in fact it had been developing since his talks with Molotov in April 1945.[10]

That said, the Truman Doctrine did set the stage for a major new phase of U.S. foreign policy. The United States was now declaring its determination to force European and Asian countries to submit to U.S. leadership in a global crusade against communism. This process would be supported by a major aid program, the Marshall Plan, and directed toward achieving the creation of an open capitalist system under U.S. leadership.

On May 8, 1947, Undersecretary of State Dean Acheson gave a speech in which he called for the economic rebuilding of both Germany and Japan as bulwarks against Soviet expansionism. He also voiced support for a major aid program to help the countries of Western Europe resist the danger of Soviet-supported communism. On June 5, U.S. Secretary of State Marshall, speaking at Harvard College, proclaimed that "the United States should do what it is able to do to assist in the return of normal economic health in the world." He added, however, that there must first "be some agreement among the countries of Europe as to the requirements of the situation." This speech triggered a prearranged plan whereby Britain organized sixteen nations into the Committee for European Economic Cooperation (CEEC). The CEEC met throughout the summer of 1947 in Paris, and in September submitted a request to the U.S. government for $20 billion in aid.

The Marshall Plan was carefully devised to achieve the goal of consolidating U.S. hegemony. It did so by forcing European countries to choose sides between the United States and the Soviet Union. To receive Marshall Plan funds, participating nations not only had to agree to coordinate their policies but to enter into bilateral agreements with the United States on the nature of those specific policies. Given U.S. insistence on financial stability, private enterprise, and an open trading system, the Soviet Union found it impossible to agree to the terms necessary to obtain assistance, even though it had been a wartime ally and sustained great material damage from the Nazi invasion. Soviet representatives left the Paris planning meeting not long after it was convened. Soon after, the Soviet Union began pressuring the Eastern European countries to join it in creating an alternative system of trade relations.

Truman sought to win congressional approval of the Marshall Plan by arguing that it was necessary to help European countries resist Soviet expansionism. In order to create the appropriate climate of distrust and hatred toward the Soviet Union, he worked to generate a red scare in the United States. For example, nine days after making his Truman Doctrine speech, he signed an executive order creating the Federal Employee Loyalty Program, which was to check the "loyalty" of all existing government employees and prevent the future hiring of "subversives." The aim was to purge the government of anyone tied, or even just sympathetic, to Communist politics. Truman also ordered the Justice Department and FBI to cooperate with investigations of the notoriously inquisitorial House Un-American Activities Committee. It is worth adding that the red scare was used not only to win support for an aggressive foreign policy, but also to create a climate within which individuals critical of capitalism, especially those active in the labor movement, could be silenced easily.

Despite Truman's efforts, Congress was initially reluctant to pass the Marshall Plan. Many congressmen worried that the aid program would lead to greater foreign spending on U.S. goods and inflation or, even worse, involvement in a new European war. The turning point for the administration's campaign came in February 1948 when, according to Truman, the Soviet Union organized a Communist takeover in Czechoslovakia. There was actually no coup. Several, but not all, conservative ministers announced their resignation from the country's Communist-dominated coalition government in an effort to create a constitutional crisis. They failed to achieve their aim. Their resignations were accepted and they were eventually replaced by individuals more sympathetic to the left.

Truman nonetheless presented this development as an ominous new threat to the peace of Europe. In a March 1948 speech before Congress, he called for passage of the Marshall Plan to help Europe defend itself and the introduction of universal military training in the United States. Other members of the administration gave similar speeches in the days that followed. Newspaper journalist Walter Lippman captured the effect of this campaign on the country when he wrote, "The President's message, the speeches, testimony, and press conferences of Mr. Marshall, Mr. Forrestal, Mr. Royall, Mr. Sullivan and Mr. Symington have put this country in the position of preparing . . . for a war."[11]

The Marshall Plan was passed in late March. It succeeded in one of its most important goals, that of tying the countries of Western Europe more closely to the United States. It failed, however, to accomplish another, that of creating the economic conditions necessary for Western European governments to embrace the open trading system desired by the United States. One reason was that Congress refused to approve the full amount of money requested by the Truman administration. Another reason was that recession in the United States, coupled with congressional refusal to lower tariffs, made it impossible for Europe to solve its trade and dollar problems.

By 1949, it had become clear to the Truman administration that a new, even larger aid program was necessary if the United States was going to achieve its European trade objectives. U.S. Secretary of State Dean Acheson and Paul Nitze, head of policy planning, began discussing a new strategy for solving U.S. economic problems, one based on greater domestic and international military spending. As they saw it, greater military spending would boost domestic demand, thereby making exports to Europe less central to continued U.S. growth. Overseas military aid would ensure that U.S. allies received a stable and substantial supply of dollars, thereby giving them the confidence to open their economies to U.S. exports.

This strategy was officially pursued when Truman, responding to the victory of the Chinese Communists in their civil war and the Soviet explosion of an atomic bomb in 1949, ordered his National Security Council to undertake a full-scale review of U.S. military and political objectives. The review lasted from January to March 1950, resulting in a document known as NSC-68. This paper argued for a major increase in defense spending, including support for a program to rearm Western Europe in order to "block further expansion of Soviet power . . . [and] induce a retraction of the Kremlin's control and influence and, in general, so foster the seeds of destruction within the Soviet System that the Kremlin is brought at least to the point of modifying its behavior."[12] The Defense Department calculated that such a policy would require an increase in defense spending from the existing $13.5 billion to $18 billion. The State Department figure was substantially higher, in the $35 billion to $50 billion range, for a simple reason: the State Department was looking to military spending to solve economic as well as security problems. NSC-68 adopted the State Department's position. The Truman administration still faced the daunting task of winning congressional support for its new policy. Past efforts to invoke the Soviet threat in defense of major spending initiatives had been successful, but there was considerable fear within the administration that this strategy had outlived its usefulness. The administration knew it needed a new crisis upon which to make its case. It found it in Korea.

The Korean War, which began on June 25, 1950, allowed the government to successfully push ahead with its plan to vastly increase U.S. military spending at home and abroad. As Joyce and Gabriel Kolko explain: "Had the Korean crisis not occurred, it would have been necessary to manufacture an equivalent or to accept a major defeat for the White House's efforts to reassert American interests in a world slipping even further beyond its grasp."[13] Seen from this perspective, it is easy to understand why Truman, desperate for a crisis that could be blamed on the Soviet Union, jumped at the chance to intervene in what was in fact a Korean civil war.

That intervention enabled the Truman administration to reorganize the Marshall Plan into the Mutual Security Administration. Congress quickly authorized more than $5 billion in military aid for NATO countries. It also supported a massive increase in defense spending abroad to construct new bases and house U.S. troops. Thanks to the Korean War, the dollar crisis in Europe was solved. In particular, the Korean War helped trigger economic recovery for two key U.S. postwar allies, West Germany and Japan. It also helped legitimate military spending as a domestic engine of economic growth. Thus, not only were the broad outlines of U.S. policy toward Korea in large measure shaped by overall U.S. foreign policy interests, but developments on the Korean peninsula proved invaluable in helping the United States realize those very same interests. To truly appreciate how much U.S. actions in Korea were a reflection of overall U.S. foreign policy rather than a particular response to Korean events, we must examine U.S. actions in Germany and Japan. As we shall see, what the United States did in Korea—allying with reactionaries and collaborators, suppressing popular movements, even promoting national division—it also did elsewhere.

Restructuring Germany

The first major policy agreement concerning Germany's postwar future was the London Protocol of September 1944, in which the United States, the Soviet Union, and Britain declared that Germany would be kept whole after the war but divided into three zones for administrative purposes. This decision was later amended to include four zones, one under French control. Berlin, the capital, was made a special area, also to be jointly administered. The Potsdam Conference in July 1945, although rearranging German borders, reaffirmed the principle of four-power control over a unified Germany. As with Korea, the "great powers" had decided to "divide up" the administration of Germany according to zones, but not to divide the country itself.

Roosevelt had agreed at Yalta to support the Soviet Union's claim to substantial reparations from Germany. Although a commission was to determine the exact amount, Roosevelt publicly endorsed a figure of $10 billion. In addition, these reparations were to come from the Western administered zones which controlled over two-thirds of German industrial capacity. Roosevelt was willing to support the rebuilding of the Soviet Union at the expense of Germany because he believed that a strong U.S.-Soviet alliance was the best way to ensure the future peace of Europe.

Truman did not share Roosevelt's commitment to U.S.-Soviet harmony or agree with his reparations policy. Convinced that the Soviets were not going to accept a secondary role in a U.S.-dominated international capitalist system, he saw no reason to weaken Germany for their benefit. He therefore began redefining the U.S. government's reparations policy, with the ultimate aim of denying the Soviets any reparations.

Truman first announced that reparations would have to be collected from an all-German economic unit. This meant that no reparations could be paid until a formal peace treaty, establishing Germany's postwar borders, was signed. Moreover, actual reparation payments would be made subject to the "first charge principle." According to this principle, the first priority of German production would be to pay for German imports. Only after the German economy became self-supporting would reparation payments begin.

At Potsdam, Truman changed the U.S. government's position again. He argued that Soviet reparations should be fixed not in dollar amounts, but as a percentage of a yet undetermined German industrial surplus based on a yet undetermined level of economic activity. The Soviets strongly objected but, desperate for money, Stalin finally agreed to a U.S. proposed compromise: each side would be free to draw whatever reparations it wanted from its own zone. The Soviet Union was also given the right to trade food or coal from its zone for industrial plants or goods equal to 15 percent of the industrial surplus in the Western zones, and promised another 10 percent of the surplus outright. The United States also agreed to a deadline of February 2, 1946, for determining the level of production necessary for German self-sufficiency and thus the size of the surplus from which reparations would be taken.

Within two months after Potsdam, Truman changed the U.S. government's position again. He now argued that Soviet reparations would have to be decided not on the basis of the calculated surplus in the Western zones, but on an all-German basis, which meant including the Soviet zone. In other words, the Soviet claim on the surplus produced in the Western zones would be reduced by the amount of reparations it took from its own zone. Pressing this new position, the United States declared, in September, that it must have access to the Soviet zone in order to monitor Soviet activities. The Soviets would be denied any role in the determination of the surplus in the Western zones if they refused. Although the Soviet Union eventually agreed to allow monitors into its zone, it held to its position that the Potsdam agreement, which stated that reparations were to come solely from Western zones, should be maintained.

The hardening U.S. position reflected not only hostility to the Soviet Union but also a new appreciation of the role a revitalized Germany could play in advancing U.S. interests in Europe. This appreciation, in turn, increased U.S. determination to secure control over German political activities in its zone. At the end of the war, German workers had spontaneously created workers' councils to run factories. Just as in Korea, the U.S. occupation viewed worker activism as a threat to its interests. Therefore, one of its first acts was to ban the councils. This ban was eventually lifted in April 1946 after the independent worker movement had been successfully crushed. Even then, severe restrictions on worker organizing and bargaining were maintained. The workers' movement in Germany was neither as well organized nor as integrated into a broader political movement as in Korea. This made it far easier to destroy.

In Germany, again as in Korea, the occupation placed a high priority on building ties with local political conservatives so that U.S. interests would have a domestic political voice. The Christian Democratic Union (CDU) was the U.S. party of choice. The U.S. State Department described it as "middle class" and "deeply concerned with the preservation of the present social order, tempered somewhat by liberal reform."[14] In the fall of 1945, the U.S. military government combined the three states in its zone into a CDU-dominated Council of Minister-Presidents and allowed it to coordinate a variety of governmental operations under close supervision.

One of the CDU's earliest leaders was Konrad Adenauer, one of the few German politicians on the right who also had a proven anti-Nazi record. Significantly, even before the end of 1945, Adenauer was arguing that Germany's future lay in division, with West Germany integrated into a broader alliance of Western European countries. For obvious reasons, then, the United States gave Adenauer, who was to become West Germany's first chancellor, strong support.

Determined to establish a stable and responsive political environment, the United States abandoned one of its most important stated priorities: de-Nazification. The U.S. had arrested a number of key Nazi leaders at the end of the war. It had also ordered those it suspected of being war criminals to complete a questionnaire detailing their past political activities. As a result of this process, some 300,000 people, most from the upper and middle classes, were designated as unemployable in positions of authority. The CDU strongly objected, and the U.S. occupation, fearful that its de-Nazification effort might allow the left to assume a dominant role in its zone, soon decided on a change in strategy. Beginning in March 1946, it gave the CDU-dominated Council of Minister-Presidents authority to determine the future of those charged with war crimes. Most Nazis, except for the top leadership, were rehabilitated. U.S. policymakers also reversed their early commitment to German decartelization. The occupation had initially ordered the breakup of all large business cartels, but with the reevaluation of U.S. policy toward the Soviet Union and Germany, it did little to promote this outcome. It was not until February 1947 that the U.S.

military government wrote a law to direct the breakup of German industry, and that law was quickly discarded.

Early Soviet occupation policies in its German zone present a sharp contrast to those imposed by the U.S. military in its zone. The Soviets were initially determined to weaken Germany's industrial and war-making potential and maximize their reparations. They therefore began rapidly dismantling and shipping materials out of their zone and into the Soviet Union. However, they stopped when it became obvious that the speed of reparations withdrawal was leading to a serious waste of resources as well as economic hardship and instability in eastern Germany. Soviet zone commanders ordered a slowdown in shipments and a series of political and economic reforms. Among the measures introduced in 1945 were a major land reform which broke up the large privately owned estates, an educational reform which not only greatly expanded opportunities but also restructured the curriculum, and labor reforms that promoted the use of workers' councils to run newly nationalized enterprises. Although the Soviets never allowed political developments to outrun their control, they were more flexible than the U.S. military command and able to support changes far more in line with local desires. The result: economic and social conditions greatly improved in eastern Germany and the Soviets were able to draw out reparations worth approximately $1 billion for three successive years, largely out of current production.[15]

U.S. authorities worried about the political effects of these changes on conditions in their own zone. According to one U.S. official, it was clear by November "that urban eastern Germany is now experiencing the beginning of social revolution. Perhaps the most important change so far is psychological. Radical workers, supported by Soviet MG . . . are taking possession of the economic instruments of power."[16] Aware that it was losing the ideological battle for the hearts and minds of Germans, the United States opposed Soviet suggestions for unified, across-zone political parties and trade unions.

Fearful that a unified Germany would likely be neutral, if not hostile to, U.S. foreign policy interests, the U.S. government decided on a policy of division. It made the first move toward achieving that end in May 1946, at the Council of Foreign Ministers meeting in Paris. There, the U.S. representative announced that no reparations would be given until the Soviets agreed to a set of common economic policies for governing Germany. This was a substantial demand. If the Soviets agreed, the United States would gain the ability to reverse the land reform, undo the nationalizations, and put an end to the workers' councils. Agreement would also give the United States access to the Soviet zone's food and coal resources, enabling it to support west German reindustrialization without having to compensate the Soviets. The Soviets were also told that if they rejected this demand, the United States would invite Britain and France to jointly create an integrated three-zone economy, a major step toward repudiation of all previous agreements and, of course, division.

The Soviets, as expected, rejected the demand, and the U.S. government followed through on its threat. In July 1946, the United States formally invited Britain and France to merge the economies of their respective zones. The British agreed in December 1946. The French, who were more worried about the implications of a revitalized Germany than the British, passed on the invitation. The U.S. government followed up its agreement with Britain by giving the Soviets a new ultimatum: accept the original U.S. offer by the March 1947 Council of Foreign Ministers meeting, or the United States would introduce a new currency into the U.S.-British economic zone. This ultimatum was made more for public relations reasons than anything else. The United States had already decided on division; there was nothing that the Soviets could do to reverse the decision. This was made clear when, only days after the start of the meeting, the presidential declaration of the Truman Doctrine branded communism, and by extension the Soviet Union, the greatest threat to world freedom.

Ignoring Truman's speech, the Soviets, who still desperately wanted reparations and to keep Germany from reindustrializing, offered the United States a final compromise. They agreed to accept a unified German economy but, in turn, wanted a common political structure, including all-German political parties and trade unions. The United States rejected the compromise. Shortly after the conclusion of the foreign ministers meeting, the U.S. and British governments agreed to create a new bizonal political structure dominated by Adenauer and the CDU.

In February 1948, the French finally agreed to join the British and U.S. governments in creating a unified west Germany. Later that month, the United States succeeded in forcing the Western European countries to accept this unified west Germany, represented by the U.S. military government, as a member of the Marshall Plan-mandated CEEC. In fact, the United States allocated to west Germany the largest single share of Marshall Plan funds. With these actions, the U.S. government made unequivocal its determination to revitalize west Germany and use it to organize Western European countries into a U.S.-dominated international economic system.

The Soviets, in recognition of U.S. intentions, made it known that if the United States continued to violate past agreements on Germany, the Soviets would no longer feel bound to respect them either, particularly the agreement guaranteeing Western access to Berlin. Disregarding the warning, the United States pushed ahead with its plan to introduce a new currency into the Western zones as part of a broader monetary reform package. The reform was initially scheduled for June 1, 1948. On May 30, the Soviets began inspecting Western troop trains as they entered Berlin. After a delay for technical reasons, the United States finally replaced the reichsmark with a new currency, the deutschemark, on June 18. The Soviets responded by refusing to allow the new currency into their zone or the western area of Berlin, and over the next week imposed an embargo on ground traffic into and out of Berlin. The United States responded with an airlift of supplies into west Berlin and a counterblockade of east Germany. On June 23, the Soviets introduced a new currency into their zone, and the following day the United States distributed the deutschemark into west Berlin.

Unhappy with the direction of events, the Soviets demanded a meeting with the United States to discuss the future of Germany. The United States agreed only to discuss the Berlin situation, and only after the blockade was lifted. The Soviet Union even tried to raise the issue of a divided Germany with the UN Security Council, but its efforts were blocked by the United States. The Soviets found themselves in a serious bind. They did not want to see Germany divided, yet their blockade of Berlin and the U.S.-led counterblockade of east Germany were effectively promoting the very division they sought to avoid.

The United States, on the other hand, found the German standoff convenient. It offered an opportunity to shape the west German political economy. In November 1948, the U.S. military government issued Law 75, which turned over management of the entire industry of the Ruhr to a handful of German industrialists, largely the same individuals who owned the industries during the Nazi regime. (In Korea, as well, the U.S. military government took enterprises away from working people and gave them to the South Korean state, which with U.S. encouragement sold many of them to former Japanese collaborators.)

Beginning in February 1949, the German Parliamentary Council, led by Adenauer, began considering the Basic Law, in essence a constitution for an independent West German state. Alarmed, the Soviets let it be known that they would lift the blockade if the United States would halt its plans to divide Germany and agree to a meeting of foreign ministers to discuss the country's future. When the United States refused, the Soviets were left with no choice but to announce, on May 4, an unconditional end to their blockade. The United States, in turn, agreed to attend a May 23 Council of Foreign Ministers meeting.

Although the United States had given informal assurance that it would take no action with regard to the division of Germany before the scheduled meeting, it encouraged the Parliamentary Council to push ahead. That it did. On May 8, it approved the Basic Law and over the following days the different state governments did the same. By the time of the meeting, the constitution for a new West German nation had already been approved. The division of Germany had gone too far to stop. The Federal Republic of Germany (West Germany) officially came into existence on September 24, 1949; the German Democratic Republic (East Germany) was founded, in response, on October 7, 1949.

This brief history shows that U.S. policymakers were willing to undermine popular democratic movements, make common cause with fascists and their supporters, and divide Germany in order to advance U.S. foreign policy interests. It should come as no surprise, then, that the United States pursued a similar course in Korea. Examination of U.S. policy toward Japan will provide additional evidence that U.S. foreign policy was guided by imperialist ambition, and that it was this ambition rather than democratic or humanitarian concerns that shaped U.S. interest and policy in Korea.

Restructuring Japan

The United States defeated Japan without the direct involvement of the Soviet Union. Thus, in contrast to the situation in Germany or Korea, the

United States was in a position to rule postwar Japan unchallenged. Truman therefore placed Japan under the command of General MacArthur, Supreme Commander for the Allied Powers (SCAP). One of the most notable consequences of the U.S. government's unchallenged rule over Japan was that MacArthur did not have to resort to dividing Japan when faced with domestic opposition to his policies.

The Japanese situation differed in yet another important way from the situation in Germany and Korea. Japanese political and economic leaders survived the war with their power largely intact, determined to maintain as much as possible of their prewar capitalist political economy. This was different from Korea where the former political and economic elite were discredited and a new government was under construction by revolutionaries. It was also different from Germany, where the government had collapsed with its military defeat and a resurgent left, with Soviet support, was attempting to fill the political vacuum. Because the Japanese government posed no fundamental threat to U.S. interests, MacArthur was perfectly content to exercise his authority through its existing structure, including the emperor, cabinet, and bureaucracy. As a result, the U.S. government saw no reason to establish a military government in Japan.

The U.S. government's Second World War allies did not approve of this state of affairs. Britain and the Soviet Union, in particular, felt strongly that Japan should be subject to some form of collective rule and occupation. To reduce tensions, the United States agreed in December 1945 to establish two consultative bodies through which the Allies could have input into the policies of SCAP. One was the eleven-member, Washington-based Far Eastern Commission. The other was the four-member, Tokyo-based Allied Council for Japan (composed of representatives from the United States, Britain, the Soviet Union, and China). The United States never intended to give either body real authority. The council, for example, did not hold its first meeting until April 3, 1946, long after SCAP had established the basic framework for the occupation and Japan's postwar political direction.

The United States initially proclaimed its commitment to democratize, decartelize, and demilitarize Japan. Because it had no fear of Soviet intervention in Japanese political affairs and (at least early in the occupation) considered China rather than Japan key to securing U.S. hegemony in Asia, its first initiatives were quite radical and far-reaching. The problem, as in Germany, was that the United States was unwilling to stand by its announced principles once it became clear that those principles led to outcomes unacceptable to U.S. interests.

In early October 1945, SCAP had issued what it called the Japanese Bill of Rights. It "abolished all laws infringing on civil liberties and trade union rights, freed all political prisoners, and dissolved the secret police."[17] SCAP took this action because it thought liberalization would promote social stability. Things did not work out as it intended. Much to SCAP's surprise and dismay, Japanese working people began using their new freedoms to challenge corporate power.

Before the end of the war, the Japanese government had transferred huge sums of money as well as goods and industrial supplies to the largest corporations. After the war, these corporations, uncertain of the future, were content to earn profits by selling their bloated inventories for inflated prices on the black market. They also assumed that the resulting economic crisis would eventually encourage the governing authorities to provide them with investment and production incentives. However, with real wages in a free fall, working people viewed the situation quite differently.[18] Led by the Japanese left, they engaged in numerous strikes, demonstrations, and takeovers of factories and offices.

This activism scared U.S. authorities. Also increasingly pessimistic about the stability of the Chinese nationalist government, they came to believe that a revitalized and reindustrialized Japan offered the most effective check on Soviet influence in the region. This new understanding of Japan's strategic value led naturally to an alliance between the U.S. occupation and the conservative Japanese power structure to suppress the efforts of those Japanese working for a radical restructuring of the Japanese political economy. By October 1946, SCAP was committed to a "reverse course." The labor movement was the first to feel the effects of this change in policy. "The police and the American Counter Intelligence Corps [began] . . . violently breaking up labor demonstrations . . . within SCAP this policy was known as 'housebreaking the labor movement.' "[19]

A similar backtracking occurred with regard to U.S. plans for restructuring the Japanese economy. The Japanese economy was dominated by a few large family-controlled conglomerates known as *zaibatsu;* SCAP initially wanted to destroy this monopoly structure, in large part to strip the country of its military capabilities. Its announced goal was the creation of a competitive capitalist economy dominated by small- and medium-sized businesses with an equitable distribution of ownership. Its plan to achieve this was ambitious. SCAP not only called for a rapid selloff of *zaibatsu* stocks regardless of price, but also a purge of top *zaibatsu* executives who would not be allowed to purchase stock for ten years. Even more notable, the plan called for giving "a decided [stock] purchase preference . . . to such persons as small or medium entrepreneurs and investors, and to such groups as agricultural and consumer cooperatives and trade unions."[20] A separate, compatible initiative called for Japan to pay reparations to the other countries of Asia, in particular China, in large part by dismantling and transferring some of its heavy and chemical industrial equipment.

The decartelization plan was never implemented. With opposition from a number of U.S. business leaders with investments in Japan, the two most important bills directing the breakup of the *zaibatsu* (the Deconcentration Law and the Anti-Monopoly Law) were not passed until early 1947. By that time, however, the "reverse course" was well underway. A new review board dominated by pro-Japanese U.S. business executives was set up in late 1947 to reexamine the original list of 1,200 firms scheduled for breakup. The board gradually reduced the number on the list to nine firms. In December 1948, after the nine had been "dissolved," SCAP declared that deconcentration had been successfully completed.[21]

The U.S. commitment to reparations also lost steam by mid-1946. In early 1947 a group of U.S. business executives was sent to Japan to review earlier reparations decisions. Their conclusion was that reparations should be limited and that most of the industries targeted for removal should instead be rehabilitated. Japan did eventually send industrial facilities to Asian countries, but it was less than 30 percent of the amount originally designated as surplus facilities.[22]

The initial U.S. plan to purge those Japanese officials associated with the war effort suffered a similar reversal. The United States allowed Japanese voters to elect representatives to a new national government in April 1946 and, soon after, gave that government complete responsibility for carrying out "The Removal and Exclusion of Undesirable Personnel from Public Office." Not surprisingly, purges soon came to a halt. What happened in Japan was limited even by comparison to the German experience. In

Germany, some 2.5 percent of the population in the U.S. zone was removed or suspended from office. In Japan it was only 0.29 percent.[23]

The U.S. government's "reverse course" also included a plan to promote Japan's economic recovery. This plan advocated that Japan adopt an export-led industrialization strategy supported by austerity policies designed to lower wages and prices. The austerity policies were harsh economic measures directed at Japanese workers that reduced average wages and created more unemployment but did little to promote growth.

Government unions, which included more than 25 percent of the country's organized workforce, called a general strike for February 1, 1947, to protest this U.S.-imposed economic plan. The day before the strike was scheduled to begin MacArthur ordered it canceled. Reluctantly, the trade union leadership complied. But with real per capita income at the end of 1947 only half of what it had been in 1934 to 1936, the unions were forced to call another general strike, this time for March 1948. MacArthur again ordered it canceled. The unions announced a new strike for August 7. This time MacArthur took more decisive action. In July, he ruled it illegal for government workers to strike or engage in collective bargaining. All existing contracts were invalidated. More than 900 workers were arrested after they struck anyway.

Fearful of the political repercussions from Japan's economic difficulties, the United States placed Joseph Dodge, a banker who had headed West Germany's economic restructuring program, in charge of the Japanese economy in 1949. He pushed a nine-point stabilization plan that involved reducing government spending, tightening credit conditions, imposing wage controls, and lengthening the work day. This plan, like the earlier one, was supposed to create an export-driven expansion. Instead, it pushed Japan into recession. Japanese workers once again demonstrated their opposition to U.S. economic policies. They rioted, attacked police stations, and seized control of many factories. SCAP eventually repressed the uprising but not before it was forced to use troops against those demonstrating for change.[24]

The U.S. decision to reinvigorate Japan had negative consequences for Korea, also. According to a March 1947 U.S. State Department report, "control of all Korea by Soviet or Soviet-dominated forces . . . would constitute an extremely serious political and military threat" to Japan.[25] A

1948 CIA paper analyzing the importance of a revitalized Japan to U.S. interests argued: "The key factor in postwar development of Japan is economic rehabilitation. As in the past, Japan, for normal economic functioning on an industrial basis, must have access to the Northeast Asiatic areas—notably North China, Manchuria, and Korea—now under direct, indirect, or potential control of the USSR."[26] In other words, the United States was willing, less than three years after Korea's liberation from Japan, to help restore Japanese dominance over Korea in order to further its own regional ambitions. As it turned out, Korea did prove to be a "key factor" in Japan's economic rehabilitation. The Korean War was a great boon to the Japanese economy. U.S. military spending, write Kolko and Kolko, "provided the essential economic stimulus and actuated the Japanese economic 'miracle' that has endured, despite periodic lapses, until this day."[27]

U.S. efforts to remake Japan as a regional power also required restoring Japan's independence. The U.S. government had delayed raising the issue of a peace treaty, in spite of pressure from the Japanese people and governments of other countries, for two interrelated reasons: it worried about the stability of the Japanese government without the presence of U.S. troops and it worried about losing its recently acquired military bases. Finally, in late 1949, after repression had weakened the left, the U.S. government decided the time was ripe for action. It announced that it would draft a peace treaty that included continuing the U.S. military presence as a requirement. The Japanese protested this arrangement to no avail.

Japan was not alone in opposing America's "peace treaty" strategy. Britain, China, and the Soviet Union strongly objected to being left out of the drafting of the treaty, as well as the requirement that Japan continue to provide bases for the U.S. military. The United States, in response, offered a non-negotiable compromise: it would write two separate treaties, one a peace treaty and the other a military security treaty. Japan, however, was required to approve both treaties on the same day. It did so at a U.S.-sponsored peace conference in September 1951, and Japan regained its independence in April 1952. Notably, the peace conference took place during the height of the Korean War. This created a political environment where the United States could speak of rewarding Japan for its assistance to the war effort and easily reject Soviet objections, as well as demand compliance from Britain and China.

In sum, U.S. foreign policy from 1945 to 1950 was consistently directed toward creating a U.S.-dominated capitalist world order. To achieve this objective, the U.S. government heightened the Cold War, promoted division in Europe and Asia, and politically restructured Germany and Japan through reprehensible means. It was Korea's ill fortune that because of geopolitical factors its domestic political choices became intertwined with U.S. economic and political ambitions. To satisfy those ambitions the U.S. government crushed the popularly supported KPR and its associated mass organizations, promoted the political fortunes of reactionaries and collaborators, and divided Korea. These actions, undertaken not out of ignorance or with the best interest of the Korean people in mind, were quite deliberate.

Chapter 5

The Korean War

The Korean War is the pivotal event shaping contemporary American understanding of political developments on the Korean peninsula and U.S. foreign policy toward Korea. Yet by focusing public attention on the Korean War as the historical starting point for U.S.-Korean relations, mainstream media and government accounts overlook U.S. actions in the region prior to 1950, including the suppression of southern Korean popular movements, disdain for independence efforts, and the promotion of Korean division. While ignoring this history makes it difficult to understand either the origins or significance of the Korean War, it certainly makes it easier to present the United States as the savior of Korean democracy.

The conventional wisdom surrounding the Korean War holds that the Soviet Union built a puppet Communist government in the North and encouraged it to invade the South in order to "Communize" the entire peninsula. Thus the United States, presented as a defender of freedom against Communist aggression, entered the war on the side of the belea-guered South as the leader of a multinational, UN-mandated force, and succeeded, although at significant human cost, in driving back the aggressors. This book has challenged elements of this conventional wisdom, showing that the North Korean regime was far from a puppet of the Soviet Union; that a majority of Koreans supported a socialist-oriented political economy in the period after liberation; and that most Koreans in the south opposed both the division and the highly dictatorial U.S.-created South Korean regime. Still, the question remains: how should we understand the Korean War?

The Korean War was not fought to repulse a "foreign" invader, it was a civil war fought to reunify the country. The United States intervened not to defend Korean democracy or independence but to protect its own political interests, represented in Korea by an unpopular South Korean government led by Syngman Rhee. The U.S. intervention prevented the likely internal outcome, quick resolution of the conflict in favor of socialist forces, and succeeded in maintaining the political status quo, including Korea's division. Even today, a peace treaty concluding the war has yet to be signed, and the Korean peninsula remains highly militarized and potentially explosive. Although North Korea is blamed for this situation, it was the United States and South Korea that sabotaged good faith efforts to peacefully reunify Korea at the Geneva Conference. The United States continued to reject North Korean overtures to replace the armistice with a formal peace agreement as a step toward normalizing relations and reducing tensions between the two countries.

The Beginning of the War

A telegram from John Muccio, U.S. ambassador to Korea, arrived at the State Department at 9:26 p.m. on June 24, 1950 (which was June 25 in Korea). It stated: "According to Korean army reports which are partially confirmed by Korean Military Advisory Group field advisory reports, North Korean forces invaded Republic of Korea territory at several points this morning."[1] In other words, Muccio was reporting that fighting was taking place and that he had yet to confirm South Korean claims of unprovoked North Korean aggression.

Secretary of State Dean Acheson, without consulting President Truman, who was vacationing in Missouri, decided that the UN Security Council should be called into session the next day, June 25. He instructed Ernest A. Gross, deputy U.S. representative to the United Nations, to telephone UN Secretary-General Trygve Lie. Gross told Lie, "The American ambassador to the Republic of Korea has informed the Department of State that North Korean forces had invaded the territory of the Republic of Korea at several points in the early morning hours of June 25."[2] Muccio, clearly, had not expressed such certainty in his cable.

At the Security Council meeting, Gross presented a resolution that described the events in Korea as "an armed attack upon the Republic of

Korea by forces from North Korea." It called for a withdrawal of those forces, as well as the cooperation of UN member states to ensure that outcome. Gross argued that since the United Nations had helped to create South Korea as an independent state, this attack was in essence an attack on the organization.

The United States placed great emphasis on the idea of UN responsibility for Korea, so it is worth recalling Soviet objections to the 1947 UN decision to become involved in Korean affairs. Among their most important objections was that the UN had no jurisdiction over postwar settlement issues. The United States, for example, refused to allow the UN to consider issues related to Germany and Japan on the same grounds. Another objection was to the UN decision to establish a temporary commission (UNTCOK) to observe elections without first giving the Korean people an opportunity to present their position on national election procedures. The UN charter required consultation with both sides in a dispute.

Overlooking both the lack of firm evidence on the origins of the fighting and Soviet objections, Secretary-General Lie worked hard to win approval of the U.S. resolution. He lobbied several countries and even allowed a South Korean representative to address the Security Council. The final vote was nine to one in favor of the resolution. The only negative vote was from the Yugoslav representative who offered an alternative resolution, which called for a cease-fire, withdrawal of all forces, and a meeting with both North and South Korean representatives. The Soviet Union, which could have vetoed the resolution, did not have a representative at the meeting. It had been boycotting the Security Council to protest its refusal to recognize the People's Republic of China.

On the afternoon of June 27, the Security Council met again to consider a second resolution, "that the Members of the United Nations furnish such assistance to the Republic of Korea as may be necessary to repel the armed attack and to restore international peace and security in the area." The Security Council had before it a June 26 United Nations Commission on Korea statement which concluded, largely on the basis of a field report by two UN field officers, "first, that judging from the actual progress of operations, the Northern regime is carrying out a well-planned, concerted, and full-scale invasion of South Korea, second, that the South Korean forces were deployed on [a] wholly defensive basis in all sectors of the parallel, and third, that they were taken completely by surprise as they had no reason to believe from intelligence sources that invasion was imminent."[3] The Security Council passed the resolution, committing its member nations to war.

The U.S. government maintains that the decision to fight in Korea was made in response to this resolution. Actually, the opposite is closer to the truth. Several hours before the Security Council meeting, Truman issued a statement, largely authored by Acheson, that said, "The attack upon Korea makes it plain beyond all doubt that communism has passed beyond the use of subversion to conquer independent nations and will now use armed invasion and war." In response, he ordered "U.S. air and sea forces to give the Korean government troops cover and support," and the Seventh Fleet to defend Taiwan from possible Chinese mainland attack. The statement also announced additional support for U.S. forces in the Philippines and greater military assistance to the Philippine government, as well as an "acceleration in the furnishing of military assistance to the forces of France and the Associated States in Indochina and the dispatch of a military mission to provide close working relations with those forces."[4] Thus Truman and Acheson, no doubt thinking about NSC-68, quickly took advantage of the fighting in Korea to promote a broader anticommunist offensive.

With Truman acting to commit U.S. forces in Korea before the UN Security Council meeting, the member states were left with no choice other than to follow the U.S. lead and pass the resolution. As Jon Halliday and Bruce Cumings explain:

> The United Nations was used to ratify American decisions. As an official Joint Chiefs of Staff study put it, "Having resolved upon armed intervention for itself, the U.S. government the next day sought the approval and the assistance of the United Nations," an accurate judgement.[5]

Three days after the UN passed its second resolution, Truman upped the ante. He ordered the bombing of specific targets in North Korea, a naval blockade of the entire Korean coast, and use of U.S. ground troops. The UN followed on July 7, passing another resolution recommending that "all Members providing military forces and other assistance . . . make such forces and other assistance available to a unified command under the United States." It also called upon the United States to "designate the commander of such forces."[6] Amazingly, the UN placed all member country forces under U.S. control without requiring accountability. In other words, the United States was given the freedom to fight the war unaccountable to any other member nation, clothed in the principles and ideals the United Nations claimed to represent.

Truman chose General Douglas MacArthur to head the unified command. Along with the United States, fifteen nations including Australia, Belgium, Canada, Columbia, Ethiopia, France, Greece, Luxembourg, the Netherlands, New Zealand, the Philippines, the Republic of South Africa, Thailand, Turkey, and the United Kingdom provided soldiers. The United States, however, provided most of the troops and paid most of the bills. It was a U.S. show wrapped in a UN flag.

Establishing Responsibility

The U.S. government succeeded in building international support for intervention in Korea, largely because it was able to convince "world public opinion" that North Korea had launched an unprovoked and well-planned invasion of South Korea. The evidence does not support this charge. It is true that the North Korean decision to cross the 38th parallel in force escalated the fighting between North and South forces into a full-scale war. But this does not mean that the North alone should be held responsible for the conflict. The Korean War was a civil war whose roots are to be found in the liberation period struggle between radical and conservative political forces. The division of the country both frustrated a peaceful resolution of these political differences and forced them into a North-South framework. Thus, primary responsibility for the Korean War should rest with those who divided the country, in particular, the U.S. government.

Moreover, the fighting, which began on June 25, 1950, was not the first cross-border battle between North and South Korea. North-South clashes had become increasingly frequent in 1949. The first major battle was initiated by the South on May 4, near Kaesong. It lasted four days; thousands of troops were involved, some 400 North Korean and 22 South Korean soldiers died. Another major clash, this time provoked by the North, took place June 26 on the Ongjin peninsula (where the June 25, 1950, fighting began). Perhaps the most serious fighting started on August 4, 1949, when North Korean soldiers attacked a South Korean force occupying a small mountain north of the 38th parallel, again on the Ongjin peninsula. Although the South Korean troops were badly beaten, the South continued to initiate small cross-border battles on the Ongjin peninsula throughout August.

The Ongjin peninsula was the scene of the heaviest fighting for important military reasons. The nearby city of Haeju, on the northern side of the 38th parallel, was the headquarters of the South Korean Workers' Party and the Southern guerrilla command. It was also directly connected by highway and rail to the North Korean capital Pyongyang, which was only sixty-five miles away. In addition, there were railway lines from the Southern border cities of Ongjin and Kaesong which converged on Haeju. Thus, if Southern forces could gain control over the northern part of the Ongjin peninsula and Haeju, they would be well-placed to disrupt the Southern guerrilla movement and launch a quick strike at Pyongyang. Recognizing its vulnerability, the North, in turn, focused its military attention on the southern part of the Ongjin peninsula and Kaesong. Control over the peninsula and territory east (including Kaesong) would enable it to strengthen its defensive position, and turning the tables, put pressure on Seoul.

It was well-known at the time that Syngman Rhee was eager for war. General William L. Roberts, the U.S. Military Advisor Group commander, was certainly aware of this, commenting: "Each [of the many clashes in August 1949] was in our opinion brought on by the presence of a small South Korean salient north of the parallel. The South Koreans wish to invade the North. We tell them that if such occurs, all advisors will pull out and the . . . [money] spigot will turn off."[7] Undeterred, Rhee publicly stated in October 1949 that it was only U.S. opposition that kept the South from taking Pyongyang in three days. Later that month, Rhee's defense minister commented at a press conference, "If we had our own way we would . . . have started up already. . . . We are strong enough to march up and take Pyongyang within a few days."[8]

The following year, Rhee and his officials began to change their public tune. Instead of threatening to march north, they began calling for U.S. help to strengthen Southern defenses against a future North Korean attack. In May 1950, for example, Rhee made an appeal for combat planes: "May and June may be the crucial period in the life of our nation." At a press conference later that month, the defense minister stated, "North Korean troops were moving in force toward the 38th parallel and that there was imminent danger of invasion from the North."[9]

Significantly, after mid-May the South Korean government made no further public statements about the danger of a North Korean attack. In fact, Rhee ordered the South Korean army to take up defensive positions and to retreat if attacked. It was this posture that the two UN field officers say they observed when they visited the 38th parallel in June 1950. However, not everyone shared their opinion of South Korean military behavior. An Australian embassy representative reported in late June:

> Patrols were going in from the South to the North, endeavoring to attract the North back in pursuit. Plimsoll warned that this could lead to war and it was clear that there was some degree of American involvement, as well as South Koreans wishing to promote conflict with American support.[10]

According to the former Australian prime minister, E. Gough Whitlam,

> Less than a week before war erupted . . . the Australian government had received reports of intended South Korean aggressions from its representative in South Korea. The evidence was sufficiently strong for the Australian prime minister to authorize a cable to Washington urging that no encouragement be given to the South Korean government.[11]

The South was not alone in spoiling for a fight. In September 1949, Kim Il Sung apparently sought Soviet support for his own offensive against the South. According to Soviet documents, the North had received information that the South was readying yet another attack on the northern part of Ongjin peninsula and Kim wanted Stalin's permission to strike first, "with the goal of seizing the Ongjin peninsula and part of the territory of South Korea to the east of the Ongjin peninsula, approximately to Kaesong, so as to shorten the lines of defense . . . [and] if the international situation permits . . . to move further South."[12] The Soviets opposed this move, arguing, among other things, that "if military actions begin at the initiative of the North and acquire a prolonged character, then this can give to the Americans cause for any kind of interference in Korean affairs."[13] Stalin did not, however, oppose a North Korean counteroffensive if the South attacked first.[14]

Both the North and the South were thus poised and eager for battle. As Bruce Cumings explains, "The 1950 logic for both sides was to see who would be stupid enough to move first, with Kim itching to invade and hoping for a clear Southern provocation, and hotheads in the South hoping to provoke an 'unprovoked' assault, in order to get American help—for that was the only way the South could hope to win."[15] Seen from this perspective, it makes little sense to view June 25 as the "start" of the Korean War or to place total responsibility on the DPRK.

In addition, there is also reason to believe that it was the South, and not the North, that actually initiated the June 25 fighting. According to the U.S.-UN-South Korean version of events, fighting began on the Ongjin peninsula at 4 A.M. with a North Korean attack on Southern positions, hours later spreading eastward along the 38th parallel (Kaesong, Chunchon, and finally all the way to the east coast). According to the North, the South had been shelling Northern positions on the Ongjin peninsula for over a day when, in the early morning of June 25, troops from the ROK Seventeenth Regiment moved north across the 38th parallel toward Haeju. The North says it responded by blocking the advance and launching its own attack south. In fact, the South does claim to have attacked Haeju, although not under the conditions asserted by the North. On the morning of June 26, the South Korean government stated that its forces had briefly taken control of the city as a result of a successful counterattack.

The chronology of events seems to support the North Korean version. The official U.S. military history of the war states that the Ongjin peninsula was not considered defensible and that the ROK Seventeenth Regiment was evacuated in response to the initial North Korean attack. The nearby city of Kaesong came under DPRK attack at around 5:30 A.M. and was taken by 9:30 A.M. In short, North Korean forces were on the offensive and South Korean forces were in retreat. Yet somehow, in the late afternoon or early evening of June 25, after South Korean troops had been evacuated, in an area under North Korean control, the South Korean government claims troops from the Seventeenth Regiment were able to mount a successful counterattack, capturing and holding Haeju for a brief period of time, before slipping back over the border.[16] This hardly seems likely. What seems more likely is that South Korean troops stationed on the Ongjin peninsula attacked Haeju first. The North, either fearing a South Korean general offensive or eager to take advantage of the Southern attack, responded in force.

This scenario, in which the South moved first, is also consistent with a comment made by John Gunther, General MacArthur's biographer. Gunther and his wife were on a June 1950 outing in Japan with two important members of the U.S. occupation staff. One was called to the phone. When he returned, Gunther claims he said, "A big story has just broken. The South Koreans have attacked North Korea."[17] Gunther dismissed the statement, deciding that the official got it backward because of his excitement.

Finally, even if the North initiated the fighting on June 25, there are reasons to doubt that its attack across the border was the planned opening salvo of an invasion of the South. For example, the North was still building its military strength. Tens of thousands of North Korean soldiers recently returned from fighting in the Chinese civil war were being slowly integrated into the DPRK military. Had the North waited several more months, it would have had an additional five divisions mobilized. The significance of this is revealed by the fact that the initial Northern attack included only 38,000 soldiers, less than half of the U.S. estimated total of 95,000 North Korean soldiers. Moreover, the South Korean military had some 50,000 troops stationed between the border and Seoul. It is hard to imagine planners of a massive invasion choosing to launch an attack under such conditions.

It was an unlikely moment for the North to launch an attack for political reasons as well. National Assembly elections were held in the South on May 30, 1950. South Koreans voted for the most left-wing candidates running, dealing Rhee and his allies a major electoral defeat. In contrast to Rhee, a majority of these newly elected officials were open to a dialogue with the North. Recognizing this, the North launched a peace offensive, calling for a meeting of political leaders to discuss holding an all-Korean election to create a unified Korean government.

Hard evidence linking the Soviet Union to the June 25 fighting is also lacking. As noted above, although Stalin knew of Kim's desire to take the offensive, Soviet documents also show that he opposed a first strike. We do know that Soviet weapons and equipment were sent to North Korea in April 1950. But the Soviet Union also greatly reduced the number of military advisors in the North to 120 as compared with 500 U.S. advisors in the South. Moreover, the Soviets did not respond to the fighting by initiating their own war mobilization or increasing military shipments to the North.

The Soviets also made the North pay for additional supplies and equipment, and most of what they were willing to sell was pre-1945 vintage. The South, in contrast, received modern military equipment from the United States at no cost. Perhaps most telling was the Soviet Union's boycott of the Security Council meetings when the actual fighting began. Had its representative been present, he could have easily vetoed the UN resolutions, thereby greatly complicating the U.S. war effort against the North. It is hard to reconcile this absence with either Soviet encouragement or direction of a prepared invasion.

The best explanation of what happened on June 25 is that Syngman Rhee deliberately initiated the fighting and then successfully blamed the North. The North, eagerly waiting for provocation, took advantage of the Southern attack and, without incitement by the Soviet Union, launched its own strike with the objective of capturing Seoul. Then a massive U.S. intervention followed.

There is also reason to believe that Rhee did not act alone and that his plan was encouraged by influential Americans who believed that war in Korea would provide the necessary justification for launching a broader crusade against communism. For example, General MacArthur and John Foster Dulles, the Republican advisor to the U.S. secretary of state, considered war between the United States and the Soviet Union inevitable and believed that, given the existing U.S. superiority in arms, the sooner this happened, the better. They were also convinced that Asia, especially China, was the logical place to confront what they believed to be a Soviet-directed, international communist conspiracy. Alarmingly, from their point of view, this movement was gaining strength in China and Korea, and still had influence in Japan. They felt that the U.S. government was not doing enough to support those Asians who opposed it, in particular Chiang Kai-shek.

In 1949, Chiang had been forced to withdraw with what was left of his army to the island of Taiwan, where he faced the threat of invasion from the mainland. He asked Truman to order the U.S. Navy to block any Chinese attack, but Truman refused. At the beginning of 1950, Truman, fed up with Chiang's corruption, said in a written statement that the United States would not give "military aid or advice" to Chiang and would not "pursue a course which would lead to involvement in the civil conflicts in China."[18] This was U.S. policy until the Korean War, a policy that people like MacArthur and Dulles tried to change.

One who recognized the possibility that the United States might be drawn into a war "against communism" was Senator John Connally of Texas, chairman of the Senate Foreign Relations Committee and the Democratic Party's main spokesperson on foreign relations. In a May 1950 interview with *U.S. News and World Report,* Connally stated that it was his opinion that the Soviet Union did not want a war, but that there were those in the United States who were looking for an excuse to start such a war. As he explained, "Well, a lot of them believe like this: They believe that events will transpire which will maneuver around and present an incident which will make us fight. That's what a lot of them are saying: 'We've got to battle some time, why not now?'"[19] And on June 25, events did transpire to present just such an incident.[20] There is no hard evidence to support this account of conspiracy, but as the journalist I.F. Stone stated in *The Hidden History of the Korean War,* "The hypothesis that invasion was encouraged politically by silence, invited militarily by defensive formations, and finally set off by some minor lunges across the border when all was ready would explain a great deal."[21]

While questions remain about which side started the fighting, there is little question about who gained and lost. The war saved Rhee from being thrown out of office, and Chiang from an invasion that would have led to the same end. It gave both Truman and Acheson the crisis they needed to implement NSC-68, and MacArthur the opportunity he wanted to launch an all-out war against communism in Asia. The People's Republic of China, on the other hand, lost an opportunity to regain Taiwan and claim its place in the UN Security Council. The Soviet Union faced a far more hostile environment as a result of the war-related reindustrialization of Germany and Japan and the remilitarization of Western Europe and the United States. It was, of course, the Korean people who lost the most, not only because of immense destruction of life and property, but also because nothing was changed by it. At its conclusion, their country remained divided into two hostile parts.

The Nature of the War: Phase I

U.S. accounts of the Korean War typically portray it as a war for freedom in which the U.S.-supported South Korea fought to repulse a brutal invasion from the North, whose aim was to create a communist dictatorship throughout the peninsula. In reality, it was a war fought to determine the political character and vision of a unified Korea. Those who wished to build a socialist-oriented Korea by restoring to power the liberation-era people's committees enjoyed majority support. The United States, opposed to this outcome, led the fight to expand South Korea's repressive, capitalist political economy into the North.

The first phase of the Korean War began as North Korean troops crossed the 38th parallel south of the North Korean city of Chorwon at approximately 5:30 A.M. on June 25. After breaking through ROK lines, they headed south toward Seoul, which they easily captured on June 28. After waiting a week, they began moving south again, down the peninsula. The Northern advance greatly benefited from the activities of Southern guerrillas. Although the United States had considered the guerrilla movement destroyed as of May 1950, it clearly played a very important role in the fighting. The fact that some 67,000 guerrillas were reported killed and 24,000 captured in the period from June 25 to August 31 provides one indication of its size and involvement in the war.[22]

As the war continued, the United States rapidly built up its forces in Korea, and by the beginning of August, U.S. and South Korean forces together outnumbered Northern forces along the front—92,000 (47,000 Americans) to 70,000.[23] Slowed by the growing military strength of the U.S. and UN forces, as well as by overextended supply lines, the Northern drive was finally brought to a halt at the end of the first week of August at the Pusan perimeter (with its northern point at Pohang on the coast, its southern point in the Chinju-Masan region, and its center just above Taegu). The North launched its last major offensive at the end of August but failed to break through U.S. defenses.

Having secured his front line, MacArthur moved to split Northern forces. On September 15, more than 260 ships successfully landed troops at the port city of Inchon, near Seoul. Unable to block the landing, the North had no choice but to withdraw from Seoul and the surrounding area. By September 28, Rhee was back in Seoul and U.S. forces were in command of the South.

Differences in the political character of the two Korean governments are readily observable during this first phase of the fighting. As the North advanced down the peninsula, the South Korean government ordered local authorities to execute their leftist political prisoners. In Seoul, there was enough time to kill only about one hundred prisoners. According to North Korean claims, based on eyewitness reports, approximately 1,000 prisoners were slaughtered in Inchon in late June. On July 14, the head of the South Korean National Police admitted that his force alone had executed 1,200 leftists since June 25.[24] In Pusan, the South Korean government set up what British reporter James Cameron called "concentration camps." He described one as follows:

> I had seen Belsen, but this was worse. This terrible mob of men convicted of nothing, untried, South Koreans in South Korea, suspected of being "unreliable." There were hundreds of them, they were skeletal, puppets of string, faces translucent gray, manacled to each other with chains, cringing in the classic Oriental attitude of subjection, the squatting fetal position, in piles of garbage.[25]

Northern forces also committed executions as they moved south; the victims were mostly captured ROK officials, KNP officers, and leaders of right-wing youth groups. There is also evidence that some American POWs were executed in spite of North Korean government efforts to stop the practice. In October 1950, the United States claimed that the North had killed 20,000 civilians and 300 P.O.W.s in the first three months of the war. The biggest number of civilian deaths, perhaps as many as 7,000, was said to have taken place in a single incident in July, the Taejon Massacre. The U.S. government described this incident as similar in hideousness to the Rape of Nanking or the Warsaw Ghetto massacre. It appears an atrocity did take place in Taejon, but the evidence points to the work of South Korean forces.[26] Many other charges made by the U.S. government against the North were also discredited. The United States was eventually forced to admit that "the probable total of murders of civilians and POWs by both Chinese and the North Koreans to June 1953 was 29,915."[27] To put that number in perspective, a U.S. official in Seoul estimated that the Rhee government probably killed more than 100,000 people "without any trial whatsoever," when U.S. forces succeeded in reimposing its rule over the South in September 1950.[28]

In contrast to the Southern reign of terror against South Koreans, which was in many ways a continuation of earlier ROK policies, DPRK units sweeping south worked with local leftists to re-establish people's committees. These committees were given considerable freedom of action, although the North did exercise "sharp procedural controls to ensure that committee membership would conform to North Korean practice and discipline."[29] The North also pursued land reform, another key postwar demand. Cumings described a law passed on July 4, 1950, which

> called for the expropriation of landlord-held land without compensation, and limited the amount of land peasants could keep to five chongbo (about twelve acres); but it allowed richer peasants who worked their own land to keep up to twenty chongbo, a rather large farm in Korea, and also did not touch Oriental Development Company land that had been redistributed to tenants in 1948 by USAMGIK.[30]

More generally, the Northern political program called for "a united free Korea, land redistribution and nationalization of industry, equal status for women, a broad program of social betterment, lower prices and assured living for workers, and more efficient and honest government."[31] This program and the North Korean presence was well-received by South Koreans. A U.S. Air Force study of the occupation of Seoul described it as a time of "music, theater, parades, huge spectacles."[32] Similarly, interviews conducted by the predecessor of the RAND Corporation revealed that North Korean officials had been "courteous and reasonable": "When orders were given, the reasons for them were patiently explained. When systematic confiscation of property took place, the new uses to which it was to be put were carefully indicated. When people were arrested it was done apologetically and always in terms of the necessity of locating some 'outside' enemy."[33] The interviews also revealed that women's organizations were especially encouraged, and women were given positions of responsibility in the general administration of the city.

In short, it appears that the North did not approach the South as a conquered country. Its policies were clearly rooted in the politics of the period following the surrender of Japan, although with some significant differences. For example, the North promoted the use of people's committees on the basis of North Korean experience; no mention was made of the Korean People's Republic. All in all, it is fair to say that the North waged a revolutionary struggle for social change during this first phase of the Korean civil war.

The Nature of the War: Phase II

Having succeeded in regaining control over the South by late September, the U.S. government faced the question of what to do next. Its choices were to halt military operations and seek peace negotiations with the North or to continue the war in an attempt to unify Korea under U.S. terms. It chose the latter, thus beginning the second phase of the war.

The U.S. government has always explained its decision to cross the 38th parallel as a response to UN policy, in particular the October 7 resolution which mandated that "all appropriate steps be taken to ensure conditions of stability throughout Korea [and] all constituent acts be taken, including the holding of elections, under the auspices of the United Nations, for the establishment of a unified, independent, and democratic government in the sovereign State of Korea."[34] But the truth is that the United States had decided to cross the 38th parallel before the UN vote.

Truman had, in late September, given MacArthur permission to cross into the North and decide the terms of DPRK surrender. Armed with this authority, MacArthur issued an October 1 call for the North to surrender unconditionally, although he knew that the North would refuse. In fact, South Korean forces, supported by U.S. air and naval units, had already crossed the 38th parallel on the morning of October 1, before the call for surrender was issued. U.S. forces made their move across the 38th parallel on the morning of October 7, before the UN Security Council meeting to vote on the resolution.[35]

U.S. actions obviously predetermined the outcome of the UN vote, but the speech given by Warren Austin, U.S. ambassador to the United Nations, in defense of the resolution, deserves careful consideration:

> Today, the forces of the United Nations stand on the threshold of military victory. . . . The aggressor's forces should not be permitted to have refuge behind an imaginary line . . . [which] has no basis for existence in law or reason. Neither the United Nations, its Commission on Korea, nor the Republic of Korea, recognizes such line. Now, the North Koreans, by armed attack upon the Republic of Korea, have denied the reality of such a line. Whatever ephemeral separation of Korea there was for purposes relating to the surrender of the Japanese was so volatile that nobody recognizes it. Let us not, at this critical hour and on this grave event, erect such a boundary.[36]

As Michael Walzer points out, "If the 38th parallel was an imaginary line, how then did we recognize the initial aggression?"[37] In other words, Austin's own speech makes clear that even the U.S. government understood that the Korean War was a civil war.

South Korean and U.S. forces met little opposition as they moved north across the "imaginary line." As cities and towns were taken, South Korean units, primarily the KNP assisted by right-wing youth gangs, were given responsibility for maintaining order. By October 10, the KNP controlled nine towns north of the 38th parallel.[38]

As U.S.-led forces continued to advance toward the Chinese border, U.S. newspapers trumpeted that the end of the war was near. The exuberant headlines were premature. The North Korean army was far from defeated; it had followed a strategy, also used by the Chinese Communists, of retreating and regrouping, and fighting only when the situation was most advantageous for doing so. Moreover, the Chinese government would soon provide direct assistance.

The Chinese government warned the UN member states that they would intervene if UN forces crossed the 38th parallel. In preparation, they began moving hundreds of thousands of troops toward Manchuria in early September. Still suffering the wounds of their own civil war, the Chinese government did not want to engage in a new war against the United States. It had begun demobilizing large numbers of its 1.4 million strong People's Liberation Army just before the fighting in Korea began. At the same time, it had good reason to feel threatened by the existence of hostile forces heading toward the Chinese border. Perhaps even more important, Mao Zedong felt an obligation to help the North, which had only recently come to his assistance during a difficult period in China's own civil war.

Its warnings ignored by the United States, China sent 250,000 soldiers across the Yalu River into North Korea on the night of October 19. When the U.S.-led drive continued, combined Chinese and North Korean forces made a number of pounding attacks against both U.S. and ROK units, inflicting significant casualties. They then broke off contact to await the U.S. response. In early November, MacArthur responded by ordering massive air attacks, with B-29s dropping incendiary bombs and napalm, destroying entire North Korean towns. The area between the front and the Chinese border was turned into a "wilderness of scorched earth."[39] Then, in late November, MacArthur launched a new general offensive that moved forward for three days until it was engulfed by a massive Chinese and North

Korean counteroffensive. UN troops were thrown back into rapid retreat. Although U.S. attention focused on Chinese involvement, the North Korean military also played a significant role in the fighting. Though thought to have been destroyed as an effective force, the North Korean army put some 150,000 troops into the field.

The Soviet Union also entered the war during this phase of the fighting, though in a limited, defensive capacity. Beginning in November, it gave air cover to Chinese and DPRK forces operating in the northern part of North Korea. Soviet pilots claimed to have shot down "tens" of U.S. planes; they also suffered heavy losses. The Soviets masked their involvement by having their pilots wear Chinese uniforms and marking their planes with Chinese emblems.[40] The Soviets also later acknowledged that they had five Red Army divisions fully outfitted and prepared for combat if the United States threatened to expand the war into either China or the Soviet Union.[41]

Faced with what seemed like a complete rout, Truman raised the possibility of using the atomic bomb during a November 30 press conference. He also made it clear that the United States would not wait upon or require UN authorization. Truman actually went so far as to order unassembled bombs to be moved to an aircraft carrier on the Korean coast; practice bombing runs were then made over the North.[42] MacArthur later asked for, but was not given, authorization to use twenty-six atomic weapons, listing such cities as Beijing and Vladivostok as potential targets.

The combined Chinese and North Korean offensive eventually succeeded in driving back U.S.-UN forces. Pyongyang was retaken on December 5, and by the end of the month the North was back in control of its own territory. It was now up to the Chinese and North Korean governments to decide what would come next, peace talks or a continued war. They, like the United States before them, chose to cross the "imaginary line" in pursuit of total victory.

Even a brief examination of U.S. and South Korean government policies in this second phase of the fighting, a period when U.S.-led forces controlled some 90 percent of North Korea, can offer considerable insight into the political nature of the war. Internal U.S. documents make clear that the South Korean forces carried out widespread killings and torture in the North; one described it as "a nauseating reign of terror."[43] One possible motivating factor was that the ROK officer corps included many Northerners who had fought against the Communists in Manchuria under the Japanese. In fact, in June 1950, all but one senior ROK commander had served in the Japanese military.[44] Northerners also tended to dominate the KNP and youth leagues. It is likely that these officers felt a special motivation to settle a score with those who resisted colonialism and chose socialism.

North Koreans accused UN forces of committing extensive war crimes, including the mass murder of more than 170,000 civilians during their occupation of the DPRK.[45] They also accused them of destroying villages and food supplies during their withdrawal, leaving many North Koreans homeless and hungry during a winter when temperatures consistently dropped below freezing. Callum MacDonald concludes his study of the UN occupation of the North as follows:

> The evidence suggests that there is more to the North Korean case than has ever been admitted in the West. . . . ROK, Army, police, and paramilitary forces were relied upon to preserve order and replicated the pattern of ferocious repression already evident below the 38th parallel. . . . Since the ROK was not recognized as sovereign in the North, the UN Command, as the legal authority, and the United States as head of that command, must bear the ultimate responsibility. Washington must also take responsibility for significant undisciplined acts by U.S. troops, which included rape and the murder or mistreatment of civilians and POWs. The full extent of these crimes awaits further investigation.[46]

On the day before ROK troops crossed into the North, Acheson said, "Korea will be used as a stage to prove what Western democracy can do to help the underprivileged countries of the world."[47] The United States may have promised liberation, but what it delivered was a deliberate and massive campaign of terror. This campaign was designed not only to crush the left, but also to impose Rhee's government on the people of the North, a government that the United States had already helped to impose on the people of the South.

The Nature of the War: Phase III

The last phase of the war began with the late December southward crossing of the 38th parallel by North Korean and Chinese forces. They recaptured Seoul on January 4, but their offensive ran out of steam by the end of the month. U.S.-UN forces launched a counterattack, retaking Seoul in mid-March. They pushed on, crossed the 38th parallel, and once more headed north toward Pyongyang. But by mid-1951, their offensive had ground to a halt.

Both sides now faced each other, as historians Stewart Lone and Gavan McCormack write, "with huge armies more or less evenly balanced on the ground seesawing back and forth across a relatively narrow band of territory in the general vicinity of where the war had begun." Accepting the new reality, both sides agreed in July to begin talks in Kaesong over how to end the fighting. Expectations on the North Korean side were that it would take only a few days to reach an accord.[48] The war, however, was to last two more years, with some the heaviest fighting taking place during that period. The war continued largely because the U.S. government refused to stop fighting until all outstanding issues, in particular the location of the cease-fire line and terms for exchange of prisoners, had been settled.

The question of the location of the cease-fire line was the first issue to be addressed at the Kaesong talks. Wilfred Burchett, an Australian writer covering the talks, called the negotiations over this issue an occasion for "one of the great hoaxes of history." The pre-meeting position of the United States was that the prewar borderline should serve as the cease-fire line. But at Kaesong, U.S. negotiators representing the UN side demanded that the line be set according to the location of the actual battlefield. This meant that Northern armies would have "to yield up a substantial slice of territory by withdrawing an average of over thirty-two miles in depth along the whole 150 miles of the battlefront."[49] The North rejected this demand and was vilified in the Western press for being unreasonably opposed to accepting a return to the 38th parallel.

In August, U.S. forces launched a major offensive in an effort to force China and North Korea to agree to the proposed armistice line. U.S. planes even bombed the Chinese and North Korean delegation headquarters in Kaesong, a "neutral" city, almost killing the delegation. The Chinese-North Korean side ended the negotiations and counterattacked. During a period of especially heavy fighting in September and early October, the United States again threatened the North with nuclear attack. Operation Hudson Harbor involved flying lone B-29 bombers over the North and dropping dummy atomic bombs.

Negotiations resumed in late October, this time at Panmunjom. The North Korean-Chinese side agreed to accept the new military line as the armistice line, but the United States again changed its demand, asking for concessions, including the transfer of Kaesong to the Southern side. The United States eventually yielded on this point and finally, on November 27, 1951, an agreement was reached on the location of the armistice line, as well as a two-mile demilitarized strip on either side.

Both sides now turned their attention to the issue of prisoner exchange. The United States, hoping to weaken North Korea's resolve, initiated a massive bombing campaign. The aerial and naval bombardment of the North Korean city of Wonsan, for example, lasted for 861 days, ending one minute before the cease-fire hour of 10 P.M. on July 27, 1953. During one period toward the end of the war, the U.S. Navy shelled the city for forty-one "straight days and nights," what Rear-Admiral Allan F. Smith called "the longest sustained naval or air bombardment of a city in history."[50]

Continuing to negotiate in spite of the bombing, the North Korean-Chinese side proposed implementation of the 1949 Geneva Convention, which called for the immediate and total repatriation of prisoners after an armistice was signed. The United States countered with the principle of voluntary repatriation. While both positions were based on widely recognized and important principles, it appears that the United States adopted its position to inflict a propaganda defeat on the North Korean-Chinese side, and not for humanitarian concerns. As Admiral C. Turner Joy, the chief U.S.-UN negotiator at Panmunjom, later wrote, "It was thought that if any substantial portion of the ex-communist soldiers refused to return to communism, a huge setback to communist subversive activities would ensue. I regret to say this does not seem to have been a valid point."[51]

The United States had given primary responsibility for administering United Nations P.O.W. camps to South Korean forces. In some cases, however, Chiang's nationalist troops were used to oversee Chinese Communist prisoners. As the bargaining over repatriation grew in intensity, so did the violence in the camps. A number of prison revolts took place after February 1952, when the United States formally declared its intention not to return all P.O.W.s. U.S. troops were given "shoot-to-kill" orders and at times used tanks and flamethrowers, killing hundreds of prisoners.[52]

In April, the United States announced that some 60,000 out of 130,000 North Korean and Chinese prisoners did not want to be repatriated. The 60,000 total was allegedly calculated through a neutral screening process, but it was far from that. In the words of one State Department official, there was a "reign of terror" in the camps. Admiral Joy wrote in his diary that any prisoner wanting to return home was "either beaten black and blue or killed ... the majority of P.O.W.s were too terrified to frankly express their choice."[53] Two translators working for the State Department told Joy that an honest screening would have likely resulted in 85 percent of the Chinese prisoners expressing their desire to go back to the mainland; not the recorded 15 percent.[54] Ultimately, approximately 22,000 prisoners did not return.

In February 1952, in the midst of the dispute over prisoner repatriation, both sides agreed to hold a political conference, within three months after signing an armistice, to discuss Korea's future. Rhee strongly opposed this agreement. In fact, he was opposed to any agreements with the North; his goal was to keep UN forces fighting until total victory was achieved. In an attempt to undermine future negotiations, Rhee declared his army independent of U.S. control. Then, in late May 1952, he declared martial law and began an intense crackdown on all political activity in the South. The U.S. government considered arresting Rhee and installing a new president. It had already prepared for this possibility in a plan called Operation Everready.

In the United States, Dwight D. Eisenhower was elected president. His campaign promise, "I shall go to Korea," was interpreted by many to mean that he would find a way to end the war. Instead, he promptly threatened to expand the war in his February 1953 State of the Union address. He announced that the Seventh Fleet would no longer position itself between the Chinese mainland and Taiwan, and he threatened China with an atomic attack.

The first ray of hope for a settlement of the POW issue came with the April exchange of sick and wounded POWs. Ground fighting increased, however, and in May, the United States launched a number of air raids on dams near Pyongyang. Massive flooding took place, destroying food crops and covering entire parts of Pyongyang. The North Koreans canceled talks and the United States once again publicly contemplated using atom bombs. In the end, allied pressure and (perhaps most importantly) the fear of Soviet retaliation held the U.S. atomic hand. At long last, on June 8, 1953, an agreement was reached on prisoner repatriation. The North Korean-Chinese side accepted voluntary repatriation. On June 17, an agreement was also reached on a final armistice line.

In one final attempt to undermine the armistice, Rhee organized a raid on P.O.W. camps, kidnapping some 27,000 prisoners. The North Korean-Chinese forces responded quickly. On June 24 and 25 their troops hit South Korean forces hard; in one week the ROK lost 7,400 soldiers. They also demanded that the United States obtain Rhee's pledge to abide by the armistice. When the United States gave no answer, they struck at Rhee's forces again, both taking and inflicting high casualties. These devastating attacks on South Korean units exposed U.S. forces to possible attack. Finally, the United States agreed to take responsibility for Rhee's compliance with the armistice.

The armistice was signed on July 27, 1953, restoring a border that gave the South more territory at the center and east, but less in the west. The agreement was signed by Chinese, North Korean, and U.S. representatives. Rhee refused to sign, but with heavy pressure from the United States he did agree to refrain from taking hostile actions for a period of ninety days. To reduce the likelihood of his restarting the war after that period, the United States signed a defense treaty with South Korea in early August 1953 that obligated U.S. forces to remain in South Korea and placed South Korean forces under U.S. command.

It is impossible to calculate the costs of the Korean War. However, the number of people killed provides one relevant indicator of the enormity of the tragedy; more than 4 million people died, including some 2 million North Korean civilians, 500,000 North Korean soldiers, 1 million Chinese soldiers, 1 million South Korean civilians, 10,000 South Korean soldiers, and 95,000 UN soldiers, of whom 54,000 were Americans. To place these figures in perspective, North Korea lost more than 20 percent of its prewar population. That is a higher percentage than either the Soviet Union or Poland lost during the Second World War. Japan suffered a total of 2 million civilian and military deaths during the Second World War, but that represented only 3 percent of its population.[55]

The Geneva Conference

Most discussions about the Korean War end with the signing of the armistice; very little attention is given to the Geneva Conference that followed. This is unfortunate, though perhaps not accidental, since what happened at the conference underscores the lack of U.S. concern for Korean democracy and reunification. The United States was willing to endorse Korean reunification but only if the reunification process was sure to guarantee a Korean government responsive to U.S. interests. Since that proved impossible to achieve either on the battlefield or in Geneva, the United States was content to maintain Korea as a divided country, regardless of the wishes of the Korean people.

The conference, called "to settle through negotiation the questions of the withdrawal of all foreign forces from Korea, the peaceful settlement of the Korean question, etc.," was the result of U.S. insistence that all talks between the two sides leading to the armistice be confined to military matters. Although it was supposed to take place within three months of the signing of the armistice, disagreements over who should attend delayed its start until late April 1954. It was finally agreed that those who fought in the war, and the Soviet Union, would be invited; only South Africa decided not to send a representative. South Korea wanted itself and the United States exclusively to have voting rights at the conference. The United States thought that this was excessive, and instead, requested and received "control of tactics."[56] In other words, the United States managed to successfully establish the same kind of unified command at the conference that it had enjoyed while fighting the war.

U.S. strategy was clear-cut: the allies were to demand full implementation of UN General Assembly resolutions on Korea, including the resolution that called for UN-supervised elections in North Korea as a prelude to reunification. Under no circumstance was the allied side to repudiate the role of the United Nations. With the North unlikely to accept UN-supervised elections (for the UN had been its wartime opponent), it was readily apparent that the U.S. strategy was designed to win an ideological victory at the conference, not advance the peace and reunification process. Sydney D. Bailey, an international mediator and the author of many books on UN peace negotiations, made this point when he reported, "The U.S. delegation showed the U.K. a memorandum on the psychological tasks in connection with the conference: the theme of this was that communist China was 'committed to the world communist conspiracy led by Moscow,' and that every effort should be made to reduce China's prestige."[57]

The South Korean representative, Y. T. Pyun, set the tone for the conference by arguing that the South Korean government was the only legal government in Korea and that UN-supervised elections should be held in North Korea to achieve reunification. Chinese forces, which were under control of Moscow, should immediately withdraw. UN forces, on the other hand, could stay, since they "were in Korea before the aggression by the Chinese communists, to take a police action in punishing the North Korean aggressors."[58]

The North Korean representative, Nam Il, took a different position. He proposed that general elections be held throughout Korea to elect representatives to a Korean National Assembly, organized by an All-Korean Commission. To encourage this process, "the All-Korean Commission should immediately take measures to establish and develop economic and cultural relations between the Democratic People's Republic of Korea and the Republic of Korea, in matters of commerce, finance, transport, frontier relations, free movement across the frontier, freedom of correspondence, scientific and cultural exchanges, and all other relations."[59] The proposed All-Korean Commission would be divided equally between North and South Korean representatives, and all issues would be decided upon "by mutual agreement." All foreign troops would be withdrawn in six months. Zhou Enlai, speaking for the Chinese delegation, proposed modifying the North Korean proposal to allow representatives from a group of "neutral nations" to supervise the proposed elections. The North accepted the modification.

The U.S. position was presented by John Foster Dulles. His opening remarks made clear his government's determination to establish both Soviet responsibility for the war and the UN's authority to shape Korea's postwar future:

> The present phase of Korea's martyrdom goes back to August 1945. Then the United States, which had for four years borne the burden of the Japanese war, agreed that the Soviet Union might move into Manchuria and Korea north of the 38th parallel to accept there the surrender of the Japanese. But the Soviets, having gotten into North Korea for one purpose, stayed on for another purpose. Their goal has been, directly or through puppets, to turn North Korea into a satellite state and, if possible, to extend their rule throughout all Korea . . . . It is important that we should constantly bear in mind that what is here at stake is not merely Korea, important as that is; it is the authority of the United Nations. The United Nations assumed primary responsibility for establishing Korea as a free and independent nation. It helped to create the Republic of Korea and

nurtured it. When aggressors threatened the Republic of Korea with extinction,
it was the United Nations which called on its members to go to Korea's defense.[60]

Dulles went on to say that the United States supported the South Korean
position that UN forces were the only foreign forces entitled to remain in
Korea, and the only way to create a democratic Korea was to hold UN-supervised elections in the North, after which a unified Korean government
could be formed.

This U.S.-South Korean position created problems for U.S. allies, who
did not think it reasonable, for example, to demand the withdrawal of
Chinese but not UN troops, or that elections should be held only in the
North. Unwilling to openly oppose the United States, most delegates chose
to remain silent. According to Bailey, "Eden [Britain's foreign minister]
refused to support the [U.S.-ROK] position because he thought that it
would be judged unreasonable by world opinion. On 29 and 30 April,
Dulles reproached Spaak (Belgium), Pearson (Canada), and Eden about the
silence of the friends of the United States."[61] The allies begged for a positive
proposal that they could endorse, but South Korea held its ground. Any
mention of all-Korea elections, even under UN supervision, was unacceptable
to Rhee.

Finally, under heavy allied pressure, the South made a new proposal on
May 21. Pyun agreed to allow UN-supervised elections throughout Korea
on the condition that they conform to South Korean constitutional procedures. He proposed that Chinese forces withdraw one month before the
election. UN personnel would be given complete freedom to move
throughout the country and would withdraw only after the new government had firmly established its authority to rule all of Korea.[62] While the
United States praised this proposal as "clear, moderate, and reasonable,"
the delegations from Britain, Canada, New Zealand, Belgium, and France
chose not to comment.

Finding it difficult to control the conference, the United States began to
fear losing at the negotiating table what it had been able to maintain
through military means: a U.S.-friendly regime in the South. It therefore
began pressuring the allies to declare the conference a failure because the
Communist side refused to accept UN authority in Korea. Above all, the
United States wanted to end the conference quickly and avoid issuing any
final statement. Most allied delegates felt uncomfortable adopting the U.S.

justification for ending the conference. It was not a UN-mandated conference, so the United Nations and its authority was not a relevant issue in the
proceedings. They were, however, reluctant to challenge U.S. leadership.

At the last meeting on June 15, Molotov, representing the Soviet Union,
submitted a draft of the final conference declaration that expressed support
for a unified, independent, and democratic Korea. Zhou submitted a similar
declaration but with the addition that negotiations to achieve the peaceful
reunification of Korea would resume at an appropriate time and place.
Bailey notes that Spaak, the head of the Belgium delegation,

> then said that, while the Conference was not going to approve the Soviet and
> Chinese proposals, that did not mean a rejection of the ideas they contained (at
> which point the previously impassive younger members of the Chinese delega-
> tion joined in a chorus of jeering laughter because a Western delegate had put
> forward a position that differed from that of the United States).[63]

Lord Reading, Britain's minister of state, then offered his own agreement
with Spaak. Eden said that in his opinion Zhou's proposal expressed the
spirit of the conference. Nevertheless, U.S. strategy prevailed and the conference ended with no final declaration or statement of principles. Allied
frustration with U.S. actions is perhaps best summarized in the following
statement by the Canadian representative, Ronning:

> The communists had come to Geneva to negotiate. . . . I thought I had come to
> participate in a peace conference. . . . Instead, the emphasis was entirely on
> preventing a peace settlement from being realized. . . . There was no excuse for
> closing the conference without a peace agreement. Molotov's resolution . . . could
> have been accepted as a basis for a settlement by most of the Sixteen [states that
> fought under the UN flag].[64]

Tragically, ignorance of the history of both the Korean War and the
Geneva Conference has continued to undermine Americans' ability to
think clearly, not only about past developments, but also about current U.S.
policy toward Korea. For example, this historical ignorance makes it difficult for Americans to understand why many South Koreans harbor resent-
ment against the United States, or why South Korea might willingly choose
an alternative political system and reunification with the North. It also
makes it difficult for Americans to understand the North Korean perspective on relations with the United States. For instance, ongoing North Korean
efforts to negotiate a peace treaty with the United States are commonly
viewed as nothing more than devious attempts to split the South Korean-

U.S. alliance. Perhaps most importantly, this collective ignorance has allowed successive U.S. administrations to continue, unchallenged, the same foreign policy that guided U.S. strategy at Geneva: support those in the South that speak for U.S. interests and seek propaganda victories over the North. This is one reason for the lack of progress toward the peaceful and democratic reunification of Korea.

III. FROM DIVISION
TO REUNIFICATION

Chapter 6

Divided Korea: The North Korean Experience

According to the experts favored by network news programs, North Korea is a dangerous copy of the Soviet Union that has outlived the original. They consider North Korea dangerous because its "unstable" leaders, having already transformed the population into "unthinking robots," seek to deflect attention away from the country's deepening economic crisis and the broader crisis of socialism by threatening a new war on the Korean peninsula. Understandably, this view of North Korea has led many Americans to support a strong U.S. military presence in northeast Asia and efforts to keep North Korea isolated until it either collapses or its people overthrow their leaders and accept absorption by the South.

North Korean economic conditions are certainly desperate. The country's leadership has also created an unattractive version of socialism, rejecting the democratic grassroots impulses that inspired Korean political activism in the period after liberation. Yet the North Korean government's original attempts at radical social transformation were genuine. While the distorted outcome of these efforts is in large part the result of decisions made by North Korean leaders such as Kim Il Sung, it is also important to acknowledge that these decisions were made under tough circumstances. Most importantly, options were often limited or foreclosed by division and U.S. hostility. In other words, U.S. actions had a significant negative impact on North Korea's political, social, and economic development.

Although the secretiveness of the North Korean state makes it difficult to interpret political trends, the current regime certainly appears stable. The North Korean leadership has pursued a surprisingly flexible foreign policy in response to the country's difficulties, especially when dealing with the United States, and military tensions on the peninsula have been generated more by aggressive U.S. policies than North Korean desperation. In contrast, the regime has shown no interest in promoting domestic political reform. Significant social change will therefore come slowly and only if North Koreans choose to explore new collective responses to current problems. A Southern-initiated, popularly structured reunification dialogue could well provide the impetus for such a development.

Kim Il Sung and the Evolution of North Korean Socialism

Throughout the first decade of its existence, the DPRK was dismissed by most U.S. and South Korean scholars as nothing more than a Soviet puppet. Their general assessment was that the Northern regime, and its leader Kim Il Sung, had no revolutionary credentials or independent political vision. The North Korean experience, even today, is largely understood as an extreme version of the Soviet experience under Stalin, with first Kim, and now his son, playing Stalin's role.

This understanding of North Korean history is mistaken. There were powerful revolutionary movements operating throughout Korea beginning in the 1920s; it is inaccurate to say that popular aspirations to socialism or Kim himself were merely Soviet exports. While the Soviets did influence North Korea's political and economic development, more important determining factors were Kim Il Sung's political experiences and vision and, closely related, U.S. foreign policy and the division of the country. This is well illustrated by an examination of Kim's rise to power and his policies.

Kim arrived in northern Korea in September 1945, approximately one month after the Japanese surrender. While he commanded the loyalties of a group of revolutionaries who had fought with him in Manchuria, other groups of Communists were also active in the north. One group included domestic Communists, who had remained in Korea during the period of Japanese colonialism. Another included Soviet-Koreans who had been living in the Soviet Union but now wished to live in Korea. The last was the Yenan group. Led by Kim Tu-bong, this group was made up of Koreans who had been with Mao on the Long March and in Yenan. The Yenan group soon established its own political formation, the New Democratic Party.

Kim Il Sung wasted little time before becoming active in Korean Communist politics. The Japanese had effectively destroyed the Korean Communist Party. With the country divided, Communist activists decided to rebuild the party by establishing separate northern and southern bureaus. Kim played a leading role in organizing the northern bureau, which began functioning in October. In December, he was chosen to lead it.

Kim disagreed with the KCP's two-bureau organizing strategy. Political conditions differed enormously in the north and south. For example, Communists in the south were on the defensive, forced underground by U.S. military government repression. By contrast, Communists in the north were able to organize and operate openly. Because of these differences, Kim believed that one party, especially one headquartered in the south, would likely hold back political developments in the north. He argued that the best way to build a socialist Korea was for those in the north to build as strong a socialist movement as possible. Such a movement would inspire all Koreans and promote more effective resistance to U.S. plans for division. However, it could only be built if northern Communists were free to form their own independent party.

While the creation of a separate Communist party in the north would obviously enable Kim to strengthen his personal power, his proposal was also based on a serious assessment of the existing political situation. As political conditions worsened in the south, a majority of those in the northern bureau eventually came to favor Kim's proposal. In June 1946, the north Korean bureau of the Korean Communist Party reformed itself as the North Korean Communist Party (NKCP).

Kim's vision included organizing the NKCP as a mass party. By August, after an aggressive recruiting drive, NKCP membership reached 270,000. Kim then approached Kim Tu-bong, leader of the New Democratic Party (with some 60,000 members), suggesting a merger, and he agreed. In late August, the founding congress of the North Korean Workers' Party (NKWP) was held. Kim Tu-bong was elected chairman and Kim Il Sung was elected as one of two vice-chairmen. A similar merger took place in the south in November, when the South Korean Communist Party joined with several southern parties to form the South Korean Workers' Party (SKNP).

There was a major debate at the second NKWP congress in March 1948, which highlighted both Kim's political inclinations and the way U.S. policy influenced North Korean political choices. Kim attacked the domestic Communists, in particular O Ki-sop, for encouraging an independent trade union movement. This policy, he argued, would lead workers to mistakenly view their interests separate from those of the party and state which, according to Kim, represented the working class as a whole. Because of U.S. intentions, he found this an especially dangerous policy. Nothing, he believed, should be allowed to weaken northern political unity. Survival itself, not to mention the reunification of Korea, was at stake. O, on the other hand, argued that it was the party's duty to champion democratic and popular participation in economic decisionmaking regardless of U.S. actions. This required promoting a strong independent trade union movement.[1]

Unfortunately, Kim's position on trade union independence carried the day. Many party members agreed with Kim that the unstable political situation required that priority be given to political centralization. This decision, however, ran counter to Korea's legacy of independent working class political action, which could have served as an alternative linchpin for building a new socialist society; in the immediate postwar period, the Korean People's Republic and its program enjoyed strong popular support from well-organized and militant grass roots organizations, including the National Council of Korean Labor Unions.

Kim faced perhaps the most serious challenge to his leadership during the Korean War. The challengers were followers of Pak Hon-yong, one of the most influential and well-known domestic Communist leaders. Facing arrest in the south by the U.S. military government, Pak went north in 1946 and became an active party member. In September 1951, after the entry of Chinese troops into the war, his supporters began preparing a coup to replace Kim with Pak. They were motivated by a general discontent with Kim's leadership style, pre-Korean War policies, and closeness to the Soviet Union. Their coup attempt, which took place in early 1953, failed. All the conspirators, as well as Pak, were arrested and eventually executed after the Korean War ended.

Kim was involved in another, less serious, intraparty dispute during the Korean War. After U.S. and South Korean forces were driven out of the North in late 1950, the party faced the challenges associated with reorganization. A major concern was party loyalty. Kim ordered Ho Ka-I, the chair of the Inspection Committee and the highest ranking Soviet-Korean, to carry out an investigation into disloyalty. Ho, ignoring Kim's advice to move with restraint, punished or expelled some 450,000 of the party's 600,000 members. He judged any member not in possession of a party card guilty of disloyalty. The problem with this determination of guilt was that many loyal party members destroyed their cards during the U.S.-UN occupation of the North so as to avoid arrest. Ho also sought to use his authority in the investigation to reduce the number of peasants in the party. According to his vision, the party should be small and overwhelmingly working class. Kim disagreed on both counts. In December 1952, Kim purged Ho and reinstated most of those who had been expelled. By April 1956, after a successful recruitment drive, the party claimed a membership of almost 1.2 million, about 12 percent of the population. This percentage gave North Korea the highest ratio of members to population of any Communist party in the world.[2]

The end of the Korean War left the country divided and the North economically and socially devastated. A debate broke out in the party over both economic and political strategy. Although the DPRK desperately needed foreign aid to rebuild, Kim called for following an economic strategy based on self-reliance. Toward that end, he advocated strong state control over the economy and the priority development of heavy industry.

Kim's economic strategy was rejected by others in the party, in particular members of the Soviet-Korean and Yenan factions. Stated in general terms, their position called for greater emphasis placed on light industry and agriculture and for a greater role for collectives and private enterprise. Many also advocated decentralized management systems, including a relatively independent role for trade unions. Most also supported immediate integration into the "socialist international division of labor," which meant joining the Soviet-led Council for Mutual Economic Assistance (COMECON). The resulting specialization, they argued, would enable the DPRK to import consumer goods in exchange for exports of such primary products as mineral ores, thereby producing an immediate and sustainable increase in the average standard of living.

There were other differences. Kim had called for military self-sufficiency, a strategy that reinforced his emphasis on heavy industry. Many of the same Koreans who opposed Kim's economic strategy also opposed his military strategy. They preferred to follow the new Soviet emphasis on "peaceful coexistence" with capitalist countries, especially the United States. Highly critical of Kim's leadership style, they charged him with trying to build a Stalin-like cult of personality and called for the establishment of collective leadership.

Kim defeated his opponents at the third party congress in April 1956 and succeeded in replacing many of them with members from his political faction.[3] Four months later, at a meeting of the Central Committee, a coalition of Soviet-Koreans and members of the Yenan group attempted to oust Kim but failed. Kim prevailed for two main reasons. First, he had aggressively rebuilt the party with Koreans who were loyal to him. Second, and more importantly, he was able to convince the great majority of party members that he alone stood for Korean independence, and that his opponents were really little more than representatives of foreign interests whose policies would leave Korea dependent on others.[4] Kim began expelling his opponents from the party in 1957. It was no coincidence that these purges coincided with the final withdrawal of Chinese troops from North Korea, a withdrawal undertaken at North Korea's request. Negotiations with the Soviet Union also led to abolishment of dual North Korean-USSR citizenship, forcing Soviet-Koreans to choose "sides."

Thus, Kim's rise to power was not simply the result of his Soviet connections. He proved himself to be a strong and successful advocate for policies that many North Koreans hoped would promote the socialism they desired. Tragically, Kim's vision of socialism became increasingly narrow and hierarchical. He encouraged an encompassing cult of adoration that was eventually to include his entire family, most importantly his son and eventual successor, Kim Jong Il. Most of the democratic impulses of the past Korean revolutionary movement were lost, as Kim and other leaders in the Workers' Party of Korea (created by a 1949 merger of the NKWP and SKWP) struggled to build a stable political formation in one half of a divided country.

The North Korean "Economic Miracle"

During the first two decades after division, many Koreans, perhaps even a significant majority, viewed North Korea more favorably than South Korea. Reflecting this sense of superiority, it was the North, not the South, that made repeated offers for greater North-South communication and exchange. The South Korean government not only rejected these offers, it refused to make any counterproposals. Perhaps even more revealing of Korean impressions of the two Koreas is the fact that in 1960, some 450,000 Koreans living in Japan officially selected North Korea as their "mother country," as compared with 165,000 that selected the South. This difference is even more impressive because the great majority of Koreans living in Japan were originally from southern Korea. Between 1959 and 1962, approximately 75,000 Koreans left Japan to permanently settle in the DPRK.[5]

One reason that North Korea was able to confidently approach the South and attract tens of thousands of Koreans from Japan was its economic superiority. While South Korea struggled with recession and high rates of unemployment during the 1950s, the North Korean economy generated full employment and rapid growth. And even though new state-dominated relations of production enabled the South Korean economy to grow rapidly over the following decade, the North Korean economy continued to outperform it in terms of employment, income distribution, and growth.

North Korea's strong economic performance was the result of a thorough state-directed transformation of Northern economic and social relations. Although Japan did "industrialize" Korea, it did so in an uneven way. In 1940, approximately 85 percent of Korea's heavy industry was in the north while 75 percent of the country's light manufacturing and almost all its agricultural production was in the south. The division of the country left each side with half an economy. The North Korean leadership responded to this historical legacy by implementing a number of sweeping reforms which radically changed workplace, gender, and ownership relations. It also launched a series of economic plans—one-year plans in 1947 and 1948, and a two-year plan covering 1949 to 1950—that were designed to create a more balanced and self-sufficient economy.[6] These initiatives were both popular and effective.

North Korea's economic progress was temporarily interrupted by the Korean War. At the end of the war, power production was only 26 percent of what it had been in 1949, fuel 11 percent, chemicals 22 percent, and metallurgy 10 percent. Agriculture was also in chaos (primarily because of the massive U.S. bombing of the country's dikes and dams).[7]

Almost immediately after the armistice, the North began an impressive rebuilding program, pursuing what Stewart Lone and Gavan McCormack call "possibly the most centralized and planned economic development strategy of any country in the world."[8] A three-year plan was produced for 1954 to 1956 that gave priority to the development of heavy industry. The plan's targets were actually met some six months ahead of schedule. A five-year plan was then drawn up covering 1957-1961, and its targets were also met ahead of schedule. According to the DPRK, its completion meant that the country had successfully built "a base for the development of an independent national economy."[9] A new seven-year plan was launched in 1961, with the aim of modernizing the country's newly created industrial base, as well as establishing more technologically advanced industries.

In the postwar period, the state also completed the task of eliminating private ownership of productive assets. Agriculture went through a process of collectivization which proceeded in stages between 1953 to 1958, a process largely driven by the destruction left by the Korean War, which made the pooling of limited resources and labor necessary for survival. Lone and McCormack describe the collectivization experience as follows:

> Despite the urgency of the task of capital accumulation for industrialization, the regime seems not to have squeezed the farmers too hard, allowing them to experience gradually rising living standards and reduced taxation levels, until the tax on the agricultural yield was eliminated entirely in 1966. Irrigation, terracing of hillsides, mechanization (large scale production and allocation of tractors) and chemicalization (use of fertilizers) were promoted on a large scale.[10]

Urban handicraft as well as small-scale, privately owned enterprises involved in commerce and industry also went through a similar process of collectivization. By August 1958, the North Korean leadership, basing its assessment on the extent of state ownership, announced that the country had achieved "the socialist transformation of the relations of production, in both the rural and the urban communities."[11]

North Korea's economic achievements were truly remarkable. Agricultural output grew by an average of 10 percent a year during the 1950s and 6.3 percent during the 1960s. By the end of the 1960s, the government was able to declare that the country had achieved food self-sufficiency.[12] Industrial growth rates were even more noteworthy. Gross Industrial Product in 1956 was almost three times what it had been in 1953; in 1960 it was almost 3.5 times what it had been in 1956.[13] As a result, industry's share of national income rose from 16.8 percent in 1946 to 64.2 percent in 1965.[14] And by

1960, machine-building had become the country's largest industrial sector.[15] These achievements were so remarkable that even Western economists began to speak of the "North Korean Miracle."[16] In fact, according to the economist Joan Robinson, writing in 1965, "All economic miracles of the postwar world are put in the shade by these achievements."[17]

The End of the Economic Miracle

North Korea's economic advance began to slow in the second half of the 1960s. The government announced in 1966 that its seven-year plan would not be completed on time, and the planning period was extended for three years, until 1970. A new six-year plan was launched in 1971. Although the North announced its successful completion in late 1975, four months ahead of schedule, no new plan was presented in either 1976 or 1977. In spite of these difficulties, even CIA estimates, as summarized by Lone and McCormack, showed that, "as of early 1976, the North Korean economy was outproducing the South in per capita terms in almost every sector, from agriculture through electric power generation, steel and cement, to machine tools and trucks (but not in televisions and automobiles)."[18] Nevertheless, the North was losing the economic race. Between 1960 to 1976, Northern per capita GNP grew by an average annual rate of 5.2 percent; Southern per capita GNP grew by 7.3 percent.[19] The South caught the North on a per capita basis sometime in the mid to late 1970s, and then continued to pull further ahead.

North Korea's economic difficulties had several causes. Among the most important were the decline in aid from the Soviet Union and the division-impelled diversion of scarce resources into the military sector. While North Korea has always prided itself on following an economic strategy based on the traditional principle of *juche* (self-reliance), the country also benefited significantly from foreign aid. For example, North Korea received substantial aid from the Soviet Union and other Eastern European countries in 1953 and 1956 that helped finance its three-year plan. According to one scholar:

> During the Three Year Plan, 75.1 percent of all capital investments of the DPRK was financed from the grants from the communist bloc. In these years 24.6 percent of the Pyongyang state budget was financed from aid from the bloc countries (including credits). Finally, aid and credits from socialist countries financed 77.6 percent and 3.9 percent respectively of all DPRK imports during the Three Year Plan.[20]

The Soviet Union also gave substantial scientific and technical aid, almost all without charge. By 1962, the Soviets had given North Korea over 2,581 technical documents; some 935 were drawings of complete plants or machinery. This technical support enabled North Korea to produce many industrial products, including trucks, cranes, compressors, agricultural machinery, electric motors, transformers, and tractors, which greatly contributed to the country's rapid industrialization.[21]

Beginning in the late 1950s, relations between the DPRK and the Soviet Union grew tense. In 1956, the Soviets started pressuring the North to give up its attempt to construct a heavy industrial base and instead concentrate on producing light manufactures and primary commodity exports as part of a COMECON-structured division of labor. The DPRK did join COMECON in 1957, but only as an observer; it refused to accept any limitations on its national planning.

Complicating the dispute over economic strategy was a growing split between China and the Soviet Union. Kim had worked hard to remain friendly with both countries and was therefore placed in an awkward position by this development, especially the increasingly frequent Soviet criticisms of China. Kim actually supported the Chinese in their confrontation with the Soviet Union. He was critical of what he saw as Soviet revisionism, especially the policy of "peaceful coexistence" with the United States, the very country that had prosecuted the Korean War. Kim believed that "peaceful coexistence" reflected a racist attitude on the part of the Soviet Union toward Asia. As he saw it, détente was a policy that was developed strictly within, and had meaning only in, a European context. It could have no meaning for Vietnamese, Chinese, or Koreans, people whose countries were divided, with the socialist halves under threat of attack from the United States.

In the early 1960s, when the Soviets started openly criticizing the DPRK for its economic plans and unwillingness to condemn China, Kim stood his ground. The result was the sudden withdrawal of Soviet aid and technical support and, from 1962 to 1965, a reduction in trade between the two countries. Not surprisingly, this had a serious impact on the North Korean economy. As Gordon White explains:

> The Korean rejection of Soviet plans for integration was not without cost; it was one of the factors, for example, which led to the postponement of the completion

of the Seven Year Plan from 1967-70. After the credibility of the Soviet military guarantee embodied in the 1961 Korea-Soviet treaty declined and military aid was shut off for several years, a greater percentage of state expenditure had to be devoted to defense. Soviet manipulation of aid and possibly trade arrangements hampered the achievement of the Plan's original targets.[22]

Soviet-North Korean relations improved in the mid-1960s, but Chinese-North Korean relations deteriorated. In 1967, Chinese Red Guards began putting up wall posters which accused Kim Il Sung of betraying the world revolutionary movement by living an aristocratic lifestyle, by failing to send North Korean troops to fight against U.S. forces in Vietnam, and by ignoring the Chinese Cultural Revolution. Relations between the governments of China and North Korea deteriorated; both sides recalled their ambassadors, and the Chinese delegation to the Korean Armistice Commission was withdrawn. Adding to the tension, a territorial dispute broke out between the two governments over their incompatible claims to Mount Paektu (which plays an important role in both Chinese and Korean origin myths). Relations between the two countries did not improve until late 1969, when Red Guard attacks against Kim were halted and the Chinese acknowledged Korean sovereignty over Mount Paektu. In early 1970, the two countries again exchanged ambassadors and the Chinese delegation rejoined the Armistice Commission.[23]

For Kim, the important lesson from this experience was that North Korea could not count on the support of either of its allies, both of whom continued to maintain hostile relations with each other. He therefore began moving North Korea toward a closer identification with the third world. The DPRK became a member of the nonaligned nations movement in 1975.

North Korea's difficulties with its allies took on added significance in light of developments in the South. Park Chung Hee had led a military coup in the South in 1961, and immediately declared anticommunism as the most important principle of his new regime. He ruled out all discussions with the North until the South was strong enough, economically and militarily, to negotiate from a position of strength. One way in which he sought to achieve this position was by linking South Korea more closely with the United States and Japan. By the middle of the decade, the South was sending troops to Vietnam in support of the U.S. war effort and receiving greater military and economic aid in exchange. Park also officially reestablished relations with Japan.

Kim's response to these trends was to build up North Korea's military capabilities. Military spending rose from less than 4 percent of the national budget in 1959, to a yearly average of 20 percent between 1960 to 1966, and to a yearly average of 30 percent between 1967 to 1971.[24] This represented a major drain on the country's resources and adversely effected the government's ability to meet its economic targets, as the DPRK itself admitted in 1970.

From this point on, international trends continued to be unfavorable for the DPRK. For example, although President Nixon actually withdrew some 20,000 U.S. soldiers from South Korea in 1971, he also made a commitment to provide South Korea with additional military aid. But nervous about U.S. intentions, Park Chung Hee secretly took steps to secure the technology necessary for the production of nuclear weapons. The United States was able to stop the most public aspects of the South Korean nuclear program in 1976, but only by increasing U.S. military support. This new support included, among other things, the start of annual joint military exercises (Team Spirit) directed against the North. These exercises began with 46,000 troops and quickly grew in size. Before long, they also included simulated nuclear attacks on the DPRK. The North Korean response was predictable. Military spending rose from approximately $800 million in 1971 to $1.4 billion in 1974.[25] According to U.S. intelligence estimates, the North also greatly increased the size of its military, from 400,000 soldiers in 1970, to 700,000 in 1975, and to 1 million by the end of the decade.[26] Ironically, while this Northern military buildup was being widely criticized in the United States, it was the South that set the pace in the arms spending race. According to the U.S. Arms Control and Disarmament Agency, North Korean military spending amounted to approximately $24.4 billion from 1970 to 1983. During that same period, the South spent approximately $30.5 billion.[27] In fact, in each and every year since 1975, the South has spent more money on the military than has the North.

To understand how instability of foreign aid and pressures of military spending were two of the main reasons for North Korea's growing economic difficulties, it is also useful to contrast the experiences of the two Koreas. The U.S. government estimates that between 1946 and 1960, the North received some $1.8 billion in foreign assistance—$700 million from the Soviet Union, $600 million from China, and $500 million from Eastern European countries. It received an additional $1 billion from 1961 to 1978—$700 million from the Soviet Union and $300 million from China. Approximately $2 billion of this $2.8 billion was economic assistance, the rest was military. The South, by contrast, got $12.6 billion of aid from the United States alone between 1946 to 1975, half of that total for economic purposes. It received an additional $1 billion from Japan and $1.8 billion from other countries and international agencies.[28] In sum, the North received $2 billion in economic aid and less than $1 billion in military aid, while the South got approximately $9.1 billion in economic aid and $6.3 billion in military aid (and in a shorter period of time).

North Korea's economic problems have worsened over the 1980s and 1990s. Although the government declared its seven-year plan covering 1977 to 1984 a success, it did not publish the output levels of key target industries such as electric power, steel, and many chemicals. Even more revealing, no new plan was announced for 1985 or 1986. The next plan, covering 1987 to 1993, included targets that were supposed to have been met during the 1980s. No new plan was announced in 1993. Instead, the government declared an unspecified period of adjustment.

Economic Initiatives

DPRK leaders have often been portrayed as resistant to change, and in important ways this is true. Despite a deteriorating economic situation, they have so far refused to alter the country's basic economic structure and institutions. At the same time, they have demonstrated a willingness to pursue more modest initiatives, including adjusting planning priorities, diversifying trade partners, mobilizing workers, and attracting foreign capital. North Korean planning efforts were directed at building a self-reliant economy. As a consequence, North Korea channeled approximately 80 percent of the country's total industrial investment from 1961 to 1976 into heavy industry.[29] Recognizing that this had left the economy unbalanced, the North Korean leadership, in the mid-1970s, sought to increase both the quantity and quality of light manufactures by shifting responsibility for their production to the provinces. This change turned out to have minimal impact on economic activity, however, as new resources never followed the new responsibilities.

The state also sought to boost the country's economic fortunes by opening up new links with the capitalist world. It purchased Western technology and capital equipment on credit, largely from Japan, Switzerland, West Germany, and France. "Between 1970 and 1974," writes Nicholas Eberstadt, "the estimated current dollar value of Western imports was permitted to grow by a factor of thirteen; in 1974, North Korea may have been importing over twice as much from capitalist countries as from its communist partners."[30] The DPRK planned to pay for these imports with earnings from exports but, when the international capitalist system went into recession in 1974, this became impossible. The export prices of DPRK goods, primarily minerals, fell sharply. North Korea, like many other countries, found itself unable to service its debts. Unlike most other countries, however, the DPRK refused to adopt International Monetary Fund structural adjustment policies. It chose instead to stop making interest payments to its creditors. Western banks, in turn, refused to extend new loans. Without new funds, the country's overall trade fell by a third between 1974 to 1976. The DPRK still has outstanding debts from this period.

The state also tried mobilizing workers to work harder and better. This was not a new strategy. Kim Il Sung first introduced the mass campaign to spur worker efforts in December 1956. During a visit to the Kangson steel mill, Kim told workers that although the Soviet Union as well as some Koreans did not want the country to have machine-building factories, these factories were needed to ensure Korean independence. He called upon the workers to produce beyond their quotas and to devise more efficient production methods. The workers responded by creating the Chollima workteam movement (named after a legendary flying horse of Korean folklore). "Chollima workers" were those who surpassed their quotas and made special contributions to production.

During the 1960s, Kim visited many factories and mines, giving "on-the-spot" guidance and urging people to work hard to build socialism. After a 1960 visit to the Chonsalli cooperative farm, he recommended national adoption of a new organizational system for agriculture which he called the Chonsalli method. After a 1961 visit to the Taean electric machine plant, he promoted national adoption of what he called the Taean work system for industry. Both approaches stressed the responsibility of party leaders to become more knowledgeable about the challenges facing workers in order to help workers overcome them. This was a top-down approach to problem-solving, but it also called for the direct involvement of "higher bodies" in the concerns of production to encourage and assist the efforts of "lower bodies" to boost productivity.

As the economy faced new challenges in the 1970s, the party leadership launched a series of new mass campaigns. In 1973, Kim Jong Il inaugurated the Three Revolutions Teams movement. Each team was composed of twenty to fifty members; their assignment was to raise productivity by stimulating ideological, technical, and cultural changes in the workplace. In the 1980s, Kim Jong Il initiated the Movement to Create the Speed of the Eighties which, like the earlier Chollima campaign, was designed to encourage workers to produce more. Similar speed campaigns, often lasting for 200 days, were used during the 1990s. Western and South Korean analysts have claimed that these mobilization campaigns were failures, but no one outside the country really knows their effectiveness. It is, however, highly unlikely that mobilization campaigns alone can succeed in reversing the country's negative economic trends.

While the government continues to pursue all of these initiatives in one form or another, its primary reform effort in the 1990s appears to be directed toward attracting export-oriented foreign investment. In 1991, it established a special free economic and trade zone in the Rajin-Sonbong area in the northeastern part of the country. It also became an enthusiastic supporter of the Tuman River Area Development Program, an initiative supported by the United Nations Development Program to create a "Northeast Asian Hong Kong" by combining the labor and resources of China, Russia, and North Korea with the technology and capital of Japan and South Korea.

North Korean efforts to attract foreign capital have so far generated little activity. South Korean firms have visited and appear eager to invest, but the South Korean government has largely blocked their plans. Both the European Community Chamber of Commerce in Korea and the American Chamber of Commerce in Korea, both based in South Korea, have held informational meetings and conducted tours of the Rajin-Sonbong economic zone for interested firms. Among the major U.S. firms which have expressed interest in doing business in the North are Motorola, General Motors, AT&T, and Citibank. It is still illegal for U.S. firms to invest in the North, however. At present the main foreign investment in the North has come from Koreans who live in Japan. According to DPRK officials, there were 130 joint ventures operating in the North as of May 1996. Seventy of these were with Koreans living in Japan and another forty were with Chinese from the PRC. The total value of this foreign investment is small: $130 million.

North Korea's decision to aggressively pursue foreign investment, a decision that in many ways runs contrary to past state pronouncements on *juche*, was largely made in response to the collapse of the Soviet bloc. Up until the late 1980s, approximately 60 percent of North Korea's trade was in the form of barter agreements with Eastern European socialist countries and (most importantly) the Soviet Union. The North had exported non-ferrous metals, steel, magnesium clinker, machine tools, coal, silk, and cement; it imported petroleum, chemicals, grains and cereals, coking coal, machinery, and capital equipment. But beginning in 1989, governments in one Eastern European country after another embraced capitalism. In 1991, the Soviet Union ceased to exist. The end of this economic bloc meant an end to North Korea's barter trade. With minimal hard currency reserves, the North was forced to sharply cut its imports; overall trade between North Korea and the countries of the former Soviet bloc (including the Soviet Union) fell by approximately 67 percent in 1991.[31] The repercussions have been severe. According to South Korean and U.S. intelligence estimates, North Korea's GNP grew 2 percent in 1989 and then declined in each of the next six years: by 3.7 percent in 1990, 5.2 percent in 1991, 7.6 percent in 1992, 4.3 percent in 1993, 1.7 percent in 1994, and a further 4.6 percent in 1995.

Kim Jong U, head of the Rajin-Sonbong free economic and trade zone, was responding to these developments when he said in 1993 that "socialist markets have disappeared" and "there is only a capitalist world market." As a result, he explained, the North has no choice but to take steps, such as the establishment of the Rajin-Sonbong zone, to attract productive foreign capital in order to generate the exports necessary to finance imports. "This plan," he added, "is a temporary bridge to connect our economy" with market economies.[32]

Most Korea experts predicted that the North Korean regime, already struggling unsuccessfully to reverse the country's economic decline, would not long survive Kim Il Sung's death in July 1994. Then came the devastating rains and floods in the summer of 1995. More than thirty-one inches of rain fell in just a few days in August. Dams broke, bridges collapsed, and food stocks, already low, were washed away. Approximately 500,000 people were left homeless, and nearly half the country's farmland was ruined. Reports from defectors to the South claimed that people were starving, in many locations down to one meal a day.

Despite these disasters, so far the experts have been wrong. Kim Il Sung's son, Kim Jong Il, has by all accounts successfully assumed control of the country. He surprised many of these same experts by aggressively appealing for international aid to help the country recover from the flooding. He allowed representatives from international agencies and nongovernmental organizations considerable freedom to travel in the most affected areas and monitor the aid distribution. These groups reported widespread and growing signs of serious malnutrition in the population. They also reported that North Korea had quickly and efficiently mobilized its resources to help the population as much as it could. There was no breakdown in discipline, and no signs of corruption or diversion of aid.[33]

North Korean policymakers appear committed to "ride out" the current crisis. They have rejected Western advice to follow the example of the former Soviet bloc and embrace market forces, pointing out that the former Soviet Union (now Russia) has suffered a worse economic collapse than North Korea, in spite of significant Western financial aid. According to the International Monetary Fund, for example, the Soviet economy shrank by 12.9 percent in 1989, 18.5 percent in 1990, and 13 percent in 1991. Russian GDP fell by 19 percent in 1992, 12 percent in 1993, 15 percent in 1994, and an estimated 4 percent in 1995.[34] In 1996, the North Korean media began showing TV programs on the situation in Russia, programs that highlighted the severe economic hardships, economic inequality, and social decay experienced by the Russian people as a result of market forces.

North Korean policymakers have also refrained from undertaking substantial economic reforms for some bad reasons, including an unwillingness to acknowledge the fact that internal structural problems, such as overly centralized and politicized planning and management practices, have contributed to the country's economic slide. Another reason they have refrained from making major policy changes is that they believe that the success of their economic recovery strategy depends more on political factors than economic ones, the most important being the state of relations with the United States. They are convinced that normalization of relations with the United States will enable them to build their "bridge" to the global capitalist system, thereby establishing the conditions necessary for a return to economic stability.

Given the importance that the North Korean government places on its relations with the United States, the question arises: how likely is normalization? The answer depends not only on North Korean intentions but even more so on U.S. foreign policy objectives. What follows, then, is a brief examination of post-1953 U.S. foreign policy toward North Korea.

U.S. Policy Toward North Korea

The Geneva Conference at the end of the Korean War concluded with the United States still determined to isolate the North. The Military Armistice Commission (MAC), established by the armistice agreement, was the only direct channel of communication between the DPRK and the United States until 1988. It included five military officers from each side and its responsibility was to supervise the implementation of the armistice and settle any violations through negotiations.

The armistice established other institutions which served to oversee U.S.-North Korean relations. One of the most important was the Neutral Nations Supervisory Commission (NNSC) comprised of representatives from Czechoslovakia, Poland, Sweden, and Switzerland. The NNSC was charged with supervising, inspecting, and investigating any violations of the armistice outside of the DMZ. The NNSC employed ten mobile inspection teams, five stationed in the South and five in the North, and was supposed to report its findings directly to the MAC. One of its main responsibilities was to make sure that neither side increased its level of military force beyond what the armistice agreement permitted. This was not easy to do and each side regularly accused the other (and, often, those countries on the NNSC considered hostile) of subverting the rules.

By 1955, wrote Sydney Bailey, "the United States and South Korea had . . . come to favor complete abolition of the NNSC supervisory system, partly because it was not working satisfactorily, but no doubt also because they wanted to modernize their forces beyond what the Armistice Agreement permitted."[35] It was not until 1957, however, that the U.S. government announced that it would no longer consider itself to be bound by the military restrictions of the armistice. Later that same year, it introduced nuclear artillery and missiles into South Korea, prominently displaying them in February 1958 at a military review.[36] The public nature of their display was clearly designed to send North Korea the message that Washington was both ready and willing to attack it with nuclear weapons.

Over the decade of the 1960s, the United States added atomic demolition munitions and Nike Hercules missiles with nuclear warheads to its nuclear stockpile in South Korea, both of which were forward-deployed near the DMZ. Such a placement meant that these weapons would have to be used in the first moments of battle. Since this nuclear buildup took place during the period when the Soviets were reducing their military and economic aid to the North, it is easy to understand why Kim Il Sung felt pressured into boosting his country's defensive capabilities. But the North's response to America's nuclear buildup was not just defensive. In 1968, during a period of growing Southern opposition to Park Chung Hee, the North sent a commando team south in an unsuccessful assassination attempt. It also seized a U.S. spy ship, the *Pueblo*, and held its crew for approximately one year despite U.S. threats of attack. The following year, the North shot down a U.S. spy plane which it claimed was part of Operation U.S. Focus Retina, a military exercise that practiced airlifting U.S. paratroopers from America to the ROK.

The 1970s brought new twists and turns but no fundamental change in the U.S.-DPRK relationship. The United States withdrew troops from South Korea in 1971. In exchange, President Richard Nixon offered Park Chung Hee billions of dollars in aid, including support for a domestic arms industry and continued nuclear protection. America also initiated Team Spirit war games in 1976. By 1983, these war games had become America's largest field training exercise with an ally. Almost 200,000 troops, including 75,000 Americans, were involved.

These war games produced more than well-trained soldiers. They also greatly increased the potential for a new Korean War. For example, two U.S. soldiers pruning a tree in the DMZ were clubbed to death in August 1976 by North Korean soldiers. The United States responded three days later with a massive mobilization, including a nuclear weapons alert. U.S. and South Korean forces entered the DMZ in force and cut down the tree. This tragedy apparently occurred not because of Northern intentions to provoke the United States, but because North Korean front line troops, edgy in the aftermath of the first Team Spirit exercise, took action on their own.[37] Kim Il Sung apologized for the incident. The United States was not, however, totally blameless. Korea expert Peter Hayes noted: "Although U.S. accounts assiduously deny any American fault in the event, U.S. military officers admit privately that those involved in the pruning did not follow normal consultative procedures and verbally heightened the animosity that led to the fighting."[38]

The United States lost an opportunity to reduce tensions with North Korea in 1979, when President Jimmy Carter reversed his previous decision to withdraw all U.S. troops from South Korea by 1980. The U.S. military and intelligence apparatuses had strongly opposed this withdrawal. South Korea was an important base for U.S. military forces and nuclear weapons. In addition, the "state of war" on the peninsula gave U.S. forces an opportunity to train under real battle conditions. The military and intelligence officialdom, joined by some in the State Department, set about sabotaging Carter's plan.

The U.S. Defense Intelligence Agency and the CIA conveniently generated new and far higher estimates of North Korean troop strength. "Overnight, the United States boosted its estimates of North Korean army personnel by 160-260,000 (including 100,000 commandos), tanks by 650, APCs by 250, field guns by 500-1,000, and anti-aircraft weapons by 2,500-3,500," wrote analyst Stephen Goose.[39] The army then used these inflated estimates to raise serious questions about the wisdom of Carter's proposed troop withdrawal. Carter found himself politically trapped. Not wanting to look "soft on communism," he agreed to a reevaluation of the proposed troop withdrawal, leading quickly to its reversal.

With Ronald Reagan's election in 1980, the U.S. military became the key component of a more aggressive U.S. foreign policy. As a consequence, the United States adopted a new military strategy known as "horizontal escalation," which called for the United States to respond to Soviet aggression anywhere in the world by "hitting" Soviet interests in another part of the world. U.S. planning focused on North Korea as a prime target. This new strategy also encouraged the development of a new U.S. military doctrine for Korea called Airland Battle. As opposed to the past, when U.S. military strategy called for halting a North Korean attack at the DMZ, U.S. plans now called for immediate counterattack against the North, with special emphasis on the use of nuclear weapons. These plans, as the North well recognized, were also consistent with a first-strike strategy.

North Korea responded to the U.S. government's more aggressive military posture with acts of terrorism. After a military coup took place in the South in 1980, Northern agents hoping to destroy the new regime set off a bomb in Burma while the new South Korean military dictator, Chun Doo Hwan, and several other government officials were there on a 1983 visit. The explosion killed four cabinet ministers, thirteen other South Koreans, and four Burmese citizens. In 1987, in an apparent attempt to undermine the 1988 Seoul Olympic Games, North Korean agents placed a bomb on a South Korean airliner. The plane exploded, killing all 115 people on board.

Somewhat inconsistently, the North also made numerous attempts during the 1980s to engage the United States in direct talks about replacing the armistice with a peace agreement. The United States rejected these overtures, arguing that peace talks must first take place between the North and the South. Finally, after being encouraged to do so by South Korean President Roh Tae Woo, the United States agreed in 1988 to hold low-level diplomatic talks with DPRK officials in Beijing.

Ignoring North Korean suggestions for improved relations, the United States quickly narrowed the scope of the talks to one item: North Korea's nuclear program. The North had begun work on a five megawatt nuclear research reactor in 1980; it had become operational in 1987. Under pressure from the Soviet Union, the North signed the Non-Proliferation Treaty (NPT) in 1985, but refused to ratify the Safeguards Agreement and allow international inspections of its nuclear facilities. The reason it gave was the presence of U.S. nuclear weapons in the South. The United States did not press the ratification issue until 1989, when it announced that satellite pictures showed the existence of a North Korean reprocessing plant capable of producing weapons-grade plutonium from spent fuel rods. The following year it charged the North with actively pursuing the development of a nuclear weapons program, a charge the North denied.

Tensions between the two countries grew, especially in the period surrounding the 1991 Gulf War against Iraq. At the very moment U.S. forces
were pounding Iraqi forces, the U.S. military was preparing for Team Spirit
war games in Korea. Shortly before the start of Team Spirit in April, South
Korea's defense minister actually called for a commando raid on the North
to destroy its nuclear facilities. The end of the Gulf War brought a steady
stream of articles in the U.S. press calling the DPRK the "next renegade
state" and Kim Il Sung a "nut case" and "vicious dictator." North Korea's
alleged nuclear weapons program was proclaimed the most serious threat
to world peace.

Emboldened by its Gulf War success, the United States seemed poised
to finish its war against the North. And yet unexpectedly, after a series of
high level talks between the prime ministers of North and South Korea, the
United States took a big step toward peace on the peninsula. In late 1991,
President George Bush announced the withdrawal of U.S. tactical nuclear
weapons from all U.S. overseas bases, including those in South Korea. North
Korea, in turn, responded by ratifying the Safeguards Agreement. Interna-
tional Atomic Energy Agency (IAEA) inspectors made six inspections of
North Korean nuclear facilities over the period May 1992 to January 1993.
In 1992, Team Spirit war games were canceled for the first time.

The improvement in U.S.-North Korean relations did not last long. In
February 1993, the U.S. government announced that new satellite photo-
graphs revealed two undeclared North Korean nuclear facilities; U.S. intelligence officials believed they were nuclear waste storage sites. The CIA went
so far as to claim that the North was already likely in possession of one or
two nuclear bombs. The IAEA responded to U.S. concerns by demanding
the right to make "a special inspection" of the two sites. The North refused,
stating that they were nonnuclear military facilities. The U.S. response was
to resume Team Spirit war games in March 1993. North Korea in turn put
its military on full alert and announced its withdrawal from the NPT. It
gave three months' notice, as required by the treaty. The United States then
threatened to punish North Korea with UN-imposed economic sanctions.

Although it was never even hinted at in the U.S. media, U.S. hostility
toward the DPRK was the underlying cause of the deepening crisis. The
United States had never shown the slightest concern over the fact that Israel,
India, and Pakistan, all known to possess nuclear weapons, had neither

signed the NPT nor opened their nuclear sites to IAEA inspection. More-over, no other signatory to the IAEA Safeguards Agreement had ever been asked to subject itself to "special inspections." The news agencies also omitted that the United States had violated the NPT during Team Spirit exercises by periodically threatening a nonnuclear North Korea with nuclear attack.

The North, well aware that the crisis was about U.S.-North Korean relations, steadfastly maintained that it could be easily solved if only the United States would join the DPRK in working toward better relations. The Northern strategy was to keep the world guessing as to the status of its nuclear program in order to draw the United States into negotiations over normalization of relations, the outcome of which it hoped would lead to a relaxation in military tensions and the country's economic recovery. Ironi-cally, the United States found itself backed into a corner while threatening to organize an international embargo against the North. Unwilling to wage war against the North but also unhappy with the precedent that would be set if the North withdrew from the NPT, it reluctantly accepted the North Korean offer for direct talks. The North, in turn, agreed to "suspend its withdrawal" from the NPT.

The talks deadlocked, largely because while the North wanted the two countries to simultaneously deal with and resolve disagreements over Team Spirit, nuclear inspections, and normalization of relations, the United States was still focused on forcing North Korean acceptance of inspections. Unable to get its way, the United States again threatened the North with sanctions and even a preemptive military strike. Finally, in March 1994, North Korea agreed to allow IAEA officials back into the country to inspect the seven originally declared nuclear sites. A new disagreement broke out, however, as the inspectors and the DPRK disagreed over the extent of the inspection process.

There appeared no way to avoid a confrontation this time around. The United States began efforts to win UN support for international sanctions against North Korea. The North declared that it would consider sanctions a declaration of war. The U.S. military responded by placing Patriot air defense missiles in the South and increasing U.S. force levels in the region. The U.S. military and intelligence leadership actually seemed eager for war. In April 1994, Secretary of Defense William Perry stated that although he would not rule out a "preemptive strike against North Korea," he preferred "considerable pressure" that "will increase the risk" that the North Koreans would respond with a military assault.[40] In other words, he wanted to push North Korea into taking action that would justify a full-scale U.S. attack. *U.S. News and World Report* ran a long cover story in early June discussing how the war would be fought. It reported that many American military planners were convinced it would be a nuclear war.[41]

Then, in late June 1994, when it appeared that war was imminent, former President Jimmy Carter accepted Kim Il Sung's invitation to come to Pyongyang to act as mediator. He was able to shape an agreement whereby the North would freeze its nuclear program, while in exchange the United States would call off its sanctions campaign and resume bilateral talks. A number of U.S. political and military leaders, as well as media figures, seemingly disappointed that there might be a peaceful resolution of the crisis, criticized the agreement and claimed that Carter had been "conned" and that a resumption of negotiations would only give the North time to build more weapons.

In spite of Kim Il Sung's death in July, the talks did go forth, eventually producing an accord in October. North Korea agreed to allow full and continuous inspection of its existing nuclear sites, to freeze the operation of and later dismantle its graphite-based nuclear reactors (which produced spent fuel capable of generating weapons-grade plutonium), and to ship its existing spent nuclear fuel out of the country for storage. The United States agreed to provide the North with supplies of heavy oil; organize a consortium of nations to build new nuclear reactors based on a less-dangerous light water technology; and gradually ease restrictions on trade, investment, and diplomatic contacts, leading to the establishment of full diplomatic relations. The accord was structured to proceed in stages. While limited, it marked a positive step forward in U.S.-North Korean relations.

Almost immediately there were small but real improvements in the economic sphere. In January 1995, the DPRK lifted its restrictions on the importation of U.S. goods and its ban on the entry of U.S. ships. The United States responded by partially lifting its economic sanctions. It agreed to allow telecommunications connections between the two countries, the use of personal credit cards in the DPRK, North Korean use of the U.S. banking system for transactions, and imports of magnesite from North Korea by U.S. companies.

The North has continued to seek bigger changes. It has expressed its wish that the United States drop all economic restrictions so that the DPRK can export goods such as zinc and textiles on a regular basis and receive U.S. direct foreign investment and loans. Although the U.S. government is not yet willing to completely lift its economic embargo, it did, in July 1996, provide millions of dollars in emergency food aid to help the North overcome the tremendous agricultural damage caused by the 1995 floods. This action was significant in that it was taken over the objections of the South Korean government.

North Korea also continues to urge the United States to sign a peace treaty, thereby formally bringing the Korean War to an end. So far, the United States has refused to directly discuss the issue with the North. The closest it has come is in an April 1996 joint U.S.-South Korean invitation to the North to join four-power talks (which would also include China). However, newspaper articles in the United States and South Korea claim that U.S. officials pledged to the South not to directly discuss the issue of a peace treaty with the North at the talks. While it is clear that the North wants to achieve full normalization of relations with the United States, it is far more difficult to interpret the significance of what appears to be a limited but real change in U.S. policy toward North Korea. In fact, there are two interrelated changes in U.S. policy that require explanation—the rapid move toward military confrontation beginning in 1991 and the equally sudden movement toward negotiation and accommodation beginning in 1994.

The rush toward war with the North was likely propelled by the collapse of the Soviet Union, which left the U.S. military establishment desperate for a new enemy. General Colin Powell, at the time chairman of the Joint Chiefs of Staff, offered a good illustration of this when he said, "I'm running out of demons. I'm running out of villains . . . . I'm down to Castro and Kim Il Sung."[42] To ensure the continuation of Cold War levels of military spending, the military and intelligence brass therefore did what it could to puff up the North Korean threat to U.S. interests by emphasizing, in particular, the nuclear dimension. As the *Wall Street Journal* reported,

Diplomats in Seoul say they suspect such reports [of the North Korean nuclear threat] are inspired by overly dire briefings given by the CIA and the Defense Department. They speculate such assessments are motivated by a desire to protect America's dwindling defense budget from further cuts or compel the South Korean government to shore up its military forces to deter the North.[43]

CIA allegations that the North had at least one functioning nuclear bomb were not sustained, for example, by the State Department, which noted that it was unlikely that the North had developed a triggering mechanism, that even if it did have a triggering mechanism the country had no test site to ensure that the alleged bomb would work, and that even if it did have a test site and had somehow succeeded in conducting a test without detection, the North did not yet have a nuclear delivery system. Yet the concern about a North Korean nuclear threat grew, because it was reinforced not only by the U.S. military but also by big businesses whose profits were directly tied to the level of military spending.[44]

This rush to create a North Korean nuclear scare fed upon itself, quickly leading to a crisis situation. Because the North did not have the capacity to destroy the United States, as had the Soviet Union, there was no internal check on the pressures building for military action against the North. When the North refused to back down in the face of U.S. demands, the U.S. political establishment, which had long allowed the military and intelligence hierarchies to shape Korea policy, found itself unable to control the situation.

Most U.S. policymakers did not want war with North Korea. Such a war would devastate South Korea, cost U.S. lives, perhaps trigger instability in Japan, and certainly sour relations with China. On the other hand, having participated in the demonizing of North Korea, there was no easy way to suddenly declare North Korea's nuclear policies acceptable. An important complicating factor was the upcoming vote on NPT renewal. U.S. officials feared that North Korea's continued refusal to accept IAEA oversight as well as its scheduled withdrawal from the treaty would lead other nations to vote against the NPT's permanent extension. That outcome was likely to encourage other countries to openly and aggressively pursue their own nuclear weapons programs, thereby creating a more complicated and dangerous international situation for the United States. The result of these conflicting concerns was a kind of policy paralysis that allowed those who supported war with the North to dominate the national policy discussion.

Carter's visit changed the terms of the debate. He made it possible for U.S. policymakers to achieve a peaceful end to the nuclear test of wills at relatively small cost: better relations with the North. The October agreement also enabled the United States to secure the permanent renewal of the NPT over the objections of some third world countries. The aftereffect is that U.S. policy now leans toward accommodation rather than confrontation with the North. At the same time, there is no consensus in the U.S. government in favor of taking active steps to significantly improve relations, such as lifting the economic embargo or signing a peace treaty. Moreover, there continues to be a significant minority that would prefer to see the United States return to its earlier position of open hostility toward the North; officials of the U.S. military and conservative think-tanks remain among the biggest boosters of this position. Thus, while the North Korean government won more than what most analysts thought possible in its high stakes nuclear confrontation, it remains uncertain whether it will succeed in achieving its goal of normalized relations with the United States.

The Distorted Nature of North Korean Socialism

The closed nature of North Korean society makes it impossible to explore the nature of its socialist system through direct examination of the experiences of ordinary North Koreans, but much can be gleaned through scrutiny of Kim Il Sung's vision of and strategy for building socialism. North Korean socialism bears little, if any, resemblance to socialism as it has been practiced elsewhere in the world. Evolving under conditions of division and U.S. hostility, it has also lost much of its democratic content and emancipatory potential, leaving North Koreans at a political as well as economic crossroads.

At the heart of Kim Il Sung's political philosophy and practice was the concept of *juche,* or self-reliance. He first used the word publicly in a December 1955 speech to party workers, in which he strongly criticized what he saw as mindless devotion to things Soviet, from culture to political practice, and promoted individual self-reliance, urging individuals to look to their own history and experience for inspiration in order to solve problems. Gradually, however, his advocacy of self-reliance took on a different meaning. He began emphasizing the importance of national self-reliance, that the Korean people needed to rely on their own national leaders and resources to solve problems. Not surprisingly, this under-standing of self-reliance came to dominate during the 1960s, a period when both the Soviet Union and China were unreliable allies. Significantly, this second understanding of self-reliance came at the expense of the first.

Kim was committed to a hierarchical notion of decision-making. His advocacy of the Chongsanri method is a good example. The top-down nature of this management approach is captured in Vice President Pak Sung Chul's 1990 speech celebrating the thirtieth anniversary of the Chongsanri method. After calling it "the best way to effectively administer society and successfully accelerate socialist construction," Pak described the method as one where:

> The higher bodies help the lower. . . . The superior assists those under him and always goes down to the workplace in order to have a good grasp of the specific conditions there and to find correct solutions to problems, gives priority to political work, works with people in all undertakings, and enlists the conscious enthusiasm and initiative of the masses so as to ensure the fulfillment of revolutionary tasks.[45]

The party resolved the apparent contradiction between hierarchical decision-making and self-reliance by using the following reasoning: according to *juche*, people can, under the right conditions, overcome any problem. The right conditions exist when people correctly understand the nature of the problems they face and when they are able to join together with others to solve them. Since it is difficult for people on their own to gain clarity as to the true nature of their situation, much less organize collectively in response to this understanding, they need the party's guidance to help them overcome their problems. The party, as a collective organization, is not only capable of correctly analyzing and proposing solutions to problems, it is also able to organize people to implement them. The party, in turn, is able to carry out its mission only when it relies on the wisdom of its leader, the chairman of the party. In this fashion, hierarchy and self-reliance were made to fit together in a manner that strengthened Kim's control over the party and the party's control over the society.

This understanding of *juche* is certainly consistent with the way Kim Il Sung practiced the Chongsanri method. He made many visits to workplaces and, after learning of people's problems, offered on-the-spot guidance to solve them, guidance which was generally directed at party leaders and which required them to take a more active role in directing worker activity. Believing that this process was capable of generating solutions to the country's outstanding problems, Kim felt no hesitation in proclaiming that under *juche* "man is the master of everything and decides everything."

As the North faced growing economic difficulties and international threats in the early 1970s, Kim once again modified his meaning of *juche*. In 1972, North Korea approved a new constitution in which the DPRK was declared to be a socialist state without class antagonisms, exploitation, and oppression. Article 4 of the constitution proclaimed that "The DPRK is guided in its activity by the *juche* idea of the KWP which is a creative application of Marxism-Leninism to our country." Not long after the implementation of this constitution, the party began a new campaign to make North Korea a "monolithic society" practicing "the unitary thoughts of Kim Il Sung."

The underlying idea behind this campaign was not new. The party had to unleash the creative potential of the people to overcome the nation's problems. This, as we have seen, could only be done through *juche* or the collective efforts of the people guided by the party under Kim Il Sung's direction. The modification to the *juche* idea came as a result of a new emphasis on securing an immediate relationship between Kim and the people rather than reliance upon the party to transmit Kim's ideas. Kim was assumed to have the correct understanding of how to build a new society. Consequently, if everyone could be encouraged to recreate his understanding, then the people would be one with their leader, thereby creating a "monolithic society." In other words, armed with the "unitary thoughts of Kim," people would be able to quickly free themselves of old ideas and creatively build a new society.

This way of thinking views all problems as political problems requiring only proper leadership for their solution. That, of course, is highly voluntaristic and totalitarian. Such thinking also leads to a political dead end. Since not all problems, especially the country's economic problems, can be solved by party-directed hard work within the existing institutional structure, this way of thinking is likely to lead to frustration and failure. Ongoing difficulties, however, can only be understood either as the fault of the people for failing to take the leadership's ideas to heart or the incompetence of the leadership. Unable to admit to the latter explanation, the party is left with no option but to offer the former. At some point, this explanation is bound to lose its popular appeal.

The 1972 constitution declared the DPRK to be socialist. If one defines socialism as a system in which a dominant party directs a strong state which organizes economic activity in a manner that ensures full employment, a relatively equitable distribution of income, and affordable and accessible health care, education, and housing, then North Korea earned that designation. At the same time, North Korea also closely resembles a corporatist state, where the ruler, state, and people are considered to be an organic whole. Certainly this vision was the motivating factor behind the party's attempt to create a monolithic society. As Bruce Cumings explains, "The application of the universal truth of Marxism-Leninism to the concrete realities of Korea, as the saying goes, has resulted in a peculiar and fascinating form of socialist corporatism, mingling classic corporatist verbiage and images, but growing out of Korean political history, with progressive rhetoric and practices of Marxism-Leninism."[46]

North Korea's socialist corporatism is defined in part by the highly organized nature of North Korean society. Mass organizations dedicated to the common goal of building a better DPRK were created to shape and give meaning to people's lives. Even the Korean Workers' Party was from its beginning designated a "mass party of a new type." Kim argued that anyone who put the nation and the revolution first was a patriot and should be able to join the party. As a result, the DPRK has always had a higher percentage of the population enrolled in the party than any other Communist country. Virtually all who are not in the party are members of some mass organization that takes direction from the party.

North Korea's socialist corporate nature is also defined by the role Kim Il Sung played in giving direction to the party and country. Kim was not merely the leader of the party, he was the father of the nation. This use of family metaphor not only ties the entire population together, it also provides a direct connection, based on filial piety, between the population and Kim. The 1981 article "The Father of the People" highlights what this parental relationship means in the North Korean context:

> Kim Il Sung . . . the great father of our people . . . possessed of greatest love for the people. Long is the history of the word "father" used as a word representing love and reverence . . . expressing the unbreakable blood ties between the people

and the leader. Father. This familiar word represents our people's single heart of boundless respect and loyalty. . . . The love shown by the Great Leader for our people is love of kinship. . . . Our respected and beloved Leader is the tender-hearted father of all the people.[47]

Thus Kim was to be obeyed not only because he was president of the country and general secretary of the party, but also because he, as the father of the nation, was one with the people and had their best interests at heart. This relationship provided additional support for Kim's central role in promoting *juche.*

This process of elevating Kim to father of the nation was, no doubt, a useful way to ensure that the country would remain strong and united in the face of external threats. Such a step had to be justified, however, and this could only be done if Kim could be shown to have qualitatively greater commitment and ability to defend the Korean national interest than anyone else. This, in turn, required rewriting Korean history to elevate Kim's accomplishments.

North Korean history proclaims Kim the originator of the Korean revolutionary movement, the founder of the Korean People's Army, and the liberator of Korea from Japan. It supports these claims by arguing that he organized Korea's first Marxist-Leninist revolutionary organization in 1926 when he was only fourteen. Then he is supposed to have organized a Korean anti-Japanese partisan group in 1932 and led it into battle against the Japanese. Two years later, this group was allegedly expanded and reorganized into the Korean People's Revolutionary Army. Kim is said to have commanded this army and fought the Japanese until they were defeated in 1945. From 1940 till the end of the war, he is supposed to have operated from bases in northeast Korea, close to Mt. Paektu. Kim Jong Il was supposedly born at a camp near this mountain in 1942.

Unfortunately, none of the above appears to be true. Those outside of the North who have studied the relevant historical materials have concluded that there is no substance to Kim's claim to have started a revolutionary group when he was fourteen. He did join the Communist Party in 1931 and was a trusted and respected fighter. However, he fought as a member of a Chinese Communist unit until 1941, after which time he and his men were forced to retreat into the Soviet Union. He remained there until the war was over. Kim Jong Il was born in Khabarovsk in the Soviet Far East.

The falsehoods told to aggrandize Kim slight the important contributions made by other Korean revolutionaries both inside and outside the country. They produce a sense of history where only the actions of one man count. By giving all the credit for the founding of the Communist movement and liberation of Korea to Kim, the North Korean state also greatly complicates the task of reunification. Koreans must be able to reclaim a common and accurate history, a history in which many different Koreans participated in the struggle to free the country from Japanese colonialism and build a new society. It is worth noting in this regard that North Korean historians are being hard-pressed to maintain the official history now that both China and Russia are opening their archives to foreign historians.

One result of this falsification of history—an intended one—was the creation of a cult of personality centered around Kim Il Sung. This cult of personality grew slowly and steadily, becoming the dominant feature of Korean political life beginning in the 1970s. It was also during this decade that the cult was extended to include Kim's family. Thus North Korean history now claims that Kim's great-grandfather was involved in the destruction of the *General Sherman*, and that his grandfather and parents were heroes in the fight against the Japanese.

There are two likely reasons that the regime decided to elevate the role of Kim's entire family in the Korean revolutionary struggle. First, it gives better grounding to Kim's elevation to almost godlike status. Second, and perhaps more importantly, it helps determine the matter of Kim's successor. The DPRK built a political system around the leadership of one special individual. Logically, the only safe way to ensure the continuity of the regime was to find another special individual. Within the North Korean context, that person would have to be a member of Kim's family. In the early 1970s, Kim began preparing his eldest son, Kim Jong Il, to succeed him. By expanding the cult of personality to include Kim's entire family line, the regime guaranteed that Kim Jong Il would be able to claim his own special relationship with Korean history. Kim Jong Il was actually given responsibility for promoting the Kim family cult of personality. Beginning in the 1970s and extending throughout the 1980s he organized a massive building campaign which left the country "littered with monuments [honoring Kim and his family], as many as 50,000 of them by one estimate, often in marble or granite."[48]

Kim Jong Il's role in the party was initially kept secret from the public; his decisions and writings were credited to the "Party Center." The sixth party congress in October 1980 was the first time he was publicly acknowledged for his past work. At that time he was also elected to the Presidium of the Politburo and the Military Commission. He was also given the title Dear Leader. In August 1984 his choice as successor was officially confirmed.

Kim Il Sung died in July 1994, and most U.S. and South Korean analysts predicted that Kim Jong Il would not have the political ability and support to replace his father as leader of the party and government. While those positions officially remain unfilled, all available evidence suggests that Kim Jong Il is fully in charge. The party is certainly hard at work building his reputation, claiming in late 1995, for example, that Kim Jong Il "has energetically guided all the affairs of our Party and State, including military and foreign affairs, for more than three decades."[49]

It is difficult to know whether the North Korean population actively embraces this cult of personality and its underlying falsified history. The regime has certainly taken nothing for granted. It carefully controls all information into and out of the country. It has also dealt harshly with those who appear to pose a challenge. According to reports from defectors, political prisoners do not get fair trials, and are regularly beaten, starved, and used as cheap labor; many die in the process. Amnesty International believes that there is a network of perhaps twelve camps within which as many as 100,000 people are held under conditions of extreme privation. The South Korean government has given similar estimates. However, since all the reports we have on prison conditions come from camp defectors who have fled south, it is difficult to know whether what they describe truly represents their own experiences or what South Korean intelligence officials want them to say. Moreover, as the *New York Times* reports, "It is striking in speaking to the defectors that for all of the horrors they portray, they do not contend that North Korea is seething with discontent. On the contrary, many suggest that ordinary North Koreans have faith in their leaders."[50]

In sum, there can be no doubt that the North Korean leadership has created an ideology and social system which are far from desirable. In trying to understand the nature and evolution of North Korean socialism it is, however, important to remember that, as Lone and McCormack remark, "Ultimately, the peculiarities of the regime were all rooted in the abnormal circumstances of the continuing militarized division of the country, and the long-sustained hostile confrontation with the superpower of the United States."[51] As long as the country remains divided and under threat from the United States, it is likely that the North Korean regime will seek to maintain, if not intensify, the cult of personality that surrounds its present leader, Kim Jong Il. In the short run, such a policy is likely to help ensure the survival of the current regime. In the long run, it can only serve to discredit any vision of a democratic socialist Korea. Even normalization of relations with the United States, which the North hopes will bring fresh capital and economic recovery, can hardly be expected to breathe new life into such a vision.

The North Korean people face a difficult period ahead. They should be encouraged to rediscover their history, regain their voice, and renew their efforts to create a democratic and egalitarian society. If their efforts are to succeed, they must not be bounded by the so-called "imaginary line." They must include dialogue with those seeking social change in the South and address the process of creating a unified Korea.

Chapter 7

Divided Korea:
The South Korean Experience

Scholars and media commentators often present South Korea as one of the U.S. government's greatest foreign policy successes. Thanks to U.S. guidance and aid, they say, South Korea has arisen like a phoenix from the ashes of the Korean War to rebuild its economy. It is now internationally acclaimed as a model of successful free market capitalist development. The United States is also said to deserve considerable credit—because of its patience and timely prodding of South Korean leaders—for South Korea's slow but steady democratization. And underpinning all of this progress, foreign policy experts claim, is U.S. vigilance against North Korean aggression. Despite its Korean War defeat, the North remains determined to "Communize" the entire peninsula. Fortunately, U.S. military strength prevents this from happening.

This analysis of the South Korean experience and U.S. foreign policy is seriously misleading. The Korean War did not significantly diminish popular opposition in the South to the U.S.-promoted division of Korea, and, as a result, the South Korean regime was sustained only by a U.S.-supported military dictatorship which ruled South Korea from 1961 to 1987. The alleged North Korean threat to South Korean liberty was used to justify its rule. The United States has declared its policies a success on the basis of South Korea's "economic miracle" and political evolution. But South Korea's post-1965 growth was no miracle for the South Korean people, for the gains were based on repression and exploitation. Finally, the country's real but constrained post-1987 democratization was the result of left-led activism, not the natural outcome of successful capitalist development.

While it is true that South Koreans currently enjoy a stronger economy and a freer political system than North Koreans do, they also face serious problems. The South Korean economy went into a tailspin in late 1997. Recession and an IMF-mandated program of structural adjustment promise to produce record levels of unemployment and declining incomes. In addition, political activity remains heavily circumscribed by state-declared "national security" considerations. As a consequence, most South Koreans seek substantial transformation of their country's economic and political institutions. However, as long as the "imaginary line" continues to divide Korea, it is doubtful that they can accomplish their goal.

The Road to Military Dictatorship

Although the U.S. government trumpets its role in advancing the democratic process in South Korea, U.S. determination to achieve its foreign policy aims was the catalyst that propelled South Korea toward military dictatorship. Edwin Pauley, Truman's special ambassador-at-large, visited Korea in June 1946 and wrote in his report to the president that Korea was "an ideological battleground upon which our entire success in Asia may depend."[1] The problem for the United States, Pauley explained, was that "Communism in Korea could get off to a better start than practically anywhere else in the world."[2] Pauley's fear that Koreans might embrace communism was well-founded. According to Donald S. MacDonald, the author of a history of U.S. policy in Korea commissioned by the State Department, "Early opinion surveys by the American Military Government established that a majority of the Korean people favored a socialist economy; but at that stage in history, no official American agency could have put itself in the position of supporting socialism."[3]

Determined to oppose socialism, no matter what the wishes of the Korean people were, the U.S. occupation had little choice but to join forces with those Koreans who also opposed socialism. And given that the United States had no hope of shaping events in the north, where leftist political forces operated under Soviet protection, it also had little choice but to pursue the division of Korea. The United States succeeded in achieving its goals of dividing Korea and creating an anticommunist South Korea in large part because of the efforts of Syngman Rhee, who became South Korea's first president in 1948. Given the unpopularity of the U.S. political project among Koreans, it should not be surprising that there was very little that was democratic about Rhee's political practice.

Rhee took advantage of every opportunity afforded him to crush popular movements and strengthen his own political position. His first opportunity came during the October 1948 Yosu rebellion, when he pressured the National Assembly into passing a rather vaguely worded National Security Law (NSL). Rhee used the NSL against what remained of the South Korean left, but it was not his only target. He also used it against a number of conservative legislators who had supported him for president with the expectation that he would share power. He refused, they tried to legislatively undermine his power, and Rhee responded by having sixteen of them arrested for "endangering" national security. By the spring of 1950, nearly 60,000 people were in prison in the South, between 50 to 80 percent on charges of violating the NSL.[4]

Rhee's actions were so unpopular that they jeopardized his re-election. The constitution gave the National Assembly the power to elect the president, and Rhee worried that few of his supporters would be chosen in the May 1950 legislative election. U.S. pressure frustrated his attempt to postpone the vote and the result was as he feared. He was saved from the political consequences of the election, however, by the June start of the Korean War.

Taking advantage of the fighting, Rhee forced the National Assembly into passing a constitutional amendment in July 1952 allowing the direct election of the president. He did so by mobilizing youth gangs to engage in violent demonstrations in Pusan, the wartime capital. The demonstrations gave him an excuse to declare martial law. When legislators voted to lift martial law, Rhee had military police surround the National Assembly building. The legislators eventually agreed to his proposed constitutional change, even setting the election date for early August so that an opposition candidate would have little time to organize a campaign. Rhee handily won re-election.

Although the U.S. government had strongly backed Rhee's rise to power, it did not always agree with his policies. U.S. policymakers felt strongly that Rhee should adopt an austerity budget in order to create an inflation-free environment for private investors. Rhee disagreed, leading the U.S. government to periodically threaten to reduce its aid program. The United States and Rhee also had strong differences over military policy. Most importantly, the United States objected to Rhee's repeated attempts to sabotage armistice negotiations with the North. Rhee even threatened to carry out independent military operations in an effort to force the United States to continue the war. The U.S. government seriously considered forcibly removing him from office.

Significantly, U.S. concern with Rhee's economic and military policies did not extend to his human rights record. The U.S. government was well-aware of the undemocratic nature of Rhee's regime; in official (at the time secret) documents it often referred to Rhee's regime as a "police state."[5] But it made no serious attempt to pressure Rhee into changing his policies. U.S. planners apparently realized that their own aims would also be threatened by a democratic regime.

Growing numbers of South Koreans did not share the U.S. government's tolerance of Rhee's repressive policies. Rhee won the presidency for a third time in 1956, after using bribery and intimidation to end the constitutional restriction limiting presidents to two terms in office. However, an opposition candidate, Chang Myon, won the vice-presidency. There was also a revival of left-wing political activity. Cho Pong-am, presidential candidate of the Progressive Party, won approximately 30 percent of the vote in 1956, running on a platform calling for socialist democracy, economic planning, and reunification.[6] Rhee gave his opposition no quarter. He had Cho arrested in 1958 on charges of being a North Korean spy, and executed him the following year. Running unopposed in the March 1960 presidential election, he rigged the balloting so that Chang Myon would not be reelected vice president.

Rhee's 1960 election shenanigans proved to be his undoing. Upon hearing that Chang had lost, students immediately began organizing demonstrations. After the body of a student who had been killed by police was found in the waters off Masan in April, student demonstrations began anew. When some 30,000 students marched toward the presidential mansion in Seoul to demand Rhee's resignation, the police attacked and many were killed. Rhee called for martial law, but the army, with U.S. support, refused to impose it. Convinced that Rhee had outlived his usefulness, the United States worked behind the scenes to remove him. On April 26, Rhee agreed to resign and seek exile in the United States.

With Rhee gone, the National Assembly began to assert its influence. It amended the constitution to reduce the power of the president by, among other things, establishing the office of prime minister. New elections were held in July 1960, and Chang was elected the country's first prime minister.

Chang found himself in a difficult situation. The United States had forced South Korea to adopt an anti-inflation program in 1957 and cut its aid program in 1958. The result was economic decline. Moreover, while Chang had been the beneficiary of the student movement, his election was not the motivating force behind student action. In the words of a slogan of the day, students sought "Democracy in Politics and Equality in Economy," and they continued to pursue their aims though direct political action. As a case in point, they invaded the National Assembly in October and demanded that laws be passed to punish those who had profited from the corruption during Rhee's time in office.

The "April revolution" opened up opportunities for South Koreans to rethink their country's political direction. Tumultuous change had occurred over the past fifteen years, so the terms of, as well as the participants in, the relevant political discussions had greatly changed since the late 1940s. Most importantly, there was no longer an organized left presence in the South to define and shape an alternative vision. Nevertheless, popular desire for radical change and reunification remained strong. The latter is especially significant in light of U.S. and South Korean government assertions that South Koreans viewed the North as their enemy because of its 1950 "invasion."

Many in the South were well aware of the social, political, and economic changes taking place on the other side of the "imaginary line," and were therefore eager to initiate a similar restructuring of the South Korean political economy, as well as build closer ties with the North. The extent of dissatisfaction with conditions in the South is reflected in the fact that there were approximately 2,000 street demonstrations involving 1 million people during the ten months Chang served as prime minister.[7] Within this new environment, the left again began to rebuild. Former members of the Progressive Party formed the Socialist Mass Party, which called for removal of U.S. troops. The Socialist Mass Party joined with student organizations, labor unions, and other newly formed progressive organizations to create the Council For Independence and National Reunification, which advocated a reunification process based on establishing trade, cultural, and educational ties between the South and North, followed by general elections to unify the country.

Chang, with no real vision of his own, was unsure how to respond to this popular mobilization and leftward shift in the political mood of the country. He was a weak leader who depended heavily on the United States for support and direction. The nature of Chang's political dilemma can easily be expressed: the United States opposed radical economic restructuring and closer ties with the North, while growing numbers of people demanded nothing less. Pressured by the United States, Chang began to move to the right. His regime began branding those seeking political and economic change as communists and even introduced a new and tougher NSL. Undeterred, students led by the National Student League for Unification passed a resolution on May 5, 1961, calling for a North-South Student Conference to be held in Panmunjom on May 20. The North welcomed this initiative and Northern students communicated their willingness to attend. However, the meeting never happened.

On May 16, 1961, Chang's government was overthrown by a military coup led by Major General Park Chung Hee. The sixteen-man military junta declared martial law, dissolved the National Assembly and all political parties, outlawed demonstrations, and instituted press censorship. It also moved quickly to win U.S. support by claiming that "anticommunism was the first purpose of government."[8] While the U.S. government initially opposed the takeover, its opposition did not last long. In a report to the National Security Council, a U.S. Presidential Task Force on Korea stated, "The government of Chang Myon had failed to win the confidence of the people in its leadership and in its ability to solve the nation's problems."[9] While accurate, this conclusion conveniently overlooks the fact that the U.S. government opposed the political changes such an outcome would require. In a very real sense, then, military dictatorship was a logical consequence of the U.S. project to create a politically responsive, capitalist South Korea.

Military Dictatorship and the "Economic Miracle"

The coup leaders aimed to stop South Koreans from joining with North Koreans to establish a socialist Korea. Park and other military leaders, having recently fought against the North to preserve an anticommunist

South, had good reason to fear the outcome of a progressive-inspired reunification. Determined that such a reunification not take place, Park's mission was to win legitimacy for his regime through the one avenue left open to him in the aftermath of the coup: economic growth. The years of Park's dictatorship, 1961 to 1979, are often described as a "golden age," a time when South Koreans rolled up their sleeves, and by working together under government direction, produced an economic miracle. As we shall see, the actual experience was quite different. With the use of a pervasive state structure, Park led South Koreans on a forced march to rapid industrial growth. However, because this growth was the result of a highly repressive and contradictory economic strategy, it produced neither political legitimacy nor stability for his dictatorship.[10]

Park's approach to economics was never based on traditional American free market theories. Experience had taught him the virtues of state control and direction of economic activity. He and the other members of the ruling military junta had all worked in an intelligence unit that monitored North Korea; as a result, they were aware of North Korea's successful use of state enterprises and planning. Furthermore, Park had attended the Japanese military academy in Manchukuo in the 1930s and received special training at a military academy in Tokyo. He had great respect for the economic accomplishments of Japan and its colonial government in Korea, neither of which was based on free market policies. Drawing upon this experience, Park moved quickly to secure state control over South Korean economic activity. He established the Economic Planning Board, which set the national budget and regulated foreign borrowing and investment, and the Ministry of Trade and Industry, which licensed business activity and regulated foreign trade. He nationalized the banking system which allowed the state to determine the allocation and cost of credit. He authorized the creation of state-owned enterprises and industrial estates, which were also used to direct private business activity. Finally, Park required all domestic businesses to join one of sixty-two industrially based business associations. Through these associations, the Economic Planning Board and the Ministry of Trade and Industry were able to monitor and regulate individual firm investment, price, and trade activities.

What made this newly created system function as a coherent whole was military power. Military leaders instituted a system of weekly meetings at which top economic planners were required to brief them on the state of the economy. They also introduced planning and control offices in every major ministry. Each office was required to make quarterly reports on the status of the planning process in its assigned ministry. The military also introduced a series of reforms which, by centralizing the recruitment and placement of administrative personnel, gave them greater oversight and control over the entire state bureaucracy. In addition, as described by George E. Ogle, Park also established his own direct chain of command:

> To make sure that commands were heard and obeyed the whole way down to the plant floor, Park had military comrades appointed as president or vice president of companies, as members of the boards of directors, as heads of the personnel department and to other key positions. To complement the military presence in industry, about 38 percent of noneconomic jobs in government also went to military appointees. This permitted Park a direct and personal supervision of the entire industrial and political complex.[11]

It is noteworthy that although Park's state-centered economic approach directly contradicted past U.S. recommendations to Rhee and Chang, the U.S. government did not actively object. Apparently, the United States was willing to accept whatever was necessary to ensure the victory of "free" South Korea over "red" North Korea. Thus, as long as the Cold War contest remained in doubt, and as long as South Korean growth was sustained, the United States was prepared to grant Park a degree of freedom to set policy that it granted few other leaders.

Growth and Its Contradictions, 1961-1979

After an initial unsuccessful attempt to create a "self-reliant" economy based on import-substitution industrialization, Park adopted a growth strategy based on the production and export of manufactures. As Byong-Nak Song, a South Korean economist who worked with the government, explained:

> Under the government export promotion strategy, "survival of the fittest" among competing firms was not determined in the marketplace, but through discretionary government actions. "Fitness" was judged in terms of the ability to expand exports, rather than based on profitability. If determined "unfit," firms were likely to face bankruptcy. Such firms were under constant threat of tax investigations and other punitive sanctions. On the other hand, firms that efficiently used their government-backed loans to expand exports were implicitly considered fit and favored with even further support.[12]

The results of this strategy were dramatic. Real export growth went from approximately 9 percent in 1963 to more than 35 percent in 1965, and remained above 30 percent in each of the next four years. The ratio of exports to GNP more than tripled from 1965 to 1975. Moreover, the composition of exports also changed dramatically. In 1961, the top six exports in order of dollar value were basic ores, iron ore, fish, raw silk, vegetables, and swine. In 1971 they were clothing, plywood, other manufactures (which included wigs and toys), electrical machinery, raw silk, and basic ores. By 1976, they were clothing, footwear, fabrics, electrical machinery, plywood, and telecommunications equipment. Powered by this rapid increase in the production and export of manufactured goods, the country's annual GNP growth rate averaged 8.3 percent between 1962 and 1967 and 12.6 percent between 1967 and 1971.

Economic conditions were far from stable, however. Among the most important problems generated by the country's economic expansion was a growing trade deficit. Economic growth, especially when produced by a rapid expansion of exports, was supposed to solve the country's balance of payments problem. In South Korea's case, the problem worsened; the trade deficit grew from $240 million in 1965 to more than $1 billion in 1971. One of the main reasons was that South Korea's new manufacturing industries were structurally dependent on imports of technology, machinery, and components from Japan.

Park was able to finance this trade imbalance and maintain growth only because he was able to secure funds from Japan and the United States. As part of the 1965 Japan-ROK normalization treaty, Japan agreed to give South Korea $200 million in loans, $300 million in grants, and at least $300 million in commercial credits. Park received money from the United States by agreeing to send South Korean troops to fight in Vietnam. Some 300,000 went, and, according to the terms of a secret arrangement, the U.S. government paid a bonus in dollars for each of them. The United States also agreed to purchase war supplies in South Korea, allow South Korean firms to act as subcontractors for construction and service work in Vietnam, and modernize the South Korean military. All together, from 1965 to 1973, South Korea earned almost $1 billion from the combination of military and civilian activities carried out in Vietnam. South Korea made an additional $1.1 billion from U.S. military activities in the country itself. The $2.1 billion represented approximately 30 percent of South Korea's total foreign exchange earnings over the period 1966 to 1969.[13]

South Korea's export strategy also generated political tensions. To guarantee the export competitiveness of South Korea's light manufacturers, Park used agricultural policy to create a low-wage labor force. In the mid-1960s, Park began lowering grain prices and denying farmers' access to credit for modernization. The result was a severe income squeeze which triggered, as the government desired, a massive rural-to-urban migration. But the large number of people arriving in the cities, especially Seoul, overwhelmed the urban infrastructure, producing a growing mass of urban poor people who sometimes engaged in violent demonstrations to demand housing and social services.

The majority of those who left the countryside were young women in search of urban industrial employment. Most quickly found work in South Korea's core export industries, primarily textiles, clothing, rubber footwear, and electronics. These women labored for long hours in unsafe conditions yet received below-subsistence wages. For example, the average manufacturing worker received $40 a month. In textiles, young women earned only $25 a month. To put these figures in perspective, the Bank of Korea calculated that an urban family of four needed $90 a month for survival.[14] In spite of a lack of employment safeguards, these women fought to improve their working conditions. One of their first important labor actions took place in 1968 at a U.S.-owned electronics firm. More strikes took place in the following years at both foreign and domestically owned firms. These strikes greatly worried Park, who was eager to attract more foreign investment in order to reduce the country's reliance on foreign borrowing.

Park's political problems were compounded by international developments. In 1969, President Nixon had declared a major change in U.S. military strategy, a change dictated by the unpopularity of the Vietnam War. The "Nixon Doctrine" called for a withdrawal of U.S. ground troops from Asia; some 20,000 troops left South Korea in 1971. In addition, a global economic slowdown in 1970 triggered a rise in protectionist sentiment, especially in the United States. In 1971, the United States forced South Korea to sign a trade agreement limiting textile exports. In 1970, textiles accounted for 38 percent of South Korea's exports. Textile exports to the

United States alone accounted for 15 percent of the country's total exports.[15]

Faced with growing urban disruptions and labor unrest, a loss of U.S. military support, and the closure of key export markets, Park had good reason to worry about whether he could defeat Kim Dae Jung in the 1971 presidential election. He had won the 1963 and 1967 elections largely because of his ability to mobilize large sums of money to bribe people or, when that proved ineffective, his use of the Korean Central Intelligence Agency (KCIA) and police to intimidate his opponents. This strategy proved insufficient for victory in 1971; he also had to falsify votes.

Recognizing that his hold on power was weakening, Park declared a state of national emergency in December 1971. Then he secured passage of a new law giving him the authority to ban public demonstrations, freeze wages, and "mobilize any material or human resources for national purposes." Park justified his actions by claiming that the new law was needed to meet the threat of a North Korean attack, but there was no real threat. Park's declaration of national emergency was motivated entirely by domestic concerns. In fact, fearful of the consequences of the change in U.S. military policy, Park had initiated secret talks between the head of the KCIA and his counterpart in the North. On July 4, 1972, the two Korean governments simultaneously issued the North-South Joint Communiqué which included the following three guiding principles for reunification:

> First, unification shall be achieved through independent Korean efforts without being subject to external imposition or interference.
>
> Second, unification shall be achieved through peaceful means, and not through the use of force against each other.
>
> Third, as a homogeneous people, a great national unity shall be sought above all, transcending differences in ideas, ideologies, and systems.

Confusion reigned in the South as to what had been agreed upon. For one thing, no one was sure what it meant to transcend differences in ideas and ideologies. Some National Assembly members argued that to be consistent with this principle, it was necessary to abolish the country's Anti-Communist Law and National Security Law. Prime Minister Kim Jong Pil, one of the leaders of the 1961 coup, disagreed, saying that "the government will carry out these laws more effectively." There was also confusion over what was meant by rejecting "external imposition or interference." The

North claimed that this meant the complete withdrawal of U.S. military forces from the South. Kim Jong Pil, on the other hand, said "the presence of the UN forces cannot be viewed as 'external' forces."[16]

On October 17, Park shocked the country again by declaring martial law for the purpose of rewriting the constitution. Park claimed that a new constitution was necessary because Western-style democracy had proven unsuitable for South Korea. His answer was the Yushin or "revitalizing" constitution. The Yushin constitution gave Park tremendous power, including the rights to appoint one-third of the National Assembly, dissolve the National Assembly at will, and appoint all judges. More generally, the new constitution gave Park the authority to take any emergency measures he thought necessary whenever "the national security or the public safety and order is seriously threatened or anticipated to be threatened." The new constitution also included a new election procedure under which the president would be elected by members of a newly created National Conference of Unification, all of whom would be chosen by a select group of citizens, all of whom would be chosen by the president.

As Park had used North Korean "hostility" to justify his December 1971 actions, now he used the North-South dialogue to justify passage of the Yushin constitution. Park claimed that he needed the new powers to negotiate with the North from a position of strength. A vote against the new constitution in the promised public referendum would, he said, be a vote against North-South reconciliation. Taking no chances, Park held the referendum under conditions of martial law; the government later announced that 91.5 percent of the people had voted in favor of the new constitution. Not surprisingly, the outcome of the vote had no influence on the North-South dialogue, which soon ended.

Park's dictatorial actions generated outrage and opposition, primarily from student and religious activists. His response was a series of repressive decrees, the most draconian being Emergency Decree No. 9. Issued in May 1975, it prohibited making "false" statements about Park or the government or publicly criticizing the constitution. The decree also prohibited any student-initiated political activity or public presentation or statement describing or discussing any action which might violate the decree. It also prohibited any action or speech which might defame or harm the "welfare" of South Korea while abroad or with a foreigner while in South Korea. In short, it became illegal to object to any government policy or action. The jails filled up with students, religious leaders, and workers, many of whom were tortured. At least eight people were executed for violating the special decrees. Park's hold on power remained secure.

None of the events surrounding Yushin appeared to upset the United States. For example, Park's imposition of Yushin was met with silence, not disapproval, by the U.S. government. A U.S. House of Representative report on South Korean-U.S. relations called this "noninterference":

> When the Yushin declaration was made, the United States had to put its policy together quickly. At that time Seoul was in considerable favor in Washington because of the economic achievements and the negotiations with the North. Therefore, the policy adopted was one of noninterference. President Nixon reiterated the policy when he told Prime Minister Kim Jong Pil in January 1973 that "unlike other Presidents, I do not intend to interfere in the internal affairs of your country."[17]

Even the exposure of Park's secret program to influence U.S. public opinion and government actions, which the press dubbed Koreagate (in obligatory homage to the Watergate scandal), did not seriously diminish his standing among U.S. policymakers. The program, made public by the U.S. Congress in the mid-1970s, included illegal attempts to ensure support for Yushin from U.S. congressmen and major universities, as well as from Koreans living in the United States (in many cases by threatening them).[18]

Park's political offensive, organized around Yushin, was matched by an equally significant change in economic strategy. To overcome trade problems caused by labor unrest and tightening markets for the country's light manufactures, Park used an aggressive program of subsidized loans, protectionism, and labor repression to shift the economy's center of gravity to capital-intensive heavy and chemical industries (including iron and steel, petrochemicals, electronics, machinery, shipbuilding, and transport equipment). One measure of its success: the share of heavy and chemical industries in total exports rose from 14 percent in 1971 to 60 percent in 1984.[19]

The main beneficiaries of this economic restructuring were a small number of *chaebol* or family-owned conglomerates. The combined net sales of the top ten *chaebol* rose from 15.1 percent of GNP in 1974, to 30 percent in 1978, and to 56 percent in 1981.[20] By 1988, the combined revenue of the top four *chaebol*—Samsung, Hyundai, Lucky-Goldstar, and Daewoo—totaled almost half of the country's GNP.[21] As the *Far Eastern Eco-*

nomic Review explained, "Virtually the whole economy has fallen under the domination of . . . [the] *chaebol* . . . they have literally left no stone unturned in their expansion and control of domestic industries and markets."[22]

While South Korea's economic model of state direction and *chaebol*-dominated production challenged conventional free market wisdom, few American economists challenged South Korea's claim to economic success. The country's GNP growth averaged 11 percent a year from 1973 to 1979. South Korea had become a major producer and exporter of steel, ships, and electronics. In 1978, it was the number one third world exporter of manufactures to the developed capitalist world. Rarely noted was the fact that South Korean manufacturing workers suffered through the world's longest workweek, under oppressive conditions, in exchange for extremely low wages. Government statistics for 1978 show that approximately two-thirds of all manufacturing workers earned monthly wages below the national average. Approximately 40 percent earned below the government-defined subsistence wage level.[23]

Although it appeared Park was firmly in control of both political and economic developments, appearances were misleading. South Korea's economy, in large part because of forces set in motion by the country's growth strategy, was heading into crisis. Park had supported the establishment of the new heavy industries with massive increases in credit. This policy not only generated substantial inflation, it also left light manufacturing starved for funds. The net result was a slowdown in export earnings. Compounding the problem was the fact that most of the newly established heavy industries were dependent on Japanese components, machinery, and technology. One example: South Korea had built one of the largest corporate shipyards in the world, but only the hulls were produced in South Korea; all the machinery, engines, and instruments were imported from Japan.

Park's heavy industry strategy thus produced both the celebrated renewal in growth as well as a less-noted, ever-expanding trade deficit and foreign debt burden. Foreign debt went from less than $6 billion dollars in 1974 to more than $20 billion in 1979. Fearful of a new debt crisis, Park was forced, by mid-1979, to slow the economy.

South Korea's economic slowdown took effect at roughly the same time that a new, more radical opposition movement was gaining strength.

Throughout the 1960s and early 1970s, opposition to Park's rule had been led by students and church leaders whose main demand was for democracy, by which they meant respect for established electoral procedures and basic civil rights. Many had suffered arrest, torture, and imprisonment for acts as simple as signing petitions calling for revision of the Yushin constitution. They had hoped that their efforts would lead to international condemnation and isolation of Park's regime, and ultimately his resignation. But, as they discovered, civil disobedience by a few could not bring down a police state that was internationally celebrated for its economic achievements. Enlightened by their experience and inspired by the increasingly active workplace struggles of women, some student and religious activists began to rethink both their vision of democracy and their strategy for achieving it. The outcome of this thinking was the realization that it was the nature of power relations, including at the workplace, not the existence of formal voting rights, that defined the extent of democracy. This realization produced a number of talented and dedicated labor advisors who contributed to the development of a much more effective labor movement.

By 1979, strikes and demonstrations had become common enough that Park was motivated to take strong action. In August, he sent the police to attack 200 women at the opposition party headquarters who were protesting their dismissal from the Y. H. Trading Company; one woman was killed. When Kim Young Sam, the leader of the opposition party, criticized Park's actions to the *New York Times*, Park engineered his removal from the National Assembly. Popular anger at Park reached the breaking point. Thousands of students took to the streets in the industrial cities of Pusan and Masan, demanding his resignation. They were soon joined by workers. Park issued a statement blaming the unrest on North Korean agents, and he mobilized special paratroopers. These paratroopers never saw action, however. On October 26, Park was assassinated by the head of the KCIA, who later claimed that he killed Park to avoid the slaughter of innocent civilians. Students celebrated Park's death with demonstrations calling for an end to Yushin and the beginning of reunification. Workers joined the demonstrations and also organized their own strikes for higher wages and better working conditions.

The long march was finally over, leaving South Koreans with the difficult but exciting task of debating and deciding their own future. At past moments of decision—during the late 1940s and in 1960—the great majority of people had endorsed a socialist-oriented vision and reunification only to be "overruled" by military action. It was unclear what direction people favored in 1979. The years of repression under Park had distanced South Koreans from socialism and North Korea. That same repression, however, had generated public disapproval of the national security state, the *chaebol,* and the country's export-first growth strategy. In short, people needed time to debate and explore alternative social arrangements. Tragically, they did not get it. The military shared none of the population's uncertainty. Determined to sustain existing political and economic institutions, it waited less than a year before once again imposing its rule over the country. And it did so with strong U.S. support.

The Restoration of the South Korean Growth Model

With Park's death, the powers of state were officially transferred to Prime Minister Choi Kyu Hah. While the great majority of South Koreans wanted an immediate repudiation of Yushin and direct election of the next president, Choi insisted that he be allowed to finish out Park's term of office. On December 6 he was elected president, according to Yushin procedures.

While public attention was focused on constitutional maneuvering, forces within the military moved quickly to foreclose democratic possibilities. Major General Chun Doo Hwan, head of Army Security Command and a close friend of the murdered president, was placed in charge of the investigation into Park's assassination. Chun, who shared Park's political vision as well as his friendship, used his position to increase his own power. On December 12, 1979, with the help of Major General Roh Tae Woo, he arrested the Army Chief of Staff, falsely charging him with involvement in the assassination. Other military officials were also arrested. Chun was now in control of the military and well-placed to halt the challenge to Yushin.

Frustrated by the lack of progress toward democracy, workers and students began to directly challenge Yushin. Within the first months of 1980, garment workers, pharmaceutical workers, machine tool workers, nylon factory workers, and miners, among others, all struck for higher pay, improved working conditions, and democratic unions. Tens of thousands of other workers forced their employers to recognize their unions without striking. Student demonstrations also grew in size and militancy, especially in May. More than 100,000 students marched in Seoul on May 15, demanding a new constitution and an end to martial law.

Yielding to the pressure, the National Assembly scheduled a May 22 meeting at which many expected it would vote to end martial law. However, Chun acted first. On May 17, he pressured President Choi into expanding martial law restrictions. Chun, speaking for the government, then ordered the National Assembly dissolved and all political and labor activity banned. Military units were sent to all major cities and universities; all major opposition politicians were arrested. Chun claimed that these actions were needed to secure order and thus safeguard the nation against a possible North Korean attack.

Workers and students responded by organizing protests across the nation, including in the southwestern city of Kwangju. On May 18, special combat forces sent to Kwangju to suppress anti-Chun demonstrations went on a rampage, indiscriminately attacking people, especially those they thought were students. Horrified by the brutality of the troops, more demonstrators took to the streets the following day. An Asia Watch report describes the response of the special troops:

> They repeated the same actions of the day before, beating, stabbing, and mutilating unarmed civilians, including children, young girls, and aged grandmothers. They forced both men and women to strip naked, made others lie flat on the ground and kicked them. Several sources tell of soldiers stabbing or cutting off the breasts of naked girls; one murdered student was found disemboweled, another with an X carved in his back. About twenty high school girls were reported killed at Central High School. The paratroopers carried out searches in side streets, fired randomly into crowds, carted off the bodies in trucks, and piled them in the bus terminal. They even took the wounded out of hospitals.[24]

The people of Kwangju reacted with anger to what they witnessed. The entire city mobilized; people set fire to TV and radio stations that refused to report what was happening, students set up machine guns on their campuses, and armed citizens occupied key buildings in the city. Intense fighting followed and, on May 22, the soldiers were forced to withdraw from the city. The media outside of Kwangju told the rest of the country that there was unrest in Kwangju because of "impure elements," the government's code word for North Korean agents.

After the troops withdrew, a Kwangju citizens' committee was formed in an attempt to stop the bloodshed. It contacted the U.S. Embassy to ask for help. U.S. officials refused, stating that the U.S. government did not wish to involve itself in the internal affairs of South Korea. However, the U.S. military commander, who under the terms of a 1978 agreement was also the head of South Korean ground troops, saw things differently. U.S. Army General John Wickham gave Chun permission to use South Korean forces to "retake" Kwangju. On May 27, 1980, tens of thousands of troops attacked Kwangju, killing more people and finally ending all resistance. The government claims that only 191 people died during the period of the uprising. Others put the number in the thousands. By carrying out a slaughter similar to that which Park had been preparing before his assassination, Chun succeeded in renewing military dictatorship in South Korea.

At the time, many South Koreans wondered what role, if any, the United States had played in encouraging Chun's actions. Chun claimed full U.S. support; he made a public statement on May 30 to that effect. The U.S. government, on the other hand, attempted to publicly distance itself from Chun's statement. It said at the time, and again in a 1989 State Department White Paper, that it had no prior knowledge that special combat forces would be used in Kwangju and was deeply shocked by the resulting violence. In 1996, however, several secret U.S. government documents were made public, revealing that the U.S. government not only was well-informed in 1980 about Chun's plans, but actually gave Chun a green light for his actions.[25] It appears that while U.S. policymakers preferred that the South Korean government maintain order through peaceful means, their main objective was to maintain the existing political and economic system. The documents make clear that U.S. policymakers viewed developments in South Korea through the lens of Iran, where in 1979 the Shah had been overthrown and replaced by a government hostile to U.S. interests. The United States was afraid to take any action that might weaken the stability of the existing South Korean regime. This was why it offered no public criticism of Chun's December military takeover.

The U.S. government's fears of instability actually led it to view the democratic movement as the "problem" in South Korea. For example, Richard C. Holbrooke, the assistant secretary of state for East Asian and Pacific affairs, dismissed those involved in the democratic movement as "a relative handful of Christian extremist dissidents." In December 1979, he ordered the U.S. ambassador to South Korea, William J. Gleysteen, to tell the democratic activists that they were pushing the government too hard.[26] On May 9, 1980, during a period when students were holding almost daily demonstrations, Gleysteen told Chun and Choi that the United States would not oppose the use of military force against the demonstrators if they thought it necessary to maintain order. He said this even though he was aware that Chun had already ordered South Korean special forces to prepare for action.[27] U.S. government support for Chun continued even after officials learned of the May 18 and 19 brutality of South Korean forces in Kwangju. As a case in point, on May 22, 1980, the Carter administration approved the further use of force by the South Korean army to retake the city. Gleysteen actually told the South Korean foreign minister that the U.S. military would, if need be, directly assist South Korean "army efforts to restore order in Kwangju and deter trouble elsewhere."[28]

Direct U.S. assistance to the new dictatorship was forthcoming, but it was financial, not military. Having achieved power, Chun faced the difficult task of reinvigorating the South Korean growth model. South Korea's GNP fell by 4.8 percent in 1980. The country's trade deficit had soared in 1979 and remained high in 1980. As a result, foreign debt had ballooned, much of it short-term. Chun desperately needed new international credits to keep the economy from a downward spiral. Without them, South Korea was likely headed into a foreign debt-driven austerity crisis much like the one that devastated most of Latin America in the 1980s. The United States provided those credits. Less than two weeks after Kwangju, President Carter gave approval for John Moore, head of the U.S. Export-Import Bank, to go to South Korea and offer Chun more than $600 million worth of import credits. Moore's visit was followed by visits from David Rockefeller, head of Chase Manhattan Bank, and William Spenser, head of First National Bank; both men assured Chun of continued U.S. financial support.

Buoyed by this support, Chun launched an intense political crackdown on all sectors of South Korean society. An estimated 40,000 people were sent to secret military camps where many were tortured. Given the precariousness of South Korea's economic situation, Chun took special aim at labor. He introduced a series of labor laws designed to break the labor movement and its growing ties with other social movements. One new labor law restricted all union activity to a single workplace. Industry-wide or regionally coordinated union negotiations with one or more employers became illegal. Another law gave the government the right to change any union agreement if it believed it to be contrary to the "public interest." Perhaps the most important new law was one restricting "third party" involvement in labor activity. As interpreted, this law made it illegal for anyone not employed at a given workplace to advise those who worked there on labor law or to offer them direct support in a labor dispute, thus enabling the government to completely and legally isolate workers from each other, as well as from students and church activists. Even fired workers were now forbidden to maintain contact with ongoing union activity at their former workplace.

The combination of U.S. financial support and Chun's antilabor offensive worked its magic. By 1983, the South Korean *chaebol* were well-positioned to take advantage of the global economic expansion. Led by *chaebol*-produced exports, the country's GNP grew by more than 11 percent that year. Foreign businesses that had been scared by the labor militancy and growing radicalism of the post-Park period were reassured. As one U.S. corporate executive noted in 1982, "It is in our own selfish interest to have a strong government [in South Korea] that controls the students and labor so that everything will blossom and grow and we can continue to make profits."[29]

Growth and Its Contradictions, 1980-1992

It seemed as if nothing had changed. Park had been a dictator and his regime had produced record growth for almost two decades. By all appearances, Chun had successfully restored Park's growth model. South Korea enjoyed its best economic performance from 1986 to 1988, with GNP growth of over 12 percent. Perhaps even more noteworthy, South Korea ran its first-ever trade surplus, $4.2 billion, in 1986, and that surplus grew in size the following two years, reaching $11.4 billion in 1988. These surpluses were achieved by massive exports of cars, computers, microwaves, and consumer electronics, most of which were sold in the United States.

In contrast to appearances, political and economic conditions were far from stable. Growth itself was generating fundamental changes in state-*chaebol* relations, the international economic environment, and South Korean labor relations. These changes would soon pose a serious threat to the continued viability of the South Korean growth model.

State control over *chaebol* activity was a defining characteristic of the South Korean growth model. The state had used its power over credit and markets to direct *chaebol* investment and production according to its plan. However, the resulting *chaebol* dominance over the economy meant that the state could no longer safely ignore *chaebol* desires. Thanks to their monopoly position, the *chaebol* had collectively established a significant veto power over state policy. The changing balance of power was first revealed in the early 1980s, when the large *chaebol* were able to resist and refashion Chun's attempt at industrial restructuring. The shift in relative power accelerated during the 1986 to 1988 period, when growing export revenue gave the *chaebol* almost complete financial independence from the state. Unfortunately for the South Korean economy, the *chaebol* poured their money into land and stock speculation instead of productive investments, driving up the cost of housing and the general rate of inflation. The government failed in both 1990 and 1991 to force the *chaebol* to sell off their land holdings and concentrate their business activity on core enterprises so as to achieve greater international competitiveness.

South Korea's export-led success contributed to instability in yet another way, by creating tensions with the United States. The U.S. government, determined to lower the growing U.S. trade deficit, demanded that South Korea take steps to reduce its sizable bilateral trade surplus. The South Korean government eventually agreed, allowing the *won*, South Korea's basic unit of currency, to rise by almost 16 percent relative to the dollar in 1988. It also bowed to U.S. pressure to further open South Korean markets to U.S. products.

Japan was also threatened by South Korea's economic gains. After being forced by the United States to revalue the yen, which rose some 70 percent against the dollar from September 1985 to mid-1987, the Japanese found themselves losing U.S. market share to South Korean producers of cars and consumer electronics. In response, Japanese firms began withholding or slowing delivery of technology and components to South Korean producers. The magnitude of this action is illustrated by the fact that in 1986, the year South Korea registered its first trade surplus of $4.2 billion, the country ran a trade deficit with Japan of $5.4 billion. Some 90 percent of South Korea's imports from Japan were targeted for use in South Korea's export industries.[30]

Perhaps the most important change threatening South Korea's growth model was the rise of a militant labor movement. The state's heavy and chemical industry economic strategy included the construction of large industrial centers which promoted the creation of large working class communities. These communities exploded into action beginning late June 1987. There was an average of forty-four new strike actions every day, from the end of June to the middle of September. The strike wave began with workers employed by the large *chaebol* in the industrial areas of Ulsan, Masan, Changwon, and Pusan, but soon spread throughout the country to include manufacturing workers at small- and medium-sized businesses and white-collar workers in health, finance, research, education, transportation, and tourism. Workers struck to gain better working conditions and union recognition. Another major strike wave took place in the first half of 1988; all the major *chaebol* were affected.

Even more noteworthy than the number of strikes was the degree of worker organization and coordination. Workers joined their newly formed unions into regional labor federations. Eight were in operation by July 1988. These regional federations then joined together to form the National Council of Labor Movement Organizations (NCLMO). In January 1990, the NCLMO, which was composed mostly of unions at small- and medium-sized industrial workplaces, launched a new organization, the Korea Trade Union Congress (KTUC). The KTUC's founding declaration called for uniting "with all the democratic peoples' movements" to fight "for democracy, self-reliance, and peaceful national reunification."[31] The organization of the KTUC stimulated the December 1990 formation of the Conference of Large Factory Trade Unions, which included sixteen of South Korea's largest workplace unions. It pledged to work for the unity of all independent and democratic trade unions and support "joint activities on popular interests including prices, housing, taxes and Uruguay Round negotiations [of the General Agreement on Tariffs and Trade]."[32] That same year, unions of workers employed in printing establishments, hospitals, schools, media, and financial institutions formed their own federation, the Korea Congress of Independent Industrial Federations. One result of this organizing was that workers received wage increases of approximately 20 percent in 1988 and 25 percent in 1989.

These changes in state-*chaebol* relations, the international economic environment, and labor relations were not without economic consequence. The rate of growth in exports fell from 28.4 percent in 1988 to 5.7 percent in 1989, and again to 3 percent in 1990. Not surprisingly, 1990 brought a trade deficit. Growth remained high in 1990 and 1991 because of unsustainable construction activity supported by government policy and *chaebol* land speculation, but fell sharply the following year. Alarm bells went off in the government as *chaebol* profits and international competitiveness steadily declined.

The Resurgence of the Left

Complicating the government's response to these economic trends was the resurgence of a left opposition movement. Events surrounding Kwangju had triggered a political reevaluation among antigovernment activists, the majority of whom previously had looked to the United States for inspiration and support. Their attempt to understand why the U.S. government had supported Chun's coup raised questions about U.S. foreign policy, including why Washington had supported Korea's division and Park's dictatorship. For many, a consistent set of answers emerged, pointing to one underlying determination in U.S. policy toward Korea: the desire to maintain regional dominance. Since regional dominance was strengthened by division and dictatorship, the U.S. government had actively supported both, despite its rhetorical support for democracy. This understanding of U.S. policy promoted a broad anti-imperialist consciousness within activist circles. It also led to a growing political division within the wider community opposing the military dictatorship, as many activists began to distance themselves from the two well-known opposition leaders, Kim Young Sam and Kim Dae Jung, both of whom continued to strongly identify with the United States and "free market" capitalism.

Those who sought answers to South Korea's problems through the building of a socialist-oriented movement became increasingly active beginning in 1984. That year, a group of workers who had been blacklisted in the early 1980s formed the Worker's Welfare Association (WWA) to help rebuild the South Korean labor movement. WWA leaders described their efforts as a continuation of the work of the left-led National Coalition of Korean Trade Unions in the 1940s. That same year, twenty-three organizations of women, workers (including the WWA), farmers, students, writers, and religious activists formed the United Minjung (People's) Movement for Democracy and Unification (UMMDU), which called for the adoption of a "people's constitution" and a supporting structural transformation of the South Korean political economy. The UMMDU also targeted the United States and Japan as the major obstacles to the achievement of Korean reunification and democracy. Two years later, students started organizations that were also based on a radical understanding and critique of imperialism and capitalism.

Activists in these organizations wanted to anchor their political movement in the working class. For this reason they strongly supported worker organizing, and played a pivotal role in starting a major labor resurgence in 1985. The two most important strikes that year were at Daewoo Motors and Daewoo Apparel. The former was the first major strike against a *chaebol*. The latter was noteworthy because it triggered solidarity strikes by other workers in the area and enjoyed the open and direct support of students and the UMMDU.

Student and UMMDU activists were also successful in challenging Chun's regime on the issue of presidential elections. With Chun's term of office ending, most people wanted to directly elect the next president. Chun, determined to have his fellow military officer Roh Tae Woo succeed him, opposed this idea. Following the ruling party's nomination of Roh for the presidency, these activists joined forces with Kim Dae Jung and Kim Young Sam, both of whom hoped to become president. Together they sparked nineteen consecutive days of massive street demonstrations. The largest included more than 2 million people who demonstrated in thirty-four cities for the release of all political prisoners, the end of tear gas use, the right of freedom of assembly, and direct election of the president. Although rumors of a new military crackdown circulated, Roh finally yielded to public pressure, making a conciliatory speech on June 29, 1987. His most important political concession was to agree to the direct election of the next president. The regime was on the defensive.

The election quickly became the central focus of political discussion throughout the country. Without its own candidate, the left found itself on the sidelines, forced to watch the political maneuverings of the two liberal challengers for the presidency, Kim Dae Jung and Kim Young Sam. Each tried unsuccessfully to force the other out of the race. In the end they both ran, splitting the opposition and enabling Roh Tae Woo to win the December 1987 election with only 37 percent of the vote.

Although widely considered at the time to be a sign of public rejection of radical change, Roh's victory had little influence on the left resurgence. In 1987, in addition to the labor organizing described above, twenty-five women's groups joined together to form the Federation of Korean Women's Organizations. Two years later, poor urban workers established their own group, the National Organization of Urban Poor. The following year, farmers organized the National Federation of Farmers Associations. Several different environmental organizations were also started in the late 1980s. Representatives from these and other organizations (including the NCLMO) convened in January 1989 and established an umbrella organization, the National Democratic Movement Federation (NDMF). Its mission was to unite the diverse social movement groups and lead a more focused political struggle to reshape South Korean society. One NDMF activist explained that the formation of this new organization "reconnects the break in continuity of the South Korean people's movement of the 1940s."[33] In 1991, as part of an effort to create a more accountable and integrated leadership, the NDMF dissolved itself in favor of a new organization, the National Alliance for Democracy and National Reunification (NADNR).

Most of those involved in this effort to build a unified movement for social change believed that democracy could not be achieved without concomitant progress toward reunification. They reasoned that as long as the country remained divided, the government had a ready-made national security justification for denying people the opportunity to learn about alternatives to capitalism and repressing opposition organizing activities. In a direct challenge to the government's policy of disallowing contact between North and South Koreans, Reverend Moon Ik Hwan, a senior advisor to the NDMF, traveled to the North in March 1989 and met with Kim Il Sung. He was arrested when he returned. The student movement also began giving reunification its highest priority. In July 1989, it sent Im Su Kyung to participate in the Thirteenth World Festival of Youth and Students being held in North Korea. After the festival, she and Father Moon Kyu Hyun, who was sent from the United States by the South Korean

Association of Catholic Priests for the Realization of Social Justice, tried to cross back over into the South at the DMZ. Their first attempt was blocked by the UN command. They were finally allowed to cross on August 15, but U.S. troops immediately arrested them and turned them over to South Korean authorities. At considerable cost to those involved, these visits succeeded in forcing reunification onto the South Korean political agenda.

Unable to reestablish its dominance over the *chaebol* or restore the past international economic environment, state efforts to preserve the South Korean growth model focused on destroying the labor movement and the left. Against the former, Roh used force. For example, he sent 2,000 riot police to break a strike of Seoul subway workers in March 1989. Then, he sent 14,000 combat police to crush a 109-day strike at the Hyundai shipyard in Ulsan. In April 1990, he ordered 10,000 riot police back to the same shipyard to break another strike. Not long after, 2,400 riot police stormed Korea Broadcasting System headquarters in Seoul to end a nineteen-day strike by workers protesting the government's appointment of a former Chun Doo Hwan official as president. According to one KTUC leader, "the repression against Chonnohyup [KTUC] compares with the treatment of workers' organizations in the 1920s under Japanese occupation."[34] Roh was able to sustain his antilabor offensive in large measure because he was able to convince the increasingly important middle class that labor activism was the main factor undermining the economy.

Roh weakened the left by turning its efforts to promote reunification to his own advantage. In a July 1989 policy address he said he welcomed reunification. He then made a number of important overtures to the North which resulted in a series of North-South prime minister meetings and the signing of two important agreements: the Agreement on Reconciliation, Nonaggression, Exchanges and Cooperation, and the Joint Declaration for Denuclearization of the Korean Peninsula. Roh used these accomplishments to show the middle class that the government, not the left, was the most appropriate vehicle for achieving progress toward reunification. Then when the United States raised charges that the North was developing nuclear weapons, Roh portrayed left efforts to make direct contact with the North as endangering South Korean national security. This reunification propaganda provided a cover for a broad crackdown on all left organizing. From 1988 to 1990, during Roh's first three years as president, approximately 4,300 people were arrested for political activities compared to a total of 4,700 during Chun's eight years. Roughly 40 percent of those arrested were charged with violating the National Security Law.[35] Unable to overcome the government's propaganda and repression, the left quickly became isolated; by 1992, it was no longer a major political force.

The middle class, which had strongly supported the 1986-1987 democracy struggle, largely abandoned the left during this period. They accepted government arguments that industrial disruptions threatened their economic future and that North-South negotiations were best handled government-to-government. In addition, Roh, in contrast to Chun, carefully targeted his political attacks. His assaults on the left were matched by a steady loosening of restrictions over the rest of society, including an end to direct media censorship. As a result, many in the middle class no longer believed that radical action was necessary to secure the political and economic changes they desired.

Roh, however, was never able to translate this middle class rejection of the left into broad-based support for his regime. In fact, the middle class soon developed its own political voice through the growth of a citizens' movement—a broad coalition of reform-oriented, grassroots organizations. With regard to economic goals, this movement rejected both the left's vision of worker control and democratic planning as well as Roh's efforts to rejuvenate the country's *chaebol*-dominated, export-led growth strategy. Its answer to the country's economic problems, as represented by the influential Citizens' Coalition for Economic Justice, was greater market competition and less government intervention.

Similarly, with regard to political goals, the citizens' movement rejected both the left's call for a radical restructuring of social relations and Roh's efforts to stabilize the existing political system. Symbolic of Roh's efforts was the ruling party's merger with two opposition parties (including one led by one-time opposition leader Kim Young Sam) to create one super-party with control over the National Assembly. Not long after its formation in 1990, this new Democratic Liberal Party passed, over the objections of the weakened opposition, twenty-six bills in only thirty seconds; there was no debate, or formal vote. The same thing happened in May 1991, when the ruling party passed a vacuous revision of the widely disliked National Security Law in only thirty-five seconds. The citizens' movement's response to this sort of power-mongering was to call for decentralization of political power, restoring the right to elect local political leaders, a right denied since 1961.

In short, the left had led a serious assault, forcing the South Korean state to give ground, but it ultimately succumbed to the state's repressive power. However, it was the middle class, a creation of South Korea's 1980s economic growth, that emerged strongest from the struggle. It was in this political environment that Kim Young Sam, former opposition leader and candidate of the ruling party, defeated Kim Dae Jung and Chung Chu-yong, the founder of the Hyundai *chaebol*, to win the presidency in December 1992. Kim's election was an important milestone in South Korea's democratization process. It marked the first time in more than thirty years that a nonmilitary leader had been elected president in a direct election. It was also momentous because, having campaigned on a platform that promised much of what the middle class sought, Kim's victory made possible a test of the effectiveness of its reform strategy. The results were not favorable.

South Korea at the Crossroads

Immediately upon taking office in February, Kim Young Sam launched his program of "reform amidst stability." He downgraded the political standing of both the Defense Security Command and the National Security Planning Agency (formerly the KCIA) by structurally limiting their access to the president. He cut into the power of the National Assembly and military elite by demanding that their members declare and defend the origins of their wealth. As a result, six legislators from the ruling party and a number of generals and admirals were eventually forced to resign. He appointed political outsiders, including professors, to key government posts. Kim also pledged to "democratize" the economy and weaken the *chaebol* monopoly over economic life by allowing market forces, not the government, to shape labor market, investment, and credit allocation decisions. Finally, he appeared to commit the country to a radically different foreign policy, saying in his inaugural speech, "No foreign ally can be equal in importance to our ethnic brethren in the North."

In response to these actions and words, Kim's popularity rating soared to almost 90 percent by June 1993. To many South Koreans, Kim was proving that it was possible to shape a democratic South Korea by working through the existing system. His early efforts even won over some leftists who joined his administration.

Kim's reform drive did not go unchallenged for long. The first challenge came from the right. As they had many times before, conservative political and military leaders counterattacked by taking advantage of division-generated tensions. When North Korea announced its withdrawal from the Nuclear Non-Proliferation Treaty in March 1993, leading to heightened fears of war between the United States and the DPRK, the right took advantage of the situation to blame Kim Young Sam's foreign policy for encouraging Northern adventurism, thereby endangering the country's national security. The right also used economic trends to put Kim on the defensive. Having inherited a bad economic situation, Kim oversaw worsening conditions in 1993. GNP grew at an annual rate of only 3.3 percent in the first quarter and 4.2 percent in the second quarter, and capital investment was down almost 15 percent over the first six months. *Chaebol* leaders and their political allies charged that Kim's anti-*chaebol* statements and weak foreign policy undermined business confidence and thus economic progress.

The right-generated pressure, coupled with middle class fears of war and economic decline, led Kim to abandon most of his promises in an effort to rebuild ties with conservative elites. He adopted a harder line against the North and those who challenged his get-tough foreign policy. When 50,000 students staged a June 1994 rally in Kwangju calling for an end to the war rhetoric against North Korea, the government charged the organizers with being North Korean agents. Troops broke up the demonstration and arrested student leaders.

Kim Young Sam deliberately sabotaged an opportunity for improved relations with the North after the July death of Kim Il Sung by calling the North Korean leader a "war criminal" for his part in the Korean War. The government also organized press conferences featuring North Korean defectors. One defector's claim that the North had five nuclear weapons was widely publicized until the United States publicly challenged it. Sogang University's president helped spark a "red scare" by making a series of unsubstantiated charges that 15,000 North Korean supporters had infiltrated political circles, the universities, and the media.

Kim Young Sam's government continued to crack down hard on student challenges to his anti-North foreign policy. In August 1996, the Federation of University Students' Councils hosted a three-day Grand Unification Festival at Yonsei University, which the government ruled illegal. Riot police were sent to break it up. It took the police, on some days totaling 10,000, seven days to capture the university. More than 3,000 students were detained, and hundreds were arrested. Student leaders at every campus that had sent representatives to the rally were arrested. The government justified its actions by charging that the students were acting on behalf of North Korea. Its evidence: students were demanding the withdrawal of U.S. troops and normalization of relations between the United States and North Korea, demands similar to those made by the North.

As Kim backtracked on pronouncements about relations with the North, he also did an about-face on economic policy. For instance, he had pledged to avoid government involvement in labor disputes. Yet, when thousands of Hyundai autoworkers walked off their jobs in July 1993, Kim sent riot police to break the strike. He did the same when workers struck the Hyundai shipyards. When Hyundai autoworkers began another work stoppage in May 1995 to protest working conditions, Kim again sent riot police to the scene. Hundreds of workers were arrested. As the minister of economy and finance said, "The government will crack down hard on any illegal labor disputes and will not hesitate in using police force. We must not miss the current economic boom because of illegal labor disputes."[36]

Industrial workers were not the only ones to face government repression as a result of Kim's policy reversal. When Korea Telecom workers demonstrated for better working conditions in May 1995, the government began arresting their union leaders, even while negotiations to solve the dispute were still ongoing. Kim warned that the government would take "stringent measures" against any striking union member. A strike would, he said, be tantamount to intent to "overthrow the government."[37]

Teachers fared no better. Kim Young Sam had spoken favorably of the teachers' struggle to unionize when he was an opposition leader, but as president, he continued the antiunion practices of past military dictators. There has been no teachers' union in South Korea since 1961 when Park Chung Hee disbanded the existing union and ruled union organizing by teachers illegal. Viewing education as a key instrument of social control,

Park, Chun Doo Hwan, and Roh Tae Woo maintained a total monopoly on curriculum, teacher placement, and teacher evaluation. They also required teachers to represent government positions in the classroom and spy on students. Finally, in May 1989, teachers defied the government and formed the National Teachers and Educational Workers Union. After failing to prevent its founding congress, Roh ordered all teachers associated with the union fired. More than 1,600 lost their jobs in the union's first year. Hundreds were imprisoned for demonstrating for the right to form a union. The stakes in this struggle were enormous. The teachers proudly celebrated their own role as workers and called for a curriculum that honored both work and social solidarity, a position that directly challenged both governmental authority and its strategy to divide white-collar from blue-collar workers.

In 1995, under intense pressure from parents who supported teachers' union efforts at educational reform, Kim finally offered a compromise: he would agree to rehire the fired teachers, but only if they agreed to sign a statement that they had withdrawn from the union and would not be involved in or support any future union activities. The union reluctantly accepted Kim's terms and encouraged a majority of its members to return to work. However, when one hundred teachers signed a statement calling for genuine education reform and offering suggestions on how to achieve it, the government declared the letter to be part of a union strategy and arrested a number of the teachers.

Kim also reneged on his promise to limit *chaebol* strength. Presenting his actions as necessary to promote market efficiencies, he removed restrictions on *chaebol* borrowing, allowed *chaebol* to purchase controlling shares in privatized state industries, and reduced government oversight and regulation of *chaebol* investment and production. As a result, the value added (as opposed to net sales) of the top thirty *chaebol* rose from 13.5 percent of GNP in 1992 to 16.2 percent in 1995.[38] A 1995 South Korean government report showed that the top five *chaebol*—Hyundai, Samsung, Daewoo, LG (formerly Lucky-Goldstar) and Sunkyong—accounted for 55.7 percent of the combined assets of these thirty *chaebol* and 66 percent of their annual sales. The report also showed that the average asset growth rate of these top five *chaebol* was 17.2 percent, compared with only 7.7 percent for the next five *chaebol*, and 5.5 percent for the remaining twenty.[39]

Kim's embrace of an antileft, antilabor, and pro-*chaebol* strategy produced some positive economic results but no long-term solutions to South Korea's economic problems. In 1994, exports and GNP grew by 17 percent and 8.4 percent, respectively; in 1995, the corresponding values were 32 percent and 9.3 percent. At the same time, however, imports grew faster than exports in both 1994 and 1995. As a result, South Korea's trade deficit rose from less than $2 billion in 1993, to more than $6 billion in 1994, and to more than $10 billion in 1995.

Kim Young Sam's reliance on the policies of the past failed to solve South Korea's economic problems, because these problems were structural in nature. In 1995, the country registered a $29 billion deficit in trade with advanced capitalist countries as compared with a $19 billion surplus in trade with the rest of the world. According to one central bank official, "This means that [South] Korean manufacturers are hard at work making money in developing countries but they are spending more than they are making in the rich industrialized countries."[40] One reason for this was South Korea's continuing dependence on Japan for technology, capital equipment, and components. In 1995, South Korea suffered a $15 billion trade deficit with Japan alone.

Economic growth slowed in 1996, but the trade deficit continued to widen, reaching a record $20 billion. The deficit continued to grow for three main reasons. First, in order to gain entry into the Organization of Economic Cooperation and Development (OECD), Kim Young Sam agreed to liberalize South Korean trade policy, thereby enabling Japanese and U.S. producers to boost their exports to South Korea. Second, because of regional overproduction, the result of other Asian countries trying to follow South Korea's export-led strategy, prices fell sharply for South Korea's main exports, including computer memory chips, steel, and petrochemicals. Third, South Korean *chaebol*, taking advantage of Kim's free market policies, began shifting production to third world countries. South Korean foreign direct investment reached over $3 billion in 1995, more than three times the level in 1990.[41]

As it became clear that Kim's only answer to the country's economic and political difficulties was to revert to the ways of the past, the labor movement and the left began to regroup. In November 1995, the KTUC, the Conference of Large Factory Trade Unions, and the Korea Congress of

Independent Industrial Federations joined together with newly formed public sector unions to form the Korea Confederation of Trade Unions (KCTU). Its founding declaration called for a united struggle to "realize reunification . . . and a democratic society, which will guarantee the inherent dignity and the equality of human beings."[42] The government made its own declaration, ruling the KCTU illegal.

Despite its illegal status, the KCTU soon pushed the government into a corner. In June 1996, workers in five state-run corporations declared their readiness to engage in a full-scale, coordinated general strike over wages, working conditions, and reinstatement of 200 fired workers. The government refused to negotiate with the unions and called for mandatory mediation, a demand the workers found unacceptable. At this point the KCTU announced that if the government attempted to force the workers into mandatory mediation it would declare a nationwide general strike. One day before the public sector unions were to begin their strike, the government capitulated, agreeing to wage increases more than two times the wage limit it had earlier demanded from the private sector. Even more importantly, it agreed to reinstate the fired workers. The private sector was stunned.

Well aware of the importance of regaining the confidence of business, Kim borrowed a page from past dictators. In a December 26, 1996, secret National Assembly meeting, with no members of opposition parties in attendance, the ruling party passed two bills. The first undid Kim's past initiative weakening the investigative powers of the National Security Planning Agency (formerly the KCIA). The second rewrote the country's labor law to make it easier for companies to fire workers and break strikes.

Within two days, the KCTU called a nationwide general strike. Hundreds of thousands of workers participated in various strike actions that lasted more than two months. Although the workers were not able to bring the government down, they did force it to modify its labor revisions. More importantly, the general strike provided an opportunity for diverse groups in the social movements to rebuild their organizational ties and confidence.

The economic and political stresses and strains finally became too great; the economy collapsed in 1997. The forty-nine largest business groups had recorded total profits of just $32 million on combined sales of $274 billion in 1996—a return of just over 0.01 percent.[43] Thousands of companies went bankrupt in the first half of 1997, including KIA (the country's third largest car manufacturer), Hanbo Steel and General Construction (part of the fourteenth-largest *chaebol),* and Sammi Steel (part of the twenty-sixth largest *chaebol).* These bankruptcies, in turn, threatened the solvency of South Korea's banking system.

As the extent of South Korea's economic problems became known, foreign investors, already wary because of the currency crises underway in Thailand, Indonesia, and Malaysia, began pulling money out of South Korea and refused to roll over existing loans. By November, the South Korean government was almost out of dollars. It gave up its defense of the *won,* which quickly lost half its value relative to the dollar. Facing some $160 billion in foreign debts, $90 billion of which required payment within one year, the South Korean government in December reluctantly accepted an International Monetary Fund (IMF) program of structural adjustment in exchange for some $55 billion in loans.

In response to IMF demands, the South Korean government immediately cut government spending and raised interest rates, thereby intensifying the economic downturn already underway. It also agreed to open up new areas of the economy, including the financial sector, to foreign corporations; to accelerate its program of tariff liberalization; and to rewrite the country's labor laws to enable companies to more easily fire workers and resist unionization. While the IMF and South Korean officials publicly endorsed this program as the only possible solution to the country's economic problems, it is hard to see how a program that encourages imports and even greater dependence on exports and foreign investment (in large part at labor's expense) will build the foundation for a sustainable and desirable economic future.[44]

Perhaps not surprisingly, Kim Young Sam's approval rating fell to a record low 30 percent in mid-1995 and never recovered. Even his reluctant permission to allow Chun Doo Hwan and Roh Tae Woo to be tried and convicted of mutiny and treason for the events of December 1979 and Kwangju did little to improve his popularity.[45] From almost any angle, the country's economic and political situation looked far less stable at the end of Kim's term in office than it had at the beginning.

While South Koreans do not face the type of crisis confronting North Koreans, growing numbers of them are, for good reason, far from satisfied with existing conditions and trends. Still, neither the left nor the citizens' movement has so far proven able to fashion and promote a workable alternative political program. The citizens' movement's attempt to reform the economy through promotion of market forces not only failed, but led to greater workplace hardships and *chaebol* dominance of economic life. The left has so far been unable to make its vision of a socially regulated, democratically controlled economy concrete; many South Koreans continue to believe that there is no workable alternative to capitalism.

Labor, environmental, women's, religious, left, and other progressive movements find themselves at a political dead end. Recognizing the need for a new strategy, especially in light of the growing economic crisis, many activists seek ways of engaging each other in discussion of strategies and goals. In particular, those active in left organizations and those involved in the citizens' movement have much to learn from one another. The left, with its base in the working class, the urban poor, and farm communities, understands the importance of organizational discipline and collective action as well as the need for structural transformation of South Korean society. The citizens' movement, with its base in the middle class, understands the importance of democratic, decentralized decision-making, as well as the need to develop practical responses to concrete social problems.

Perhaps the most important factor limiting the necessary dialogue and exploration of alternatives is the division of Korea. As we have seen, the so-called "imaginary line" has provided a series of South Korean governments with a convenient justification for using force to crush political organizing and activity. It has also enabled them to create a climate of fear, a climate which has made it all but impossible for South Koreans to draw upon their own history and the lessons it offers for building a majority movement for social change. Progress in envisioning and making change in the South (as well as in the North) therefore depends in large part on a successful challenge to the North-South division.

Chapter 8

The Challenge and Promise of Reunification

The division of Korea, one of the defining features of both the North and South Korean experience, has kept millions of Koreans separated from family members and provided justification for denying millions more their democratic rights. The tensions associated with this division still have the potential to trigger a new and more devastating Korean war. Therefore, it should come as no surprise that a majority of Koreans strongly support reunification. What perhaps is surprising is the fact that the governments of North and South Korea, although creations of division, proclaim reunification as their goal. Even the U.S. government, whose policies caused and have prolonged division, advertises its support for Korean reunification.

There is only one conclusion to draw from this "universal" endorsement: reunification means different things to different people. As a result, abstract talk about reunification, even to endorse it, does little to clarify the political issues and tasks involved in creating what most Koreans want—a democratic, egalitarian, and independent Korea. This is a serious problem because, although the division of Korea continues to undermine efforts at social change, it is not necessarily true that reunification, regardless of how it is achieved, will be beneficial. The only answer to this problem is to begin thinking about "reunification" as a historically specific political task.

Reunification has re-emerged as a "live" political issue during the decade of the 1990s, because of South Korean students' efforts, German reunification, and North Korean economic and political difficulties. Taking advantage of its superior economic and political position, the South Korean government has been able to dominate inter-Korean relations, thereby shaping the way most people in South Korea and the United States think about reunification. Therefore, it is South Korean reunification policy that we must directly confront in our examination of the challenge and promise of reunification.

Contrary to what many South Korean and U.S. officials claim, Korean reunification is not a zero-sum game between two governments. Thus rejection of South Korean policy does not require endorsement of North Korean policy. There are alternative policies, and this book concludes by highlighting ways that Koreans and Americans can work together to advance an independent reunification process, one that has the potential to empower people and promote the peaceful establishment of a democratic, egalitarian, and independent Korea.

The German Reunification Experience

The South Korean approach to reunification has been heavily influenced by the 1990 German reunification experience. German reunification was driven by the rapid economic and political collapse of East Germany and achieved through the incorporation of the East into the West German system. But East Germany did not collapse solely because of internal problems, as the conventional wisdom holds. West German leaders, in an attempt to ensure the dominance of existing West German political and economic institutions in a unified Germany, deliberately and aggressively promoted both the collapse and absorption of the East. Although it has claimed otherwise, the South Korean government seems determined to replicate the achievement of the West German government and accomplish reunification through absorption. Its strategy for achieving this outcome is also the same: first bring about the collapse of the North and then absorb it. However, reunification by absorption was a disaster for the German people, and it would be a disaster for the Korean people as well.

Most explanations of the collapse of the German Democratic Republic (GDR) and its absorption into the Federal Republic of Germany (FRG) appropriately begin with state socialism's growing economic problems and loss of popular legitimacy during the 1980s. Mikhail Gorbachev's rise to power in the Soviet Union encouraged efforts at reform in a number of Eastern European Communist countries. However, in East Germany, the ruling Socialist Unity Party (SED) actively resisted even the notion of reform. Frustrated by their government's hard-line position, growing numbers of East Germans decided to leave the GDR. More than 2,000 East Germans escaped to West Germany through Hungary in June 1989. They were followed by 30,000 more in September. Unable to stop the flight of its citizens, the SED was finally forced to grant the right of free travel to the West on November 9. More than 5 million people crossed through the Berlin Wall to visit West Germany in the following four days. According to Western accounts, this opening of the Berlin Wall marks the beginning of the end for the GDR. By this analysis, as large numbers of East Germans gained personal experience of life in the FRG, popular sentiment in favor of the West German system grew uncontrollably. Fearing the consequences of social breakdown in the GDR, the West German government agreed to the fastest form of reunification—reunification through absorption.

While this conventional understanding of the German reunification experience is endorsed by most South Korean and U.S. policymakers, it is inaccurate. It is true that demands for reform of East German society did grow during the decade of the 1980s. What is not adequately acknowledged is that while some East Germans, having concluded that change was impossible, looked to escape to West Germany, others worked to create a dynamic civic movement as part of a broader struggle for socialist renewal in the GDR. This civic movement had three main roots: a church-supported peace movement, a secular human rights movement, and an environmental movement. Each began in the early 1980s as small, grassroots efforts at reform. Frustrated by their lack of progress, activists from all three movements gradually began building ties and working together to promote more broad-based political reform. When the government refused to address the root causes of the growing exodus of people from the country, many activists decided the time had come to directly challenge their government's political practice and vision. Their efforts gave rise to a number of new political organizations, including the United Left, New Forum, Democracy Now, and Democratic Awakening in September; the Social Democratic Party in October; and the Green Party in November.[1] While these new organizations represented diverse political philosophies and strategies, most of their members shared the goal of creating a vibrant civil society. They also shared an opposition to both capitalism and reunification with West Germany.

Significantly, these groups succeeded in giving birth and direction to a powerful protest movement. This movement started in Leipzig on September 4, 1989, when a small group demonstrating for the right of free travel was attacked by police. In response, new demonstrations were held on successive Mondays, each one attracting more people than the last: 5,000 people on September 25, 20,000 on October 2, 70,000 on October 9, and 110,000 on October 16. The demonstrations also became increasingly national. More than 675,000 East Germans demonstrated on October 23 and more than 1 million marched on October 30. Significantly, the demonstrators' demands grew over time, from the right to travel to fundamental political reform. The police, overwhelmed by the size of the demonstrations, were eventually forced to yield the streets to the protesters. The biggest demonstration took place in Berlin on November 4. Approximately 1 million people attended, most chanting slogans calling for "revolutionary renewal." The East German media televised the entire protest. Clearly, more was happening in East Germany than an exodus. A civic revival was taking place as growing numbers of people demonstrated their willingness to struggle to create a political system based on the principle of direct democracy and an economic system based on the principles of worker control, social solidarity, and ecological sustainability.

The West German political elite was initially unsure of how to respond to the East German civic movement. To support it meant encouraging its attempt to breathe new life into socialism, something the elite did not want to see happen. Opposing it, however, meant siding with the SED in its struggle to maintain power. West German Chancellor Helmut Kohl led the way out of this quandary. By changing the focus of the East German public debate from reform to reunification, he was able to weaken both the civic movement and the SED. Kohl first advocated pursuing reunification in early September 1989 during a parliamentary debate over the appropriate response to the flight of East Germans. He did so again on November 8 (which was after the Berlin rally but before the opening of the Berlin Wall), this time in a major public address. After praising the East German demonstrators for their courage, he called for "free self-determination of all Germans." His message was clear: the West German government wanted East Germans to renounce revolutionary renewal and seek relief through reunification.

Both the East German government and its civic opposition rejected this appeal for reunification. The newly elected prime minister, Hans Modrow, did, however, express his willingness to explore "cooperative coexistence" or "a treaty community between two independent states." The civic movement made its position public in a November 26 statement: "Either we can insist on GDR independence" and work to "develop a society of solidarity, offering peace, social justice, individual liberty, free movement, and ecological conversion" or "we must suffer . . . a sell-out of our material and moral values and have the GDR eventually taken over by the Federal Republic."[2] Within two weeks, 200,000 people had signed the statement.

Undaunted, Kohl pressed ahead with his plan to promote reunification. In response to Modrow's call for closer ties, on November 8 he offered a "Ten-Point Plan for German Unity." Under the terms of the plan, West Germany would provide the GDR with economic assistance, but only after the GDR committed itself to free elections and a market economy. The plan also called for German unity to be firmly grounded in "a common European house," by which Kohl meant that a united Germany would become integrated into Western Europe. In short, this was a plan for East Germany to surrender to West Germany.

The East German civic movement struggled to find an alternative to reunification with the West and the status quo of East German state socialism. In an attempt to chart what it called the "Third Way," the civic movement agreed to participate in a national Round Table with the government and other established political parties. The Round Table's work, however, was greatly complicated by the country's growing economic crisis, caused in large part by population flight. The East German government had allowed approximately 30,000 people to emigrate in 1988. Approximately 40,000 had been allowed to leave in the first half of 1989. The total grew to almost 350,000 by the end of the year. Two-thirds of those leaving were skilled workers, and one-sixth had completed college. The loss of so many skilled workers caused a devastating decline in industrial production as well as a breakdown in the country's ability to provide basic social services.[3]

Hoping that a freely elected government would have sufficient popular support to halt the outflow of people and resulting economic slide, Modrow announced in February 1990 that the date for national elections would be advanced from May to March. He also invited grassroots leaders to join him in an interim government of "national responsibility." The new government quickly proposed a series of political and economic reforms and called upon the West German government to provide financial assistance. Kohl, however, refused to consider giving any aid to the Modrow government, saying that all questions of money would have to wait until after the March elections.

Confident that events were moving his way, Kohl continued to raise the specter of East German collapse, hoping to frighten the French and Soviet governments as well as the East Germans into endorsing reunification by absorption. As one measure of his success, Kohl won foreign support for a German currency union which would require the East German government to agree to a market-based economic transformation supported by the introduction of the West German deutschemark (DM). The terms of this proposed currency union were such that the East German government would lose not only its control over the economy, but also its ability to engage in meaningful political negotiations over the terms of reunification.

The Round Table, recognizing the political significance of Kohl's proposal, responded by demanding that West Germany stop destabilizing the East and start providing funds to support economic reform. It also made plain its position on reunification: it should be the end result of a gradual process. The final treaty should include a social charter to protect the rights of East Germans, and the new Germany should be committed to the principle of disarmament. The West German government, not surprisingly, rejected the Round Table's demands and reaffirmed its previous position that there would be no economic support until after the March election and that monetary union should be the next step.

In effect, Kohl offered East Germans a simple electoral choice: vote for parties favored by the West and receive DMs, followed by a rapid reunification, or vote against the West and receive no assistance. Leaving nothing to chance, West German political parties (with the exception of the Greens) also took steps to directly influence the outcome of the election. Each adopted and directed their opposite number in the East, providing it with speakers, consultants, money, and equipment. Even West German media were used to broadcast election propaganda back to the East.

Kohl traveled to the GDR many times to campaign for the Christian Democratic Union (CDU)-led alliance of conservative parties that he helped form. This alliance supported reunification under the terms of Article 23 of the West German Basic Law, which allowed former states or regions to rejoin (West) Germany. Kohl promised East Germans that a vote for the CDU and its allies would be a vote for "instant prosperity." Kohl's hard work paid off; the Christian Democratic Union and its allies won the election, receiving approximately 48 percent of the vote. Kohl would now be negotiating reunification with his opposite number, Lothar de Maiziere.

On July 6, at the first meeting to negotiate the terms of reunification, de Maiziere sought to modify the previously agreed-upon reunification process. He proposed that representatives from both the GDR and the FRG jointly write a "reunification treaty" which would include a statement of the new unified Germany's constitutional goals and economic arrangements. The response of the West German negotiator was as follows: "This is the accession of the GDR to the FRG and not the reverse. We have a good Basic Law that is proven. We want to do everything for you. You are cordially welcome. We do not want to trample coldly on your wishes and interests. But this is not the reunification of two equal states."[4]

German reunification officially took place on October 3 and it was achieved by the absorption of the East by the West. This process meant that East Germans were denied any opportunity to help create a more democratic Germany. Significantly, the same was true for West Germans. Unification by absorption foreclosed attempts by many West German social groups to secure greater constitutional guarantees for gender equality, multiculturalism, and workers' rights.

This history of the German reunification process runs counter to the more widely held view that the collapse of the East left the West with no alternative but to pursue a rapid reunification through absorption. Quite the opposite was true. Kohl had many opportunities to pursue a gradual union of the two Germanys. He rejected several East German initiatives which would have contributed to that goal, the first from the Communist-dominated East German government, the second from the Round Table, and the last from the leader of the eastern CDU. In short, Kohl aggressively pursued a policy designed to ensure the impossibility of a slow and structured reunification process. He achieved his goal of reunification through absorption.

The Economic and Social Costs
of German Absorption

All accounts of German reunification agree that it has been costly. Most analysts say that the East German economy was far weaker and thus needed considerably more support than was expected. However, the reality is that the high costs associated with reunification were largely a consequence of the West's insistence on achieving reunification through absorption.

The flight of East Germans to the FRG made economic stabilization difficult for the East German government. Those who remained grew more desperate and envious of West German prosperity. Having rejected previous East German requests for financial support, Kohl announced in February 1990 that the FRG was willing to provide East Germans with DMs, thereby boosting eastern purchasing power, but only if the East German government would agree to his proposed Monetary Union. Although the currency conversion received the greatest attention, the Monetary Union was much more than an agreement regulating the introduction of DMs into East Germany. It actually mandated a complete economic takeover of the GDR by the FRG, requiring the GDR to abolish its planned economy, introduce private enterprise, and accept the West German legal system.

The Monetary Union was agreed to by the newly elected CDU-dominated East German government in March 1990. On July 1, East Germans started receiving wages and salaries in West German marks in equal number to what they had been paid in East German marks. Personal debts, on the other hand, were converted at the rate of 2 East German marks to 1 DM. The conversion of East German personal savings was made according to a sliding scale. Children under fifteen years of age were allowed to exchange up to 2,000 East German marks at parity. The level was raised to 4,000 marks for adults under sixty, and to 6,000 marks for those over sixty. Savings held above these levels was exchanged at the rate of 2 East German marks to 1 DM.

This conversion plan initially appeared advantageous for East German consumers. The official exchange rate before the monetary agreement was 4.4 East German marks to 1 DM. The agreement, therefore, not only made West German goods more available to those in the East, it also reduced their price. As it turned out, this "advantage" was overwhelmed by other aspects of the agreement. For example, the agreement called for reducing the East

German budget deficit by eliminating state subsidies for basic goods and services. Without the subsidies, prices of these goods doubled and in some cases tripled. The agreement also required East Germans to pay new income taxes and contribute to insurance and retirement funds. With both prices and social payments rising, average real disposable income in the East actually fell.[5] Most East Germans also experienced a decline in their wealth. Because of the high level of personal savings in East Germany, the effective exchange rate turned out to be approximately 1.8 East German marks to 1 DM; nearly half the value of personal savings was lost in the currency conversion.[6]

East Germans lost even more as workers than as consumers. East German firms were being forced to compete against their more modern West German counterparts at the same time that the relative cost of West German goods to East German consumers was being reduced. To make matters worse, West German suppliers pressured East German retailers to stock only West German goods. Perhaps not surprisingly, most East Germans used their new DMs to purchase West German goods, causing a noticeable increase in West German production and East German unemployment.

East German firms were additionally hampered by the fact that they faced a different currency conversion formula than did individuals. Their liquid assets were converted at the rate of 2 East German marks to 1 DM while their debts were converted at the rate of 1-to-1.[7] The resulting financial squeeze forced many firms into bankruptcy.

An even more significant blow to the East German economy was the West German insistence on immediate privatization of East German firms. The Round Table had tried to restructure the East German economy by creating a holding company whose mission was to transform state firms into joint stock companies and divide the assets into shares for the government (federal, state, and local), foundations, and individuals. On July 1, following the implementation of the monetary agreement, the holding company was ordered to privatize its assets as quickly as possible. West Germans were put in charge of the process, and they organized it in ways that benefited West German investors at East German expense. For example, they instituted a system of closed bidding, allowing West German firms to purchase the best East German firms at attractive prices. Many of these firms were later shut, having been purchased only to ensure that they would not become competitors.[8] Firms that could not be quickly privatized were usually dissolved by the holding company.

Business Week described the economic impact of the Monetary Union on eastern Germany as follows:

> Across the eastern landscape, the dismantling of communism has swept 3.5 million people into the ranks of the jobless. With 70 percent of its productive capacity shut down, the old industrial star of the Soviet bloc remains a heartbeat away from economic collapse.
>
> . . . True, after plunging 50 percent from 1989 to 1991, eastern Germany's economy turned up 9.7 percent in 1992 and will likely maintain a 7 percent to 8 percent growth rate in coming years. But at that rate it will still take until the turn of the century to achieve 1989 levels of gross national product.[9]

Kohl's promise to West Germans that reunification would not be costly, and therefore would easily be financed out of economic growth, turned out to be no better than his promise to East Germans that they would enjoy "instant prosperity." The acceleration of eastern Germany's economic decline after the completion of the monetary treaty greatly reduced government revenues in the east, at the same time that the growing unemployment and poverty generated greater demands for assistance. Kohl was finally forced to take action in 1991. He began an Eastern Recovery Program financed by an income tax surcharge of 7.5 percent on west Germans. Additional funds were obtained by large-scale public borrowing.

This strategy hit west German workers hard. The borrowing forced interest rates to increase, driving the western German economy into recession in 1993. Moreover, the combination of the recession and desperation of eastern workers gave west German corporations the leverage they needed to break previously binding labor agreements and force western workers to accept lower wages and more "flexible" work rules. Many corporate leaders hoped that the fallout from reunification would eventually enable them to achieve the complete dismantling of the country's social welfare system.[10]

Most studies of the German reunification experience have been content to define the costs of absorption in narrow economic terms. There was, however, a far uglier side to the absorption process. Central to that process was the deliberate destruction by the FRG of any potential social or ideological threat to the existing West German political economy. For example, all East German universities were ordered to close their departments of Marxism-Leninism and restructure their departments of history, law, economics, philosophy, and education. All faculty in these departments were fired. All East German faculty, regardless of their host department, lost their tenure. Moreover, all faculty members, research associates, and technical administrative personnel were required to complete questionnaires that asked about their political opinions and activities as well as past and present party affiliations. Many were dismissed as a result of their answers. Public school teachers, even daycare and kindergarten teachers, were subjected to a similar "evaluation" process, with similar results.[11]

Those working in the civil service were also dealt with harshly. The entire East Berlin judiciary was dismissed. In all, approximately 550,000 civil service employees were terminated. The Constitutional Court ruled such actions legal, finding them "necessary in order to construct a modern, efficient administration in accordance with the rule of law quickly."[12] In many cases, west Germans, often commuting daily or weekly, were hired to fill administrative positions in eastern Germany.

The (West) German state justified these actions by cleverly modifying its traditional anticommunist propaganda. In the past, East Germans had been portrayed in West Germany as helpless victims of communist totalitarianism. After reunification, the German state and media quickly transformed these same victims into active supporters of the past Communist system. Destroying GDR public institutions became insufficient; those who had worked in them also had to be punished. This strategy also enabled the German state to argue that east Germans had only themselves to blame for whatever suffering they experienced after reunification.

Although there is no simple way to calculate the costs of reunification by absorption, statistics reveal that they have been enormous. From 1989 to 1993, the birth rate per 1,000 people in eastern Germany fell by 60 percent. From 1989 to 1991, the fertility rate of east German women aged twenty-five to thirty-four fell by over 45 percent. It fell further in 1992, when the number of marriages per 1,000 people was less than half what it had been in 1989. Finally, death rates for men and women aged thirty-five to forty-four rose 20 to 30 percent between 1989 and 1991. As *Business Week* noted in reporting on these statistics, "Such changes are unprecedented for an industrial country at peace. The drops in births and marriages even eclipsed those that occurred in Germany in the final years of World War II."[13]

Three main points stand out from the above examination of the German reunification experience. First, the collapse of the GDR was encouraged by deliberate West German state policy. Other outcomes, in terms of both the direction of political change within East Germany and the reunification process, were possible. Second, the West German state pursued reunification through absorption because it wanted to ensure the economic and political hegemony of existing West German institutions in a new unified Germany. Third, absorption has been an economic and social disaster for working people in eastern Germany, as well as politically and economically costly for working people in western Germany.

Despite the significant historical and political differences between the German and Korean situations, the German reunification experience is pertinent to discussion of Korean reunification. At a minimum, it provides a useful starting point for developing criteria for evaluating Korean reunification strategies. But its relevance is far greater than that. South Korean leaders, motivated by political imperatives similar to those of their West German counterparts, also seek reunification through absorption. South Korea's reunification strategy is designed to maintain maximum economic and political pressure on the North, in hopes of precipitating its collapse. Such a strategy, given the outcome of the German experience, holds no promise of producing results compatible with the desires of most Koreans.

The Evolution of South Korean Reunification Policy

South Korea's reunification strategy has always been influenced by the relative balance of power between it and North Korea. Until the early 1970s, South Korea rejected outright all North Korean initiatives to advance inter-Korean relations and reunification because, being less stable than the North, it feared the outcome of negotiations. For example, after the end of the Korean War, North Korea made several proposals to increase North-South contact, including political conferences, economic and cultural exchanges, mutual visiting privileges, and the signing of a peace treaty. In 1960, Kim Il Sung offered a plan for achieving reunification through the formation of a confederation of the two Koreas. According to the plan, North and South Korea would continue to maintain their own distinct socioeconomic systems but the increased contact made possible by confederation would eventually allow for Korea-wide elections and the establishment of a unified Korean government. Park Chung Hee, after he took power in the 1961 coup, specifically opposed any negotiations with the North, citing the need to first develop South Korea's economic and military strength.

South Korea's rapid economic growth eventually shifted the economic and military advantage away from the North, enabling Park to offer the North a negotiating challenge. He called for a North-South Competition of Good Will in the early 1970s, offering a set of proposals for "normalizing" North-South relations. These involved humanitarian, cultural, and economic exchanges, and perhaps most importantly, the simultaneous admission of both North and South Korea into the United Nations. The North rejected these proposals, arguing that they were designed not to advance the reunification process, but to allow the South to secure a stable division of the peninsula. The North called for the withdrawal of U.S. forces from the South, the signing of a peace treaty between North and South, the formation of a confederation, and the establishment of a single, shared UN delegation. Park, in turn, rejected these proposals, arguing that North Korea's unwillingness to agree to "confidence-building measures" showed that it was not serious about reunification, but only interested in dominating the South.

Kim Il Sung's 1980 proposal for achieving reunification through confederation (which he called the Koryo Democratic Confederated Republic) went largely unanswered by the South until 1989, when Roh Tae Woo presented his Korean National Community Unification Formula. Roh's proposal called for confidence-building measures leading to the adoption of a Korean National Community Charter that would include ground rules for the establishment of a Korean Commonwealth. The Korean Commonwealth was expected to create an environment where agreement would eventually be reached on a constitution for a united Korea and a Korea-wide voting process to approve it.

The Korean National Community Unification Formula, adopted with slight modification by Kim Young Sam, was designed to close the negotiating gap between the North and South. In spite of its greater detail, it remained true to the basic structure of previous South Korean initiatives, all of which demanded that cultural, social, and economic exchanges take place before the start of negotiations to settle political and military issues.

This basic structure was the reverse of the North Korean approach. For example, the Korean Commonwealth arrangement was designed to encourage North and South Korea to develop closer social and economic relationships while operating as two independent states when dealing with political and military issues. In contrast, the Koryo Democratic Confederated Republic arrangement was designed to encourage North and South Korea to develop unified political and military policies while maintaining separate socioeconomic systems.

With each side restating, in more elaborate form, the same proposal that had already been rejected by the other side, it is not surprising that little progress was made during the 1970s and 1980s in furthering inter-Korean relations or reunification.[14] The stalemate reflected the fact that neither Korean government was seriously interested in promoting an open reunification process. Each thought of itself as the only legitimate government in Korea. Each therefore offered new reunification proposals largely in order to boost its own domestic and international standing at the expense of its rival. This stalemate also reflected the fact that neither side was economically or politically powerful enough to force the other to give diplomatic ground.

The first serious departure from this relative equilibrium in the balance of power between the two Korean governments came in the late 1980s with South Korea's successful promotion of its Northern Policy. The roots of this policy, which helped to lay the groundwork for the later pursuit of reunification through absorption, are found in Park Chung Hee's 1973 initiative to "open [South Korea's] doors to all the nations of the world . . . [and have] those countries whose ideologies and social institutions are different from ours to open their doors likewise to us."[15] This new approach to the socialist world, loosely based on West Germany's *Ostpolitik* (Eastern Policy), was adopted in part because earlier attempts to isolate the North had failed and in part because of U.S. pressure.[16] However, in spite of numerous South Korean initiatives, the Northern Policy produced few benefits for South Korea during either Park's or Chun's rule.

The breakthrough for the Northern Policy finally came in 1988. The conventional wisdom is that it was achieved largely because of President Roh Tae Woo's decision that, in contrast to the past, the country's overtures to the socialist world would no longer be motivated by an attempt to strengthen the South at the expense of the North. In a July 7 address, he said that South Korea was "willing to co-operate with North Korea in its efforts to improve relations with countries friendly to us, including the United States and Japan; and in tandem with this, we will continue to seek improved relations with the Soviet Union, China, and other socialist countries." [17] Hong Chul Yum, Roh's presidential secretary, described the difference between Roh's approach to reunification and those of past South Korean presidents as follows:

> Whereas our government's Northward Policy in the past had been primarily either for security concerns, or for the assurance of superiority to and isolation of North Korea, the Northward Policy of the Sixth Republic was now based on the spirit of the July 7 Declaration. This marked a great turning point when viewed from South Korea's shift in its position toward the North—from an adversarial confrontation toward that of national community and the welcoming of the North. [18]

Actually, the only thing new about South Korea's Northern Policy was its effectiveness. During the second half of the 1980s, many socialist countries were actively pursuing greater foreign trade and investment as part of a broader program of market-based economic reforms. South Korea was able to take advantage of this development and use the many contacts generated by its hosting of the 1988 Olympics to negotiate a number of new economic agreements with these countries. Full diplomatic relations followed soon after: with Hungary, Poland, and Yugoslavia in 1989; with Czechoslovakia, Bulgaria, Romania, and the USSR in 1990. In return, Hungary received $450 million in aid, Poland $500 million, and the Soviet Union $3 billion. South Korean relations with China developed more slowly but, by 1990, each country had opened an official trade office in the other's capital; full diplomatic relations were established in 1992.

South Korea's diplomatic success was not, public pronouncements to the contrary, coupled with any fundamental change in the government's approach toward North Korea. As in the past, it sought to use its diplomatic gains to isolate and weaken the North. The issue of UN membership offers perhaps the best illustration of this—and of the changing balance of power between the two Korean governments. South Korea had proposed, as early as 1973, that both North and South Korea become members of the United Nations. The North, with support from the Soviet Union and China, had firmly opposed this plan. In 1990, South Korea announced that it would pursue its own membership in the United Nations and that it had no interest in discussing the issue with the North. This time, primarily because of its new international connections, it was able to convince both the Soviet Union and China to support its application. The North was left with no choice but to announce, as it did in May 1991, that it would also seek membership in the United Nations. South Korea achieved its victory in September with the simultaneous entry of both Koreas into the United Nations.

Pursuing Reunification by Absorption

When Roh made his 1988 declaration calling for a new and more cooperative relationship with the North, it is unlikely that the South Korean government had any real interest in or expectation of greater contact with the North. The declaration was made to offset domestic pressures and to support the Northern Policy. An openly hostile policy to the DPRK would have made it more difficult for socialist countries to accept closer relations with South Korea. However, developments over the next two years caused South Korean planners to rethink their policy toward the North. Between 1988 and 1990, South Korea's international gains were matched by North Korean setbacks, including the disappearance of the Eastern European socialist community. Then came the single most important factor encouraging the change in South Korean attitudes about contact with the North: the 1990 reunification of Germany. As a professor at the South Korean National Defense College noted:

> South Korean politicians, scholars, journalists, and business leaders wasted no time in traveling to unified Germany to observe its experience, and universities and research institutes in Seoul have invited many Germans to South Korea to lecture and conduct seminars on such topics as the "German Experience of National Reunification and Its Implications for the Korean Case."[19]

South Korean policymakers drew two conclusions from these developments. One, reunification by absorption was also possible in Korea. Two, this outcome required maximum contact between North and South to "open up" and destabilize the North.

Knowing that the North was in need of foreign investment to reverse its economic decline, the South Korean government held out the promise of substantial economic support if the North would agree to humanitarian, cultural, and economic exchanges with the South and open its nuclear program to outside inspection. This offer of assistance had nothing to do with implementing Roh's Korean National Community Unification Formula. Rather, it was an offer inspired by the German experience. South Korean planners hoped that a policy of "engagement" could be used to create opportunities for undermining the North Korean regime, thereby producing majority support in both the North and South for reunification by absorption.

The North rejected the proposed exchanges and international nuclear inspections. In response, Kim Il Sung issued a call for negotiations to settle key political and military issues, a "Grand National Congress" to lay the groundwork for reunification through confederation, and an end to the U.S. military presence in the South. Well aware of South Korean governmental thinking, he also declared in his 1991 New Year's address that the South should have no illusions about achieving a German-style reunification.

By late 1991, some South Korean policy analysts, having had more time to study the "economic" costs of German reunification, began to voice their own doubts about the desirability of replicating the German experience. For example, the Korean Development Institute, a South Korean government-affiliated think tank, determined that a sudden and unplanned Korean reunification, such as took place in Germany, might come with a ten-year price tag of $800 billion. The South Korean government would have added yearly expenses of approximately $47 billion for each of the first four years, an amount approximately equal to the government's yearly budget at the time. A slower, planned reunification would, according to the institute, greatly reduce these costs; estimated government expenditures would be cut by more than half.[20]

By mid-1992, the Roh administration appeared to have been won over. Officials publicly announced their support for a gradual, as opposed to rapid, reunification by absorption. Kim Young Sam adopted a similar line, expressing his willingness to work with the North to help it stabilize and reform its economy. Significantly, analysts of almost all political persuasions in South Korea took the government at its word. One result is that popular discussion of reunification strategies largely ended. Most South Koreans, fearing the potential chaos and cost of a North Korean collapse, seem content to leave the policy initiative in government hands. This is a serious mistake.

One of the important lessons of the German reunification experience is that while gradual reunification is possible, gradual reunification by absorption is not. The FRG was able to absorb the GDR only because of the prior collapse of the East German regime. A viable East German government would not have accepted its own total destruction. It would have demanded, as part of a gradual process of reunification, the creation of new German institutions. That, however, is precisely what the West German elite did not want, and that is why the West German government repeatedly refused to offer economic support to the GDR and why the economic costs associated with absorption were of secondary concern to the West German government. (To the extent that those costs are expressed through lower wages and weaker unions, moreover, they are being paid disproportionately by German workers, not West German political and corporate leaders.)

South Korean policymakers seem well aware of this lesson. Recognizing that gradual reunification by absorption is impossible, they remain committed to absorption at the expense of gradualism. For the South Korean elite, the potential economic and social costs associated with the collapse of the North Korean regime pale in significance with the benefits, most importantly, the strengthening and expansion of existing South Korean political and economic relations and institutions. *Business Korea* makes this point by highlighting one reason the South Korean elite fears gradualism:

> [I]f South and North Korea move closer to genuine reconciliation, or even reunification, the social atmosphere will be loosened with less rigid government controls and social norms, which could contribute to more active labor movements [in the South]. The infiltration of socialist principles into the country's labor unions may increase, leading to a toughened stance toward management and authorities.[21]

An examination of South Korean government policy toward the North provides the best proof that the collapse and absorption of the DPRK remains the official policy goal of the ROK.

South Korean Economic Policy Toward the North

As part of its Northern Policy, the South Korean government lifted its embargo on (indirect) trade with North Korea in October 1988. Total trade (indirect and processing) rose from $1 million in 1988 to between $200 and $300 million a year during the first half of the 1990s. At the same time, the South Korean government continues to disallow the kind of inter-Korean economic cooperation that has the potential to transform the North Korean economy: large-scale South Korean *chaebol* investment and technology transfer.

In February 1989, the group chairman of Hyundai, with South Korean government encouragement, visited North Korea. While there he negotiated several agreements, including one to develop a major tourist resort. Shortly after his return to Seoul, however, the South Korean government withdrew its permission for the project. Similarly, in January 1992, the group chairman of Daewoo visited the North, again with government encouragement. While there he negotiated a number of agreements, including participation in several joint ventures to produce light manufactures in the Nampo industrial estate. Yet within a month of his return, the South Korean government ordered a halt to Daewoo's participation in these ventures. In November, it went further, ordering a total ban on all inter-Korean economic cooperation projects. The official reason given for the ban was North Korea's unwillingness to open its nuclear facilities to International Atomic Energy Agency inspection. Yet, North Korea did allow the IAEA to make six separate inspections during 1992. It did not announce its intention to withdraw from the Non-Proliferation Treaty until March 1993. Even then, according to an economic consultant writing in *The Korea Economic Weekly*, "Throughout the crisis over North Korea's withdrawal from the NPT, Southern companies detected no change in their Northern counterparts' willingness to do business."[22]

Significantly, it is the South Korean government that seeks to place limits on inter-Korean economic cooperation. It will readily allow only indirect and processing trade, not the substantial investments sought by the North Korean government. Such limits clearly run counter to South Korean government pronouncements: the South Korean government argued for economic exchanges before political and military negotiations, and it had announced its desire to support economic reform in the North in order to avoid its economic collapse.

South Korean government claims that its ban on inter-Korean economic cooperation was caused by North Korea's unwillingness to clarify its nuclear intentions were put to the test by the October 1994 U.S.-North Korean agreement to freeze North Korea's existing nuclear program and replace its old graphite-moderated reactors with militarily less dangerous light-water ones. In response to this agreement, South Korean president Kim Young Sam announced a partial lifting of restrictions. But while this policy change allowed Southern firms to visit the North to conduct feasibility studies, encouraged more reprocessing trade, and allowed Southern companies to train Northern workers, actual investment remained carefully controlled.

If granted permission, South Korean firms are allowed to invest in the North, but with an upper limit of approximately $5 million a project. The first approvals were issued in May 1995. Kohap was given permission to invest $4.5 million in four projects for the manufacture of toys and textiles, and Daewoo won permission for a $5 million investment in three projects designed to produce shirts, bags, and jackets. By comparison, Daewoo announced, almost at the same time, plans for a $300 million consumer electronics factory in Vietnam. In April 1996, three additional firms were give permission to enter business deals with North Korean enterprises. But as before, the approved investments were limited in scope and size. Moreover, it remains to be seen whether the government will allow these projects to move beyond the permission stage.

South Korea has also sought to limit investment in the North by other countries. For example, when the European Community Chamber of Commerce in (South) Korea expressed interest in exploring investment possibilities in North Korea, the South Korean government refused permission for a North Korean trade official to come to Seoul to make a presentation.[23] Actions such as these support only one conclusion: the South has no real interest in stabilizing the North Korean economy.

South Korean Policy Toward Japanese-North Korean Relations

Roh claimed, in his July 7 declaration, that he was ready to "cooperate with North Korea for improving its relations" with the United States and Japan. The Japanese government responded by declaring that it was ready to negotiate with North Korea on all issues related to Japanese-North Korean relations. Unofficial talks between North Korean and Japanese officials began in Pyongyang in September 1990. The talks concluded with an informal understanding that the two governments would meet soon and that as part of the normalization process, Japan would apologize for its past colonial exploitation and pay compensation to the North Korean government.

Official talks did begin in 1991, but rather than encourage their success, South Korean authorities did what they could to limit their significance. The South Korean government, with strong U.S. support, got the Japanese government to agree not to offer any money to North Korea until relations between the two countries were fully normalized, to press the North to allow IAEA inspections of its nuclear facilities, and to do nothing to threaten "meaningful progress" in North-South relations.[24] It is worth emphasizing that South Korea's attempt to slow the normalization process between Japan and North Korea occurred after the South had already normalized relations with the Soviet Union and was well on its way to establishing full diplomatic relations with China.

The South Koreans hoped that by linking payment of compensation to normalization of relations, they could keep North Korea from receiving Japanese funds for a considerable period of time. The North Koreans, however, surprised both the South Koreans and Japanese by expressing interest in a quick settlement of all outstanding issues between Japan and North Korea and the establishment of full diplomatic relations as soon as possible. The Japanese, under U.S. pressure, raised the issue of IAEA inspections in response. The North approved the nuclear safeguards agreement in January 1992. The Japanese then demanded implementation, and IAEA inspections began in May. The Japanese then demanded information about a Japanese woman allegedly kidnapped by the North. Convinced that the Japanese were stalling, the North withdrew from the talks in November 1992.

While Japan appears to have respected South Korea's wishes when dealing with North Korea, it was primarily U.S. pressure that secured Japanese compliance. Almost immediately after the United States and North Korea signed their October 1994 agreement ending the controversy surrounding North Korea's nuclear program, the Japanese declared their interest in renewing their dialogue with the North Korean government. However, South Korea's opposition to such talks has not lessened.

In October 1995, in response to Japanese moves to provide rice aid to the North and resume normalization talks, Kim Young Sam warned, "If Japan seeks to improve ties with North Korea by dealing over the head of South Korea, this will give [the South Korean people] the impression that Japan is obstructing reunification of the two Koreas.... The Japanese moves to improve ties with North Korea ahead of us will not be in Japan's best interest."[25] The South Korean government continues to actively oppose any Japanese initiatives to normalize relations with North Korea. Such efforts, which are contrary to official South Korean claims that it desires to help North Korea emerge from its diplomatic isolation, make sense only as part of an overall strategy designed to keep North Korea under crisis.

South Korean Policy Toward U.S.-North Korean Relations

The U.S. government responded to Roh's July 7 declaration by announcing that it would allow U.S. diplomats to meet with their North Korean counterparts, limited academic and cultural exchanges, and the sale of humanitarian goods to the North. North Korean and U.S. diplomats engaged in twenty-three counselor-level talks between December 1988 and May 1992, most often to discuss U.S. charges that North Korea was pursuing the production of nuclear weapons.

In 1990, the United States accused North Korea of pursuing a nuclear weapons program. The North denied the accusation and refused to accept unconditional international inspection of its facilities. Over the following years, the United States attempted to organize a UN-sponsored embargo of the North and threatened military action. Both the embargo and war were averted, however, when Jimmy Carter visited North Korea in June 1994 and won agreement for a new round of high-level U.S.-North Korean talks. In spite of Kim Il Sung's death in July, these talks led to the previously discussed October agreement that was designed to guarantee the nonmilitary nature of the North's nuclear program as well as encourage better U.S.-North Korean relations.

Since the South Korean government had publicly stated its desire to help the North avoid economic collapse and improve its relations with the United States, and would presumably not want a new Korean war, it should have been pleased with the agreement. The opposite was true. In an article headlined "South Korea President Lashes Out at U.S.," the *New York Times* reported that Kim Young Sam:

> said that the North Korean Government was on the verge of an economic and political crisis that could sweep it from power, and that Washington should therefore stiffen, not ease its position in pressing Pyongyang to abandon its

suspected nuclear weapons program. . . . Mr. Kim explained that compromises might just prolong the life of the North Korean Government.[26]

The *Financial Times* (London) described Kim's actions as follows:

> It appeared at times during the past year that the South Korean president, Kim Young Sam, was hindering, rather than helping, the process to find a solution to the international dispute over North Korea's nuclear program. . . . He suggested at one point that the troubled North Korean economy should be allowed to collapse rather than being bolstered with international aid that would be granted in return for Pyongyang's compliance.[27]

The South Korean government reacted sharply to U.S. willingness to negotiate with the DPRK because a thaw in U.S.-DPRK relations would make it virtually impossible for the ROK to keep the North isolated and in crisis. The South Korean government believes, as does the North Korean government, that normalization of relations between the United States and the DPRK would likely unlock both American and Japanese loans and investments. It could also reduce the need for the North to spend such a higher percentage of its GDP on defense.

As a result of the October agreement, the U.S. government followed the North in dropping a number of restrictions that formally limited exchanges between the two countries. But these first steps toward better U.S.-North Korean relations, while noteworthy, are still largely of symbolic value. Moreover, the October agreement between the two countries is sufficiently vague on a number of key points that differences of opinion leading to renewed tensions between the United States and North Korea remain a serious possibility. Taking no chances, the South Korean government appears determined to establish a veto over U.S. policy initiatives toward the North. Its strategy is to demand that the United States make any further improvements in U.S.-North Korean relations conditional on prior improvements in North-South relations. Only if Washington agrees to this demand can the South hope to sustain its strategy for achieving the collapse and absorption of the North.

The South Korean government's latest worry is the North Korean campaign to replace the armistice agreement that ended the Korean War fighting with a peace treaty. The South is in a relatively weak position to oppose this campaign; having refused to sign the armistice in 1953, it has no clear legal foundation from which to demand a role in its revision or replacement. Nevertheless, the South Korean government adamantly opposes any U.S.-North Korean talks on the subject. As the *Korea Times* explains:

> Obviously, Pyongyang is aiming to liquidate its antagonism with the United States . . . . by concluding a peace agreement for the Korean peninsula, to the exclusion of South Korea from all negotiations. . . . Replacing the Korean Armistice Agreement with a peace accord is an issue that affects each and every Korean. . . . It is ridiculous for Pyongyang to state that it will negotiate only with the United States, which signed the Korean truce agreement as its counterpart . . . South Korea should be the only nation to negotiate with the North over changing the Armistice Agreement to a peace accord between the two sides.[28]

Worried about its ability to sustain this position, given what appears to be a shift in U.S. foreign policy toward accommodation with the North, the South Korean government worked with the United States to frame a counterproposal. Presented in April 1996, this counterproposal called for North Korea to join the United States, South Korea, and China in four-power talks aimed at "replacing the armistice with a permanent peace settlement." This call for talks appeared to represent a new South Korean willingness to accept a North Korean-U.S. dialogue as part of a broader effort to resolve tensions on the peninsula. In reality, however, it represented little more than a clever repackaging of the status quo. The South Korean government won U.S. agreement that the ROK would be the sole negotiator with the DPRK in matters relating to peace and security on the peninsula. The U.S.-DPRK conversation would be limited to bilateral issues such as North Korean missile exports and the return of the remains of U.S. soldiers killed during the Korean War.[29] Not surprisingly, the North Koreans have found the ground rules for the four-power talks unsatisfactory.

It is unclear how long the United States will continue to back South Korea's foreign policy. What is clear is that South Korea continues to publicly misrepresent the aim of its own policy toward the North. On March 1, 1996, for example, Kim Young Sam said, "What our republic wants is cooperation and common prosperity with North Korea to pave the way for reunification, not the collapse of North Korea."[30] But South Korea's policies have been designed to achieve the exact opposite—the collapse and absorption of the North.

An Alternative Approach to Reunification

There are two main reasons for opposing South Korea's reunification by absorption strategy. First, as the German experience reveals, reunification by absorption is designed to strengthen existing class relations and institutions, not promote economic, political, or social reform. While the South Korean elite may be satisfied with existing arrangements, the majority of South Koreans are not. Significantly, even official South Korean government surveys on citizen attitudes toward reunification show a high degree of "support for reunification, and support for a system different from the current South Korean system . . . a sign that reunification may be viewed by some citizens as an opportunity and a method for bringing about system change."[31] Reunification by absorption would only make it harder to achieve the desired systemic change.

The second reason is that even though it is unlikely that the South Korean strategy will succeed, the government's continuing effort comes with a high price tag. The strategy has greatly increased the economic suffering and international isolation of those who live in the North. By ensuring a continuation of hostile relations with the North, it has also enabled the South Korean government to continue using the existing National Security Law to repress those who seek educational, workplace, and political reform in the South. In fact, NSL arrests are on the rise. During the 1980s, an average of 220 people were arrested each year for violating the NSL. During the first half of the 1990s, yearly arrests averaged well over 300.[32] In addition, the continuing tension on the Korean peninsula, which the South Korean strategy helps to sustain, provides a cover of legitimacy for militarists throughout the region, not to mention greatly increasing the risk of a new Korean war.

There are things that can be done to force the South Korean government to change its strategy. Within South Korea, those who favor reunification without absorption must find ways to help people better understand the nature of the German experience. They must also help expose the ways that their government, despite its public statements, continues to pursue reunification by absorption.

Within the United States, people must find ways to pressure the U.S. government to pursue a more independent and balanced policy toward North Korea, including ending war games (which continue even though

Team Spirit has ended), signing a peace treaty, withdrawing U.S. troops from South Korea, and normalizing economic and political relations. The chances for success are greater than they have been in the past because of the current lack of consensus among U.S. policymakers. A more independent U.S. policy toward North Korea is also likely to encourage the normalization of relations between Japan and the DPRK. If achieved, these developments can be expected to enable the North to stabilize its own political and economic situation and approach the reunification dialogue with the South on more equal terms.

If the Southern strategy for reunification by absorption were abandoned it would not, of course, necessarily mean that the governments of North and South Korea would end their mutual hostility and agree to implement a reunification process responsive to the needs and desires of all Koreans. Both governments will still want to control the reunification dialogue for their own purposes, and as long as they are able to resist popular participation in it, meaningful progress toward the creation of a democratic, egalitarian, and independent Korea is unlikely. This resistance must therefore be challenged and overcome.

Overcoming this resistance in the South will require the same kind of popular mobilization that eventually forced the military dictatorship to grant political concessions. But that mobilization must still be organized. At present, most South Koreans remain confused about North Korean intentions and the consequences of reunification. Believing that further progress can be made in democratizing South Korean society regardless of the state of the reunification dialogue, they therefore direct their energies toward achieving the former, allowing the government to pursue the latter at its own discretion. Activists can change this situation only by making visible the strong and direct link between democratization and popular involvement in the reunification process.[33] Educators, for example, should strive to show those who support educational reform that their efforts will always be bounded as long as national security concerns are used to limit what scholars can study and teachers teach. For labor activists, likewise, workplace democracy will always be frustrated as long as national security concerns are used to limit worker organizing and collective action.

As a part of this process, ways must be found to connect popular reform efforts directly to the reunification process. Growing numbers of South

Koreans have become involved in movements to protect the environment, for example. Those involved must be encouraged and supported in their efforts to meet with North Koreans who share similar concerns, so that both groups can begin discussing ways to ensure that reunification will strengthen respect for the environment rather than open up new areas to be despoiled. One such meeting did take place in Thailand in May 1996. Such discussions can lead to connections that strengthen environmental movements in both the North and South, and can provide insights into how an environmentally sustainable development strategy can be shaped as part of the reunification process.

Similarly, members of the South Korean teachers union should be encouraged to meet with their North Korean counterparts to discuss educational reform—in particular, ways to develop and implement a curriculum capable of promoting a new national identity based on respect for the principles of democracy and social solidarity. Women should also be encouraged to continue their existing inter-Korean dialogue over the meaning of women's rights and ways to structure a reunification process that protects and deepens those rights. Greater contact between South Korean social groups and North Korean officials and organizations will certainly make it harder for either government to restrict or narrow the reunification dialogue.

This strategy will not be easy to implement. The South Korean government continues to use "national security" fears to restrict contacts between South Koreans and individuals and groups in the North. Following the government's May 1996 declaration that student and labor organizing had reached a "critical point," the *Korea Herald* editorialized against "the increasingly vehement and irrational nature" of student activism. It singled out for special notice the open exchanges of letters and faxed messages between North and South Korean students. The editorial went on to call for an immediate halt to contacts, arguing that "reunifying the divided peninsula is a matter to be resolved between governing powers, not between individuals."[34]

Likewise, when a Canadian university student opened a web site in June 1996, on which he posted material obtained while on a trip to North Korea, the South Korean government took immediate steps to block access to it on national security grounds. The *New York Times* quoted the assistant defense minister as follows: "If we don't do anything about North Korean propaganda, then maybe our high school or university students can be ill-informed by their articles. Ordinary people do not have the information and knowledge and understanding to know what is working and what is good."[35]

South Korean activists continue to risk imprisonment for trying to overcome government opposition to their participation in the reunification dialogue. People living in the United States can extend their solidarity to South Korean activists and make a difference in the struggle by becoming better informed and more outspoken about the repressive nature of the South Korean government and its use of the National Security Law. They can pressure the U.S. government to depart from its historical pattern and foster a more open political environment in South Korea.

The strategy outlined above for the South will not work in the North. The DPRK has few, if any, autonomous social groups. All organizations appear to be under tight government control and thus do not have the independent perspective of the social movement groups in the South. This fact does not, however, lead to the conclusion that pursuing the kinds of meetings suggested above is a waste of time.

As long as people from the DPRK are willing to participate in the dialogue, the process will be useful. At a minimum it will help those in the South better understand North Korean perspectives, thereby enabling them to participate more effectively in reunification discussions in the South. These meetings become even more valuable if South Korean government planners and U.S. military officials are correct that the Northern regime will soon collapse. Then only Southern movement groups and the popular understanding of reunification possibilities they are able to communicate will stand in the way of an absorption process designed to limit progressive social change. If the North is not about to collapse (a more likely scenario), then these meetings can also promote more independent thinking on the part of North Korean social groups. North Koreans are not robots incapable of reasoning and feeling. The more opportunities they have for dialogue with those seeking progressive social change in the South, the more their own understandings of progressive possibilities are bound to grow. Those living in the United States can also help encourage both the development of more independent social groups in the North and their participation in the reunification dialogue. One way is to work to dismantle the South Korean NSL; this would make North-South contacts much easier to arrange. Another way is to create opportunities for North Koreans (including environmentalists, teachers, leaders of women's groups, health care professionals, students, and professors) to meet with Americans who are working for social change. Such contacts are bound to contribute to the creation of a more open and productive environment for North-South communication. They are also likely to contribute to a reduction in U.S.-North Korean military tensions.

Achieving Korean reunification will not be simple. However, Korean history is rich in telling experiences, including many heroic attempts by Koreans to build a more humane and democratic society. Alternative visions for Korean society, including those which have enjoyed majority support, were often crushed by one or both of the governments that claim to represent Korea. These experiences also make clear that the U.S. government bears enormous responsibility for Korea's division and current political situation. Finally, and perhaps most importantly, they teach that there are no shortcuts; progress requires building strong and democratic social movements whose practice can also inspire international solidarity.

At this moment in history, combined efforts may significantly advance the process of creating a democratic, egalitarian, and independent Korea. The benefits that would follow—especially reduced military tensions in Asia, and the inspiration of successful social change—extend well beyond Korea and would be to the decided advantage of most Americans, as well. After more than fifty years of division, it is time to erase the "imaginary line."

NOTES

Introduction

1. Department of State, *The Record on Korean Unification 1943-1960*, Far Eastern Series 101 (Washington, D.C.: U.S. Government Printing Office, 1960), 1.
2. Lena H. Sun, "Korea Remembered; Veterans of 'Forgotten War' Get Their Memorial," *Washington Post*, 28 July 1995, A1.
3. Laurence McQuillan, "Clinton Dedicates Korean War Memorial," *Reuters World Service*, 27 July 1995.
4. Charles Krauthammer, "Korea Sits Opposite Vietnam," *Cincinnati Enquirer*, 11 August 1995, A10.
5. As quoted in John W. Spanier, *The Truman-MacArthur Controversy and the Korean War* (Cambridge: Harvard University Press, 1959), 88.
6. Les Aspin, *The Bottom-Up Review: Forces for a New Era*, Department of Defense (Washington, D.C.: U.S. Government Printing Office, 1993).
7. Stan Crock, "Why the GOP Has Star Wars in Its Eyes—Again," *Business Week*, 7 October 1995, 117-18.
8. Bill Gertz, "N Korean Missile Could Reach U.S., Intelligence Warns," *Washington Times*, 29 September 1995, A3.
9. Daniel B. Schirmer, "North Korea: The Pentagon and Issues of War and Peace in the Asia-Pacific Region," *Monthly Review* 46 (July-August 1994): 68.
10. Daniel B. Schirmer, "Military Access: The Pentagon Versus the Philippine Constitution," *Monthly Review* 46 (June 1994): 24-25.
11. Nicholas Kristof, "U.S. Apologizes to Japan for Rape of 12-Year-Old in Okinawa," *New York Times*, 2 November 1995, A7.
12. Valerie Reitman, "U.S. Will Consider Relocating Troops from Okinawa," *Wall Street Journal*, 2 November 1995, A15.

Chapter 1: U.S. Foreign Policy and Korea

1. As quoted in Bruce Cumings, *The Origins of the Korean War, Liberation and the Emergence of Separate Regimes, 1945-1947* (Princeton: Princeton University Press, 1981), 126.
2. Department of State, *The Record on Korean Unification 1943-1960*, Far Eastern Series 101 (Washington, D.C.: U.S. Government Printing Office, 1960), 1.
3. Howard Zinn, *A People's History of the United States* (New York: Harper and Row, 1980), 124.
4. Ibid., 149.
5. For a useful discussion of the treaty port system see "The Treaty Port System and Japan," in W. G. Beasley, *Japanese Imperialism, 1894-1945* (New York: Clarendon Paperbacks, 1991).
6. Department of State, *A Historical Summary of United States-Korean Relations*, Far Eastern Series 115 (Washington, D.C., 1962), 45.
7. Ibid., 46-47.
8. As quoted in Zinn, 242.
9. As quoted in ibid., 306.
10. Raymond Bonner, *Waltzing With a Dictator: The Marcoses and the Making of American Policy* (New York: Vintage Books, 1988), 29.
11. Beasley, 6.
12. As quoted in Alfred Whitney Griswold, *The Far Eastern Policy of the United States* (1938; reprint New Haven: Yale University Press, 1962), 90.
13. As quoted in ibid., 96-97.
14. As quoted in ibid., 97.
15. Zinn, 353.
16. Department of State, *Historical Summary*, 56.
17. As quoted in Edward Boorstein and Regula Boorstein, *Counterrevolution: U.S. Foreign Policy* (New York: International Publishers, 1990), 67.
18. As quoted in ibid., 69.
19. Griswold, 468.
20. Beasley, 188.
21. Ibid., 214.
22. Ibid., 212.
23. Ibid., 222.
24. Bong-youn Choy, *A History of the Korean Reunification Movement: Its Issues and Prospects* (Peoria: Research Committee on Korean Unification, Institute of International Studies, Bradley University, 1984), 10.
25. As quoted in ibid., 10.

26. As quoted in Boorstein and Boorstein, 41.

27. Peter Calvocoressi and Guy Wint, *Total War: Causes and Courses of the Second World War* (New York: Penguin, 1979), 853.

28. As quoted in ibid., 858.

29. As quoted in Gar Alperovitz, *The Decision to Use the Atom Bomb and the Architecture of An American Myth* (New York: Alfred A. Knopf, 1995), 178.

30. As quoted in Choy, 11.

31. As quoted in ibid., 11.

32. As quoted in ibid., 12.

33. Alperovitz, 4.

34. As quoted in ibid., 3.

35. Department of State, *Historical Summary*, 11.

Chapter 2: The Korean Struggle for Independence and Democracy

1. Stewart Lone and Gavan McCormack, *Korea Since 1850* (New York: St. Martin's Press, 1993), ix.

2. As quoted in David H. Satterwhite, "The Politics of Economic Development: Coup, State, and the Republic of Korea's First Five Year Economic Plan (1962-1966)" (Ph.D. diss., University of Washington, 1994), 208.

3. As quoted in Carter J. Eckert, Ki-baik Lee, Young Ick Lew, Michael Robinson, and Edward W. Wagner, *Korea Old and New: A History,* (Seoul: Ilchokak Publishers for the Korean Institute and Harvard University, 1990), 197.

4. As quoted in ibid., 215.

5. Lee Ki-baik, *A New History of Korea* (Cambridge: Harvard University Press, 1984), 287.

6. As quoted in Bong-youn Choy, *A History of the Korean Reunification Movement: Its Issues and Prospects* (Peoria: Research Committee on Korean Unification, Institute of International Studies, Bradley University, 1984), 6-7.

7. Ibid., 45.

8. Eckert et al., 256.

9. Ibid., 259.

10. Ibid., 261; Lee, 314.

11. Eckert et al., 266.

12. Lone and McCormack, 61.

13. Bruce Cumings, "The Origins and Development of the Northeast Asian Political Economy: Industrial Sectors, Product Cycles, and Political Consequences," *The Political Economy of the New Asian Industrialization,*

ed. Frederic C. Deyo (Ithaca: Cornell University Press, 1987), 45.

14. Eckert et al., 310.

15. Lee, 349.

16. Lone and McCormack, 74.

17. Eckert et al., 311.

18. Dae-Sook Suh, *The Korean Communist Movement, 1918-1948* (Princeton: Princeton University Press, 1967), 202.

19. Nym Wales and Kim San, *The Song Of Ariran: A Korean Communist in the Chinese Revolution* (San Francisco: Ramparts Press, 1972), 21. Kim San was a pseudonym; his real name was Chang Chi-rak.

20. Ibid., 25.

21. Eckert et al., 293.

22. Ibid., 286.

23. Lone and McCormack, 63.

24. Ibid., 64.

25. Urban Industrial Mission, *Short History of South Korea's Labor Movement: Historical Overview and Some Information on Current Developments* (Inchon: Urban Industrial Mission, 1988), 2.

26. Ibid., 2-3.

27. Eckert et al., 301.

28. Kazuko Watanabe, "Militarism, Colonialism, and the Trafficking of Women: 'Comfort Women' Forced into Sexual Labor for Japanese Soldiers," *Bulletin of Concerned Asian Scholars* 26:4 (1994): 9.

29. As quoted in Bruce Cumings, *The Origins of the Korean War, Liberation and the Emergence of Separate Regimes, 1945-1947* (Princeton: Princeton University Press, 1981), 83.

30. Ibid., 88.

31. Eckert et al., 331.

32. Cumings, *Origins, 1945-1947,* 91.

Chapter 3: Occupation and Division

1. Department of State, *A Historical Summary of United States-Korean Relations,* Far Eastern Series 115 (Washington, D.C.: U.S. Government Printing Office, 1962), 1.

2. As quoted in Bruce Cumings, *The Origins of the Korean War: Liberation and the Emergence of Separate Regimes, 1945-1947* (Princeton: Princeton University Press, 1981), 126.

3. Ibid., 127.

4. Jon Halliday, *A Political History of Japanese Capitalism* (New York:

Monthly Review Press, 1975), 168.

5. Cumings, *Origins, 1945-1947*, 171.

6. Ibid., 196-97.

7. See ibid., Chapter 10, "The Autumn Uprising," for an extended discussion of the events of the period.

8. As quoted in Bruce Cumings, *The Origins of the Korean War: The Roaring of the Cataract, 1947-1950* (Princeton: Princeton University Press, 1990), 205.

9. Ibid., 217.

10. Carter J. Eckert, Ki-baik Lee, Young Ick Lew, Michael Robinson, and Edward W. Wagner, *Korea Old and New, A History* (Seoul: Ilchokak Publishers for the Korean Institute and Harvard University, 1990), 336.

11. Cumings, *Origins, 1945-1947*, 388.

12. Ibid., 403.

13. As quoted in Cumings, *Origins, 1947-1950*, 20.

14. Ibid., 305.

15. As quoted in ibid., 314.

16. Jon Halliday and Bruce Cumings, *Korea: The Unknown War* (New York: Pantheon Books, 1988), 62.

17. As quoted in Cumings, *Origins, 1945-47*, 232.

18. Cumings, *Origins, 1947-1950*, 65.

19. As quoted in Bong-youn Choy, *A History of the Korean Reunification Movement: Its Issues and Prospects* (Peoria: Research Committee on Korean Unification, Institute of International Studies, Bradley University, 1984), 52.

20. As quoted in ibid., 52.

21. Ibid., 56.

22. Stewart Lone and Gavan McCormack, *Korea Since 1850* (New York: St. Martin's Press, 1993), 102.

23. Cumings, *Origins, 1947-1950*, 258.

24. Ibid., 266.

25. Ibid., 283.

26. Halliday and Cumings, 54.

Chapter 4: U.S. Foreign Policy and Korea, 1945-1950

1. Donald S. MacDonald, "South Korea's Politics Since Liberation," in *Korea Briefing, 1993*, ed. Donald N. Clark (Boulder: Westview Press, 1993), 21-23.

2. Joyce and Gabriel Kolko, *The Limits of Power: The World and United States Foreign Policy, 1945-1950* (New York: Harper and Row, 1972), 2.

3. As quoted in Richard M. Freeland, *The Truman Doctrine and the Origins*

of McCarthyism: Foreign Policy, Domestic Politics, and Internal Security, 1946-1948 (New York: New York University Press, 1985), 30.

4. As quoted in ibid., 33.
5. As quoted in Edward Boorstein and Regula Boorstein, *Counterrevolution: U.S. Foreign Policy* (New York: International Publishers, 1990), 47.
6. Ibid., 242.
7. As quoted in ibid., 246.
8. While the Truman Doctrine specifically referred to Greece and Turkey, Korea could not help but be affected by this declaration. As one of the few areas in the world where both U.S. and Soviet troops were stationed, it would have been surprising if the United States did not pay careful attention to events there. A May 7, 1947, State-Navy-War interdepartmental meeting recommended that the Truman administration ask Congress for a one-year military and economic aid program for Korea immediately after funds for Greece and Turkey had been approved. A request for $215 million was made but rejected by Congress. Undeterred, the State Department succeeded in establishing a Marshall Plan aid mission and a military advisory group in Korea that was the largest in the world.
9. Kolko and Kolko, 228-29.
10. Bruce Cumings, *The Origins of The Korean War: The Roaring of the Cataract, 1947-1950* (Princeton: Princeton University Press, 1990), 37.
11. As quoted in Freeland, 275.
12. As quoted in Boorstein and Boorstein, 257.
13. Kolko and Kolko, 65.
14. As quoted in ibid., 126.
15. Ibid., 133.
16. As quoted in ibid., 134.
17. Ibid., 309.
18. Ibid., 313.
19. Ibid., 314.
20. As quoted in ibid., 321-22.
21. Ibid., 516-17.
22. Jon Halliday, *A Political History of Japanese Capitalism* (New York: Monthly Review Press, 1975), 177.
23. Ibid., p. 172.
24. Kolko and Kolko, 528.
25. As quoted in Cumings, 46.
26. As quoted in ibid., 168.
27. Kolko and Kolko, 528.

Chapter 5: The Korean War

1. As quoted in Department of State, *The Record on Korean Unification, 1943-1960*, Far Eastern Series 101 (Washington, D.C., 1960), 86.

2. As quoted in I. F. Stone, *The Hidden History of the Korean War* (New York: Monthly Review Press, 1952), 46.

3. As quoted in ibid., 50.

4. As quoted in Department of State, 99.

5. Jon Halliday and Bruce Cumings, *Korea, The Unknown War* (New York: Pantheon Books, 1988), 75.

6. As quoted in Department of State, 100-101.

7. Bruce Cumings, *The Origins of the Korean War, The Roaring of the Cataract, 1947-1950* (Princeton: Princeton University Press, 1990), 388.

8. As quoted in Stone, 64.

9. As quoted in ibid., 7.

10. As quoted in Cumings, *Origins, 1947-1950*, 547.

11. As quoted in ibid., 547.

12. "Ciphered Telegram from Shtykov to Vyshinsky, 3 September 1949," Document II, *Cold War International History Project Bulletin* No. 5 (Spring 1995): 6.

13. "Politburo Decision to Confirm the Following Directive to the Soviet Ambassador in Korea, 24 September 1949," Document II, ibid., 8.

14. "Ciphered Telegram from Shtykov to Vyshinsky, 19 January 1950," Document VI, ibid., 8.

15. Bruce Cumings, *Korea's Place in the Sun: A Modern History* (New York: W. W. Norton and Company, 1997), p. 251.

16. Karunakar Gupta, "How Did the Korean War Begin?," *The China Quarterly* 52 (1972): 706.

17. As quoted in Stone, 45.

18. As quoted in ibid., 20.

19. As quoted in ibid., 21-22.

20. A fact worth pondering in this regard: Bruce Cumings reports that one week before the start of the Korean War, "the Pentagon 'approved, printed and distributed' a plan called SL-17, which assumed a KPA invasion, a retreat to and defense of a perimeter at Pusan, followed by an amphibious landing at Inchon." *Origins, 1947-1950*, 614-15.

21. Stone, 44.

22. Halliday and Cumings, 84.

23. Ibid., 82.

24. Cumings, *Origins, 1947-1950*, 698-99.

25. As quoted in ibid., 701.

26. Stewart Lone and Gavan McCormack, *Korea Since 1850* (New York: St. Martin's Press, 1993), 122.

27. Callum MacDonald, "So Terrible a Liberation: The U.N. Occupation of North Korea," *Bulletin on Concerned Asian Scholars* 3:2 (April-June 1991): 8.

28. Gregory Henderson, *Korea: The Politics of the Vortex* (Cambridge: Harvard University Press, 1968): 167.

29. Halliday and Cumings, 87.

30. Cumings, *Origins, 1947-1950*, 677.

31. As quoted in Lone and McCormack, 112.

32. As quoted in ibid., 112.

33. As quoted in Cumings, *Origins, 1947-1950*, 670.

34. As quoted in Department of State, 106.

35. Stone, 131-32.

36. As quoted in John W. Spanier, *The Truman-MacArthur Controversy and the Korean War* (Cambridge: Harvard University Press, 1959), 88.

37. Michael Walzer, *Just and Unjust Wars, A Moral Argument with Historical Illustrations* (New York: Basic Books, 1977), 118.

38. Halliday and Cumings, 107.

39. As quoted in ibid., 115.

40. Lone and McCormack, 114.

41. Halliday and Cumings, 132.

42. Lone and McCormack, 115.

43. As quoted in ibid., 119.

44. MacDonald, 10.

45. Ibid., 3.

46. Ibid., 19.

47. As quoted in Cumings, *Origins, 1947-1950*, 715.

48. Lone and McCormack, 122.

49. Gavan McCormack, "Korea: Wilfred Burchett's Thirty Years' War," in *Burchett Reporting the Other Side of the World 1939-1983*, ed. Ben Kiernan (New York: Quartet Books, 1986), 166.

50. As quoted in Halliday and Cumings, 156.

51. As quoted in Lone and McCormack, 123.

52. Halliday and Cumings, 179.

53. As quoted in ibid., 178.

54. Ibid., 179.

55. Cumings, *Origins, 1947-1950*, 770.

56. Sydney D. Bailey, *The Korean Armistice* (New York: St Martin's Press,

1992), 152.

57. Ibid., 156.

58. As quoted in Department of State, 156.

59. As quoted in ibid., 159.

60. As quoted in ibid., 160.

61. Bailey, 163.

62. Bong-youn Choy, *A History of the Korean Reunification Movement: Its Issues and Prospects* (Peoria: Research Committee on Korean Unification, Institute of International Studies, Bradley University, 1984), 76-77.

63. Bailey, 167-68.

64. As quoted in Halliday and Cumings, 211.

Chapter 6: Divided Korea:
The North Korean Experience

1. Dae-Sook Suh, *Kim Il Sung, The North Korean Leader* (New York: Columbia University Press, 1988), 83-89.

2. Ibid., 125.

3. Barry Gills, "North Korea and the Crisis of Socialism: the Historical Ironies of National Division," *Third World Quarterly* 13:1 (1992): 112.

4. Ibid., 112.

5. Aidan Foster-Carter, "North Korea, Development and Self-Reliance: A Critical Appraisal," in *Korea North and South, The Deepening Crisis*, ed. Gavan McCormack and Mark Selden (New York: Monthly Review Press, 1978), 147-48.

6. Young Whan Kihl, *Politics and Policies in Divided Korea: Regimes in Contest* (Boulder: Westview Press, 1984), 38.

7. Stewart Lone and Gavan McCormack, *Korea Since 1850* (New York: St. Martin's Press, 1993), 184.

8. Ibid., 184.

9. As quoted in Kihl, 47.

10. Lone and McCormack, 185.

11. As quoted in Kihl, 46.

12. Lone and McCormack, 185.

13. Erik van Rhee, "The Limits of juche: North Korea's Dependence on Soviet Industrial Aid, 1953-76," *The Journal of Communist Studies* 5:1 (1989): 57.

14. Joseph Sang-heon Chung, *The North Korean Economy: Structure and Development* (Stanford: Hoover Institution Press, 1974), 146-47.

15. Van Rhee, 57.

16. Ibid., 57.

17. Joan Robinson, "Korean Miracle," *Monthly Review* 16 (January 1965): 541-549.

18. Lone and McCormack, 187.

19. Kihl, 142.

20. Van Rhee, 57-58.

21. Ibid., 60-61.

22. Gordon White, "North Korean Chuch'e: The Political Economy of Independence," *Bulletin of Concerned Asian Scholars* Vol. 7, No. 2 (1975): 48.

23. Dae-Sook Suh, Chapter 10, *passim.*

24. Gavan McCormack, "Kim Country: Hard Times in North Korea," *New Left Review* No. 198 (March-April 1993): 35.

25. Kihl, 146.

26. Nicholas Eberstadt, *Korea Approaches Reunification* (Armonk, NY: M. E. Sharpe, 1995), 22.

27. Stephen Goose, "The Military Situation on the Korean Peninsula," in *Two Koreas—One Future?*, ed. John Sullivan and Roberta Foss (Lanham: University Press of America, 1987), 59.

28. Kihl, 154-55.

29. Van Rhee, 61.

30. Eberstadt, 21.

31. Ibid., 134.

32. As quoted in Mark Clifford, "Send Money," *Far Eastern Economic Review* (September 30, 1993): 72.

33. Teresa Watanabe, "Lawmaker Finds Face of Famine in North Korea," *Oregonian,* 9 April 1997.

34. International Monetary Fund, *World Economic Outlook, May 1996* (Washington, D.C.), 125.

35. Sydney D. Bailey, *The Korean Armistice* (New York: St. Martin's Press, 1992), 177.

36. Ibid., 178.

37. Peter Hayes, *Pacific Powderkeg: American Nuclear Dilemmas in Korea* (Lexington: Lexington Books, 1991), 132.

38. Ibid., 132.

39. Goose, 72-73.

40. As quoted in John M. Swomley, "Carter's Diplomacy May Thwart Pentagon's Plans," *Facts for Action* No. 164 (June-July 1994): 1.

41. *U.S. News and World Report,* "Korea the Next War?," 20 June 1994, 40-56.

42. As quoted in "North Korea: Creation of a Demon," *The Defense Monitor* 23:1 (1994): 4.

43. Steve Glain, "U.S. Envoy to Seoul Aims to Meet Needs of Security Without Provoking the North," *Wall Street Journal*, 8 August 1994.

44. Any Borrus with Eric Schine, "The Pentagon's Real Readiness Crisis," *Business Week*, 19 December 1994; Stan Crock, "Why the G.O.P. Has Star Wars in its Eyes—Again," *Business Week*, 7 October 1995.

45. As quoted in Gills, 114.

46. Bruce Cumings, "The Corporate State in North Korea," in *State and Society in Contemporary Korea*, ed. Hagen Koo (Ithaca: Cornell University Press, 1993), 204.

47. As quoted in ibid., 221.

48. McCormack, "Kim Country," 35.

49. As quoted in Samuel Kim, "North Korea in 1995," *Asian Survey* 36:1 (January 1996): 63.

50. Nicholas D. Kristof, "Survivors Report Torture in North Korea Labor Camps," *New York Times* (July 14, 1996): 6.

51. Lone and McCormack, 199.

Chapter 7: Divided Korea:
The South Korean Experience

1. As quoted in David H. Satterwhite, "The Politics of Economic Development: Coup, State, and the Republic of Korea's First Five Year Economic Plan (1962-1966)" (Ph.D. Dissertation, University of Washington, 1994), 176.

2. As quoted in ibid., 208.

3. Donald S. MacDonald, *U.S.-Korean Relations from Liberation to Self-Reliance: The Twenty Year Record* (Boulder: Westview Press, 1992), 230.

4. Carter J. Eckert, Ki-baik Lee, Young Ick Lew, Michael Robinson, and Edward W. Wagner, *Korea Old and New: A History* (Seoul: Ilchokak Publishers for the Korean Institute and Harvard University, 1990), 349.

5. Satterwhite, 30.

6. James B. Palais, "'Democracy' in South Korea, 1948-72," *Without Parallel: The American-Korean Relationship Since 1945*, ed. Frank Baldwin (New York: Pantheon Books, 1974), 116.

7. Alexander Joungwon Kim, *Divided Korea: The Politics of Development, 1945-1972* (Cambridge: Harvard University Press, 1976), 209.

8. Bong-youn Choy, *A History of the Korean Reunification Movement: Its Issues and Prospects* (Peoria: Research Committee on Korean Unification, Institute of International Studies, Bradley University, 1984), 86.

9. As quoted in Satterwhite, 42.

10. See Martin Hart-Landsberg, *The Rush to Development: Economic Change and Political Struggle in South Korea* (New York: Monthly Review Press, 1993), for a critical examination of the origins, structure, and nature of the South Korean growth model.

11. George E. Ogle, *South Korea: Dissent within the Economic Miracle* (New Jersey: Zed Books Ltd. in association with International Labor Rights Education and Research Fund, 1990), 31-32.

12. Byong-Nak Song, *The Rise of the Korean Economy* (New York: Oxford University Press, 1990), 101-2.

13. James Stentzel, "Seoul's Second Bonanza," *Far Eastern Economic Review,* 30 July 1973, 43.

14. Bernie Wideman, "Korean Chauvinism," *Far Eastern Economic Review,* 5 March 1973, 5.

15. Jung-en Woo, *Race to the Swift: State and Finance in Korean Industrialization* (New York: Columbia University Press, 1991), 105.

16. As quoted in Bong-youn Choy, *A History of the Korean Reunification Movement: Its Issues and Prospects* (Peoria: Research Committee on Korean Unification, Institute of International Studies, Bradley University, 1984), 104.

17. U.S. House of Representatives, *Investigation of Korean-American Relations* (Washington D.C.: U.S. Government Printing Office, 1978), 39.

18. See Robert Boettcher with Gordon L. Freedman, *Gifts of Deceit, Sun Myung Moon, Tongsun Park and the Korean Scandal* (New York: Holt, Rinehart and Winston, 1980).

19. Alice H. Amsden, *Asia's Next Giant: South Korea and Late Industrialization* (New York: Oxford University Press, 1989), 55.

20. Ibid., 116.

21. Walden Bello and Stephanie Rosenfeld, *Dragons in Distress: Asia's Miracle Economies in Crisis* (San Francisco: Institute for Food and Development Policy, 1990), 63.

22. "Industrial South Korea," *Far Eastern Economic Review,* 19 July 1984, 43.

23. Jang Jip Choi, *Labor and the Authoritarian State: Labor Unions in South Korean Manufacturing Industries, 1961-1980* (Seoul: Korea University Press, 1989), 302-4.

24. Asia Watch Committee, *Human Rights in Korea* (Washington, D.C.: Asia Watch, 1985), 37.

25. These documents came to light as a result of Freedom of Information Act requests by Tim Shorrock. See his article "Ex-Leaders Go On Trial in Seoul," *Journal of Commerce,* 27 February 1996, and his Web posting on *Korea WebWeekly* (www.kimsoft.com/korea.htm), "The U.S. Role in Korea in

1979 and 1980."

26. Shorrock, *Journal of Commerce*, 27 February 1996, 1A.

27. Ibid.

28. As quoted in ibid.

29. As quoted in "Buying Time for Change," *Far Eastern Economic Review*, 19 July 1984: 40.

30. Paul Ensor, "Two Way Trade-off," *Far Eastern Economic Review*, 6 March 1986.

31. As quoted in "Korea in the 80's: Decade of the Workers," *Asian Labor Update*, No. 1 (February-April 1990): 9.

32. As quoted in "Unions of the 16 Large Plants Form Alliance," *Korea Labor: Monthly Newsletter of the Korea Research and Information Center* (Seoul), No. 4 (Dec. 1990): 6.

33. As quoted in Miriam Louie, "South Korean Mass Movement Mushrooms," *Frontline*, 3 July 1989.

34. As quoted in "Korea: An Achievement That We Still Exist," *Asian Labor Update*, No. 6 (January 1992): 2.

35. "1991 Korea Human Rights Situation," *Korea Update* No. 105 (Jan. 1992): 7.

36. As quoted in Human Rights Watch/Asia, *South Korea, Labor Rights Violations Under Democratic Rule* (Washington D.C.: Human Rights Watch, November 1995), 19.

37. As quoted in ibid., 21.

38. Andrew Pollack, "South Korea's Growing Pains," *New York Times*, 4 February 1997, C8.

39. "Super Chaebol," *Korea Times*, 7 April 1995.

40. As quoted in Sah Dong-seok, "Deficit With Advanced World Surging," *Korea Times*, 24 June 1995.

41. "Exodus of Local Industries," *Korea Times*, 28 June 1996.

42. "Income Gap Between Poor, Rich Widens in 1993-1995," *Korea Times*, 18 June 1996.

43. "Seoul is Still Teetering on the Edge," *Business Week*, 29 December 1997.

44. See Martin Hart-Landsberg, "The Asian Crisis: Causes and Consequences," *Against the Current* 73 (March/April 1998).

45. See James M. West, "Martial Lawlessness: The Legal Aftermath of Kwangju," *Pacific Rim Law and Policy Journal* 6:1 (Jan. 1997), for a comprehensive examination of the trial and its significance.

Chapter 8: The Challenge and Promise of Reunification

1. For a brief history of the civic movement and discussion of ideological and strategic differences between these newly formed political groups, see Konrad H. Jarausch, *The Rush to German Unity* (New York: Oxford University Press, 1994), esp. Chapter 2, "Protesting for Freedom."

2. As quoted in ibid., 67.

3. Ibid., 240.

4. As quoted in ibid., 170.

5. Ibid., 149.

6. Dorothy Rosenberg, "The Colonization of East Germany," *Monthly Review* 43:4 (September 1991): 17.

7. Ibid.

8. "Germany: Is Reunification Failing?," *Business Week*, 15 November 1993, 48-49.

9. Ibid.

10. "Finally, Germany is Paring The Fat," *Business Week*, 17 October 1994.

11. Rosenberg, 25-29.

12. As quoted in ibid., 27.

13. Gene Koretz, "The Population Plunge That's Wracking Eastern Germany," *Business Week*, 29 August 1994, 20.

14. Bong-youn Choy offers a detailed presentation and discussion of North Korean and South Korean reunification proposals from the division of Korea until 1983 in *A History of the Korean Reunification Movement: Its Issues and Prospects* (Peoria: Research Committee on Korean Unification, Institute of International Studies, Bradley University, 1984).

15. As quoted in ibid., 107-108.

16. Martin Hart-Landsberg, "Korean Reunification: Learning from the German Experience," *Journal of Contemporary Asia* 26:1 (1996); Kim Hak-Joon, "The Republic of Korea's Northern Policy: Origin, Development, and Prospects," in *Korea Under Roh Tae-Woo: Democratization, Northern Policy, and Inter-Korean Relations*, ed. James Cotton (Australia: Allen and Unwin, 1993).

17. Roh Tae Woo, "July 7, 1988 Special Declaration in the Interest of National Self-esteem, Unification, and Prosperity," in *Korea Under Roh Tae-Woo*, 317.

18. Hong Chul Yum, "The Unification Dialogue Between the Two Koreas in the 1990s," *Asian Perspective* 14:2 (Fall-Winter 1990): 78-79.

19. Kang Suk Rhee, "Korea's Unification, The Applicability of the German Experience," *Asian Survey* 13:4 (April 1993): 360.

20. Ibid., 372-373.

21. Sohn Jie-Ae, "Older, But Wiser," *Business Korea*, July 1994, 25.

22. Michael Breen, "Trade and its Impact on Korean Unification," *Korea Economic Weekly*, 6 December 1993.

23. Kim Chang-young, "Foreign Domination of N. Korean Market Worries Business Circle," *Korea Times*, 21 October 1994.

24. Perry Wood, "The Strategic Equilibrium on the Korean Peninsula in the 1990s," in *Korea Under Roh Tae-Woo*.

25. "Kim Hits Japan's Rash Moves to Improve Ties With P'yang," *Korea Times*, 11 October 1995.

26. James Sterngold, "South Korea President Lashes Out at U.S.," *New York Times*, 8 October 1994.

27. John Burton, "On the Front Line: Kim's Balancing Act—War and Peace," *Financial Times*, 31 December 1994.

28. "Preconditions for Peace," *Korea Times*, 16 September 1994.

29. Han Dong-soo, "Seoul Will Solely Be Responsible for Setting Up New Peace Regime," *Korea Times*, 16 April 1996.

30. "Kim Calls for Resumption of S-N Talks," *Korea Times*, 2 March 1996.

31. Jin Min Chung and John D. Nagle, "Generational Dynamics and the Politics of German and Korean Unification," *Western Political Quarterly* 45:4 (December 1992), 857.

32. Michael Baker, "N. Korea Threat Prods Seoul to Muzzle Internal Dissent," *Christian Science Monitor*, 14 November 1996, 6.

33. See Paik Nak-chung, "South Korea: Unification and the Democratic Challenge," *New Left Review* No. 197 (January/February 1993), for an insightful discussion of the relationship between democracy and division.

34. "Risk in Campus Activism," *Korea Herald*, 18 May 1996.

35. Nicholas D. Kristof, "At Crossroads of Democracy, South Korea Hesitates," *New York Times*, 10 July 1996, A3.

INDEX